Praise for *THE NATURE OF SOUTHEAST ALASKA*

"Unlike the standard nature guides th[...] on animals, Nature stresses the web of interr[...] flora and fauna. This affectionate examination o[...] of North America's most spectacular surviving old-growth forests will delight backpackers and armchair naturalists."

—*Los Angeles Times Book Review*

"This is one book you must have along if you're planning to get marooned on a deserted Southeast Alaskan island. Since the authors—longtime Southeast teachers and biologists—have pondered everything in the Tongass from giant glaciers to the smallest no-see-ums, this book is probably the most comprehensive treatment you can get of the flora, fauna, and habitat of Southeast."

—*Ketchikan Daily News*

"*The Nature of Southeast Alaska* does a good job at weaving together scientific research, personal observations, and down-to-earth writing."

—*Sitka Sentinel*

"The authors write with humor and insight on a range of natural topics—from banana slugs and slime mold to glaciers, old-growth forests, and the reproductive problems of blueberry bushes. . . . This witty reference book goes beyond the traditional field guide, offering in-depth and entertaining insights."

—*Fairbanks Daily News-Miner*

"[This book is] the best Alaska regional nature guide. . . . Unlike some more technical field guides, this one can be read with pleasure by nonspecialists. Without sacrificing their concern for facts, the authors conspire to make their text readable by describing their own field ventures in a lively fashion that conveys their enthusiasm."

—*Anchorage Daily News*

The *Nature* of Southeast Alaska

A GUIDE TO PLANTS,
ANIMALS, AND HABITATS

THIRD EDITION

Richard Carstensen • *Robert H. Armstrong*

Rita M. O'Clair

Illustrations by Richard Carstensen

Photos by Robert H. Armstrong

ALASKA
NORTHWEST
BOOKS®

Third Edition 2014
Second Edition 1997
Second printing (updated) 1998

Library of Congress Cataloging-in-Publication Data

Carstensen, Richard, 1950-.
The nature of Southeast Alaska: A guide to plants, animals, and habitats / Richard Carstensen, Robert H. Armstrong, Rita M. O'Clair; illustrations by Richard Carstensen. — Third edition.
    pages cm
Includes bibliographical references and index.
ISBN 978-0-88240-990-0 (pbk.)
ISBN 978-0-88240-929-0 (e-book)
ISBN 978-1-941821-21-3 (hardbound)
1. Natural history—Alaska, Southeast. I. Armstrong, Robert H., 1936- II. O'Clair, Rita M., 1945- III. Title.
QH105.A4O35 2014
508.798'3—dc23

                                    2013045235

Alaska Northwest Books®
An imprint of Turner Publishing Company
4507 Charlotte Avenue, Suite 100
Nashville, TN 37209
(615) 255-2665
www.turnerbookstore.com

Cover designer: Elizabeth Watson
Interior designer and cartographer: Richard Carstensen
Illustrations: Richard Carstensen

All photographs by the authors unless otherwise indicated.
Front cover: Bald eagle and chick. **Inset**: Nootka lupine and Mendenhall Glacier. Robert H. Armstrong.
Back cover: Young black bear with sockeye salmon. Robert H. Armstrong.

Alaska Geographic is a nonprofit publisher, educator, and supporter of Alaska's parks, forests, and refuges. A portion of every purchase at Alaska Geographic bookstores directly supports educational and interpretive programs at Alaska's public lands. Learn more and become a supporting member at: www.alaskageographic.org

*Your Connection to Alaska's Parks,
Forests, and Refuges*

Alaska
Geographic

CONTENTS

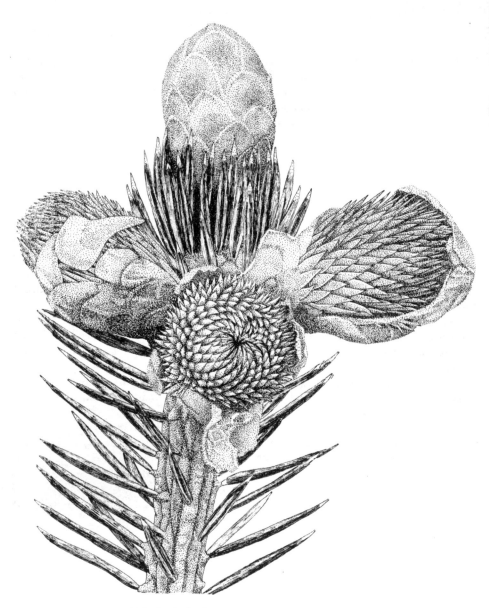

Unfurling buds of
Sitka spruce in
May. Southeast
Alaskans gather
these edible tips
for preserves and
beer-making.

PREFACE · FIRST EDITION

Our collective enthusiasm for the natural history of Southeast Alaska precipitated this book. It started with the nature hikes. One of us would collect specimens; another would photograph them or take notes. Identifying things was the most pressing need initially. Then came the questions. How are plants such as yellow skunk cabbage and early blueberry pollinated, since they often bloom before the snow melts and before we see insects flying about? What do short-eared owls eat? Why do some places support towering spruce forests, while others produce only scrubby pines and sphagnum bogs? Whether emerging together or singly from bog or forest, we came to wonder how each small piece fit into the greater puzzle of Southeast Alaska's natural history.

We pored over the available scientific literature, often collecting all the information we could find on a subject. We interviewed resident experts on tree physiology and pathology, landslides, brown bear denning behavior, and marine plankton. As capital of Alaska and headquarters of many state and federal research agencies, Juneau has a pool of professional biologists and geologists perhaps unmatched by any other city its size. And

Wolf scat on alpine ridge crest, with toe bone, claw, and sun-bleached hair of hoary marmot.

when local knowledge was insufficient, Rita O'Clair prompted the University of Alaska Southeast to bring in authorities on fungi, lichens, mosses, and insects to teach classes so intensive that our heads would swim dizzily for months afterward with new names and new insights. On a few occasions we set up our own research studies, but mostly we just observed and speculated.

We complemented each other well. Rita had a background in invertebrates and plants, Bob Armstrong in fish and birds, Richard Carstensen in mammals and habitats. Our illustrative skills also dovetailed; Rita and Bob amassed encyclopedic photographic files, while Richard concentrated on ink drawings. We enjoyed teaching each other and dabbling in subjects new to us. We resisted the tendency to specialize, feeling that good generalists were sorely needed, we needn't be embarrassed to be dilettantes, and, finally, being generalists was fun! Slowly we realized we had become naturalists.

Eventually our interests and increasing knowledge evolved into the rewarding task of teaching others. We taught courses and workshops in landforms, general biology, ecology, botany, zoology, habitat mapping, postglacial succession, natural history of Glacier Bay, old-growth forests, alpine and subalpine communities, wetlands, intertidal and marine habitats, bird identification, biology of freshwater fish, migration of Alaska's fishes, nature photography, animal tracks and sign, wild edibles, kayaking, and outdoor survival. We found that teaching others was also the fastest and surest motivation to teach ourselves, and with each class we learned perhaps more than most of our students.

Our strongest motivation in writing *The Nature of Southeast Alaska* was to extend our teaching beyond the classroom to residents and visitors. The study of natural history is the first step in repaying our debt to the earth. We believe that to take our natural inheritance for granted is tantamount to ensuring its destruction. From teaching, we've learned that appreciation awakens a sense of stewardship. Our grandchildren deserve to inherit the sea lion rookeries, cedar groves, sedge flats, and sockeye runs we are privileged to enjoy today.

PREFACE • THIRD EDITION

More than twenty years have passed since first publication of *The Nature of Southeast Alaska*—years that have seen huge advances, not only in understanding of northwest-coast natural history, but also in the world of publishing. We're still getting requests for this little guide, and are pleased that it remains a text in high school and college classes, a traveler's companion on the marine highway, a stowaway in kayakers' dry bags, and a well-thumbed reference on Alaskan naturalists' bookshelves. Clearly, *Nature* needs to stay in circulation. But what should a third edition look like?

For starters, we've retained the scope and structure of earlier editions, resisting the temptation to turn the third edition into an encyclopedia. We deleted color plates of earlier editions, but more than doubled the amount of Carstensen line art—much of it previously unpublished—and integrated graphics more fully with the text.

Some topics, such as old-growth forest studies and issues, have evolved so much we had to expand these sections. Other descriptions are shortened—such as details more systematically treated in Armstrong's *Guide to the Birds of Alaska* (2008), or Pojar and MacKinnon's *Plants of the Pacific Northwest Coast* (1994). Those guides tell you what you've seen out there in the woods and waters. Back home on the couch, or around the campfire, *Nature* explores how they fit into the bigger picture. Two decades after the first edition, we're still learning—still entranced by these species, habitats, and connections.

To avoid confusion in a three-author book, earlier editions were written in the 'royal we' voice. While that's still mostly the case, you'll find first-person accounts in sidebars throughout this third edition, signed by either Bob or Richard. These typically report on recent findings or experiences, breaking news from the rain-forest frontier.

ACKNOWLEDGMENTS

Many people helped us by providing information through interviews, by editing selected articles or chapters, and by the identification of specimens we had collected or photographed. We offer special thanks to the following individuals: Paul Alaback (old-growth forests, plants), Nancy Barr (assistance with field work), Dan Bishop (habitats, hydrology), Sam Bledsoe (mycorrhizae), Richard Bottorff (insects), Terry Brock (peatlands), Fenja Brodo (insects), Irwin Brodo (lichens), Richard Carlson (fish), Joseph Cook (mammals), Richard Gordon (birds, habitats), Tom Hanley (deer, skunk cabbage), Al Harris (habitats), Lyle Hubbard (small mammals), Mike Jacobson (bald eagles), Jan Janssens (mosses, wetland ecology), Jim King (sea ducks, Vancouver Canada goose), Matt Kirchhoff (old-growth forests), Gary Laursen (fungi, mycorrhizae), Donald Lawrence (plant succession), Dave Lubin (plants), Stephen MacDonald (mammals), Tom McCarthy (mammals), Mark Noble (alpine, succession), Chuck O'Clair (marine invertebrates), John Schoen (bears), Mark Schwan (birds), Charles 'Terry' Shaw (dwarf mistletoe), Greg Streveler (habitats, mammals), Doug Swanston (surficial geology), Gus Van Vliet (marbled murrelets), and Mary Willson (plant dispersal).

Bonnie Lippitt, Linda Mills, Catherine Pohl, and Graham Sunderland reviewed all or most of the manuscript and offered many useful suggestions. In the beginning, Nikki Murray Jones provided encouragement and editorial help when many of our ideas first appeared in the columns "Nature Southeast" and "The Southeast Naturalist" in the *Southeastern Log*. Ellen Campbell first suggested that we write this book. Ellen Wheat's encouragement helped make the book a reality. Lorna Price's editing improved our writing and kept us on track.

Acknowledgments, third edition—Many people contributed to this latest edition, especially our partners at Graphic Arts Books: Doug Pfeiffer, Kathy Howard, Vicki Knapton and Michelle Blair. The staff and board at Juneau's *Discovery Southeast* have been steady supporters throughout the long evolution of

Edition 3. This book is in many ways a reflection of our membership in *Discovery's* multigenerational network of Alaskan naturalists.

Several colleagues have helped us across a wide range of topics and disciplines: Koren Bosworth, Bob Christensen, Rich Gordon, Marge Hermans, Kathy Hocker, John Hudson, Hank Lentfer, Steve Merli, Richard Nelson, Catherine Pohl, Greg Streveler, and Mary Willson.

For specific improvements to this third edition, many thanks to: Jim Baichtal (geology), Aaron Baldwin (invertebrates), LaVern Beier (bears), Karen Blejwas (bats) John Caouette (forests), Nora and Richard Dauenhauer (Tlingit history and culture), Chiska Derr (lichens), Jim Geraghty (history), Wayne Howell (archaeology), Kitty LaBounty (plants), Jim Mackoviak (history), Kristin Munk (groundfish, mollusks), Dave Person (wildlife), Kenelm Philip (butterflies), Lynn Schooler (marine mammals), Tim Shields (amphibians), Derek Sikes (insects), and Liana Wallace (Tlingit culture).

Raven's view into Mount Edgecumbe caldera. The Tlingit name L'úx means *blinking, opening of the eyes.* The more customary side view of 'Sitka's Mt. Fuji'—jewel of storm-swept Kruzof Island— dominates the horizon in the direction of Japan.

THE WILD SOUTHEAST

Southeast Alaska extends from Icy Bay, just north of Malaspina Glacier, to the southern end of Prince of Wales Island. Some 525 miles long and 120 miles from east to west, Southeast is composed of a narrow strip of mainland mountains and over a thousand offshore islands in the 13,800-square-mile Alexander Archipelago. Those islands are so diced and convoluted that 80 percent of the land is within three miles of an ocean beach.

The defining features of Southeast are its wetness, its intimate interfingering of land and sea, its isolation from major human thoroughfares, and its wildness. Even our village boat harbors are half wild, with sea lions breathing among the slips at night, rich with sea smells and gull cries by day, and only a moment from uncrowded waterways and wild coastal forests, which rise abruptly into even wilder subalpine parkland. To help preserve this wildness, Congress has established National Parks and wilderness areas at Glacier Bay, Admiralty Island, and Misty Fiords.

About 77 percent of Southeast Alaska is Tongass National Forest, at 16.8 million acres, the nation's largest. Within this forest lie the biggest tracts of old-growth trees left in the United States. Southeast contains higher densities of both brown bears and bald eagles than any other place in the world.

The wildness of Southeast is further enhanced by small human population and relative lack of environmental destruction, a hallmark of thickly settled areas. About 73,500 people, of whom 22 percent are Alaska Native, live in one of our thirty-five communities. With about 32,000 residents, Juneau is the largest. The next two largest cities are Sitka (about 9,000) and Ketchikan (about 8,000).

Above: Sitka black-tailed deer on Kupreanof Island in July, with soft-tipped antlers still in velvet. High-pointing rack indicates mature-but-young buck, probably 3.3 years old.

The climate of Southeast Alaska is moderated by maritime influences. The area is bathed by the Alaska Current, an eddy off the North Pacific Drift, which crosses the ocean from Japan. It buffers winter sea temperatures, which average 42°F, a full ten degrees above freezing. On the other hand, the sea cools the area in summer, when water temperature rises to only 55°F. A thick cloud blanket obscures the sun for 85 percent of the year.

The same clouds inundate our area with precipitation, estimated to reach four hundred inches per year in some places, such as higher elevations on southern Baranof Island. Average precipitation in Skagway is only twenty-seven inches (it lies in the Glacier Bay rainshadow), and at Ketchikan about 160 inches. One consequence of high rainfall is that wildfire is less pervasive here than in most of North America. Only northern Lynn Canal has extensive forests dating to fires about a century ago.

Abundant precipitation translates into countless streams and lakes. The US Forest Service database totals 50,000 miles of mapped streams on the Tongass alone, and our ground-truthing suggests an even greater length of important unmapped channels, hidden under forest canopy and undetectable by desk-bound cartographers. Over 25,000 mapped lakes and ponds cover almost 500 square miles. Rivers tumble down mountains and out from beneath glaciers, spewing 180 square miles of sediment into our fifty largest estuaries. The Stikine Flats near Wrangell (thirty-four square miles) and the Mendenhall Wetlands at Juneau (six square miles) are good examples of such wetlands crucial to migrating waterfowl and shorebirds, and also essential as nurseries for commercially important fish.

The structural backdrop of Southeast Alaska is rugged mountains. You can climb from sea level to perpetual ice fields over a distance of just a few miles and an elevation gain of just 4,000 feet. Summits of islands usually range from 2,000 to 4,000 feet, but much larger peaks define the Canadian boundary. Kate's Needle at 10,023 feet dominates the Stikine Icefield. Mount Saint Elias north of Yakutat rises to just over 18,000 feet.

Big mountains spawn big events. In 1986, the Hubbard Glacier, which flows from ice fields near 15,300-foot Mount Hubbard, made world news by advancing to the mouth of Russell Fiord, damming it and creating a lake for about four months. When this lake finally burst through the ice dam, it produced probably the largest water discharge in North America of the past few centuries.

Major volcanic eruptions occurred between 14,000 and 12,000 years ago, when Mount Edgecumbe, on Kruzof Island west of Sitka, spewed forth ash that covered much of Southeast and can still be found in bog sediments a hundred miles away. The most recent volcanic activity in Southeast was a lava flow down the Blue River, tributary to the Joonák, *dreaming,* (Unuk River), about two hundred years ago. Several hot springs occur, ranging from remote and rarely visited to community centers such as the tubs at Tenakee.

Large and beautiful caves on Prince of Wales and neighboring islands are formed by water dissolving limestone and marble. On the surface this landscape, called karst, is equally spectacular; fluted spires and bottomless sinkholes adorn island summits. Karst also holds secrets from the deep past. Bones of bear, deer, and marmot who stumbled into pits or died in their dens have awaited paleontologists for as long as 45,000 years. Carbonate bedrock once supported Alaska's most magnificent forests. Unfortunately, most karst old growth has been logged, not only on Prince of Wales but on the carbonate rocks of Kuiu and Chichagof Islands and Lynn Canal.

Of course, what Southeast Alaska *doesn't* have is also important; this includes rattlesnakes, poison ivy, and frequent lightning storms!

The Nature of Southeast Alaska is about a place—its geology, glacial history, landforms, natural communities, species interrelationships, and the roles played here by a suite of emblematic plants and animals. Instead of dipper, sand lance, and devil's club, we might have chosen Pacific wren, herring, and salmonberry. Our selection includes those species we know best, as well as some that we wanted to learn more about.

Salmonberry
(*Rubus spectabilis*).

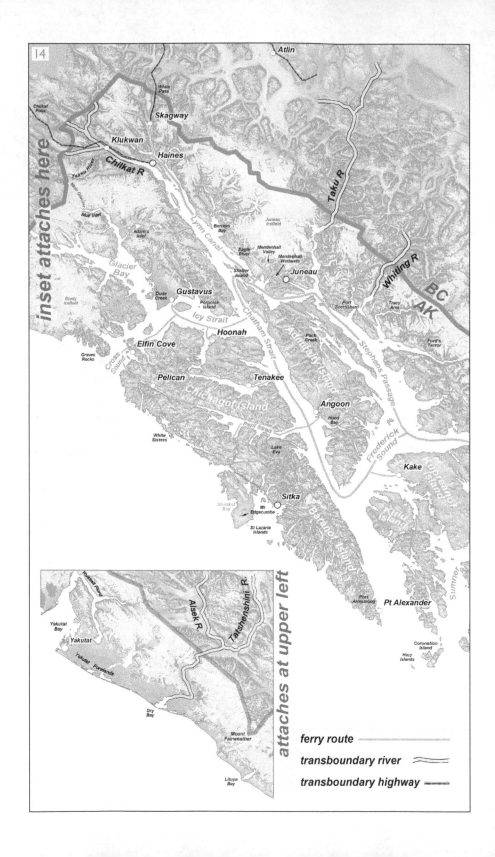

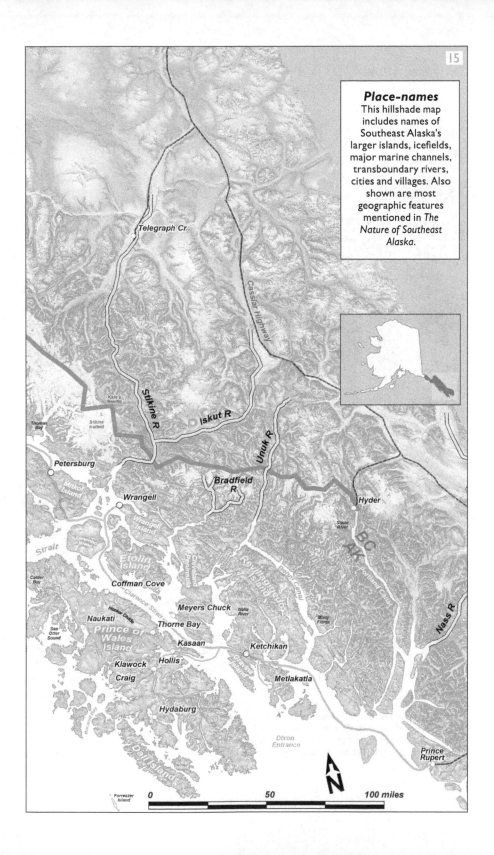

Place-names
This hillshade map includes names of Southeast Alaska's larger islands, icefields, major marine channels, transboundary rivers, cities and villages. Also shown are most geographic features mentioned in *The Nature of Southeast Alaska.*

Telegraph Cr

Cassiar Highway

Stikine R

Iskut R

Unuk R

Kate's Needle

Thomas Bay

Stikine Icefield

Petersburg

Bradfield R

Hyder

Wrangell

Soule River

Mitkof Island

Wrangell Island

BC AK

Strait

Etolin Island

Cleveland Peninsula

Revillagigedo Island

Portland Canal

Calder Bay

Coffman Cove

Clarence Strait

Meyers Chuck

Naha River

Misty Fjords

Nass R

Sea Otter Sound

Naukati

Harbor Docks

Thorne Bay

Prince of Wales Island

Kasaan

Ketchikan

Klawock

Hollis

Craig

Metlakatla

Hydaburg

Dixon Entrance

Prince Rupert

Forrester Island

0   50   100 miles

N

Canoeists on the Honker Divide canoe trail, spanning from tidewater to tidewater across Tàan, *sea lion* (Prince of Wales Island). From Sweetwater Lake, the route threads streams, rivers, ponds, lakes, and estuaries, with a portage over Honker Divide into Thorne River. On the Honker trip we slept on an island in a lake on an island—immersed in the amphibious personality of Southeast Alaska.

View northwest up Lynn Canal from Eagle River near Juneau.

HABITATS

The overriding and underlying theme of Southeast Alaska is water, and inescapable moisture is the unifying feature of nearly all its habitats. From whales' permanent immersion to banana slugs' damp haunts, all our plants and animals contend with water. Only when droughts shrivel the rest of North America do Southeast residents count their soggy blessings.

Amount and distribution of water is the logical way to differentiate Southeast's many natural habitats. These range from ocean, lakes, ponds, and rivers, to frequently submerged salt marshes and stream flood zones, to perennially saturated bogs and other freshwater wetlands, to the usually drenched rain forest and alpine tundra. After a rare two-week drought, it's sometimes possible to sit in the forest understory without soaking our pants. Then rain resumes.

Some habitats are defined by solidified water—glaciers and high-country snowfields. The term "terrestrial" as applied to certain Southeast Alaskan habitats is somewhat generous; it actually means "occasionally free of water."

The Pacific rain forest—Southeast Alaska is a geographic unit defined by the open Pacific Ocean on the west and the boundary with Canada on the north, east, and south. In some cases the lines on maps are ecologically as well as politically significant. For example, if you climb eastward over the crest of the Coast Range into British Columbia (an expeditionary venture!), you enter more

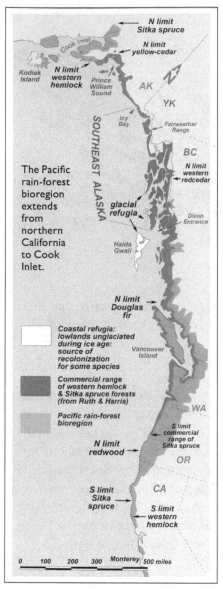

N limit
Sitka spruce

N limit
yellow-cedar

Kodiak   N limit
Island   western
         hemlock   Prince
                   William   AK
                   Sound

YK

Icy
Bay   Fairweather
          Range

BC

The Pacific   N limit
rain-forest   western
bioregion   redcedar
extends   glacial
from   refugia   Dixon
northern   Entrance
California
to Cook   Haida
Inlet.   Gwaii

N limit
Douglas
fir

Coastal refugia:
lowlands unglaciated
during ice age:
source of   Vancouver
recolonization   Island
for some species

Commercial range
of western hemlock
& Sitka spruce forests
(from Ruth & Harris)

Pacific rain-forest
bioregion
                              WA
N limit   S limit
redwood   commercial
                              range of
                              Sitka spruce
                              OR

S limit
Sitka   CA
spruce   S limit
             western
             hemlock

0   100   200   300   Monterey 500 miles

SOUTHEAST ALASKA

than just a different nation. Precipitation declines suddenly in the mountains' rainshadow. Flora and fauna are dramatically different. You've crossed a border in every sense of the word.

In other cases our political boundaries are ecologically arbitrary. Traveling southeastward across Dixon Entrance into northernmost coastal British Columbia, one detects no sudden differences in natural communities. In fact, many biogeographers would describe the immense North Pacific rainy coastline from Kodiak Island to Monterey, California, as a single ecologic unit or bioregion—a geographic area with a distinctive plant community and climate. This unit extends as far inland as the influence of oceanic rain and humidity, from less than a mile in parts of coastal California to several hundred miles in Oregon and Washington.

Cool in summer and warm in winter, the Pacific rain-forest bioregion is dominated by dense, wet, coniferous forest, with some of the greatest biomass (weight of living material per unit area) of any natural community in the world. Forest dominance grades from redwoods in California to Douglas fir, western redcedar, and western hemlock in Oregon, Washington, and southern British Columbia, to western hemlock and Sitka spruce in northern British Columbia and Southeast Alaska. The western hemlock-Sitka spruce forest also forms the seaward edge of the Pacific rain-forest bioregion as far south as Coos Bay, Oregon, where coastal fog supplements summer rainfall, preventing drought.

While western hemlock extends inland to the Rockies, Sitka spruce is intolerant of drought, and hugs the humid coast. Southward and inland from the coastal hemlock-spruce forest, the rest of the Pacific rain-forest bioregion dries out enough in summer to be influenced by periodic fires. These fires need occur no more often than every five centuries or so to maintain dominance of Douglas fir and, to the south, the coastal redwoods.

Relatively few new species of plants or animals are encountered as you travel northward from California to Alaska through the Pacific rain-forest bioregion. Many species drop out, however, as they encounter climatic restraints or geographic barriers to colonization, or lose their favorite foods. Spotted owl and Douglas fir extend northward roughly to the latitude of Vancouver Island. Bigleaf maple reaches the latitude of BC's Haida Gwaii Islands. Southern red-backed vole and western redcedar fade out on the southern Tongass. A few species, such as red-breasted sapsucker and shore pine, reach the northern tip of Southeast Alaska but are missing in Prince William Sound. Finally, range limits are not static. In Misty Fiords some of the northernmost Pacific silver firs grow to four feet in diameter. Such trees are certainly not at the limit of environmental tolerance, but are actively extending their range.

Bedrock geology

Geologically, Southeast Alaska is one of earth's most dynamic regions. The Fairweather Ranges rise abruptly from sea level to more than 15,000 feet. No place in the world—including Everest, where base level is higher—has greater elevational relief. These geologically youthful mountains are rising faster than glaciers can wear them down.

Very little of the bedrock in Southeast Alaska could be considered native to our region, in the sense of having originated here. Most was formed hundreds of millions of years ago in far-away volcanic island arcs with surrounding coral reefs, in shallow marine basins, or on the deep seafloor.

These alien rock groups—called geologic terranes—shifted thousands of miles by seafloor spreading and plastered onto the Southeast coast where plates overlapped and collided, creating intense heat and pressure that formed granitic rocks in deep magma chambers. Tremendous uplift and erosion has exposed these deep-sea sediments, solidified magma, and coral reefs in a northwest-southeast-oriented linear array of terranes.

Within each Southeast terrane there are many different bedrock types, but certain patterns may be detected. For example, the highest-grade limestone and marble rocks that host our famous caves and karst features are found mostly within the Alexander and associated Wrangellia terranes. Extending from Glacier Bay through the center of the archipelago to Prince of Wales Island, the Alexander is oldest of the island terranes, where rocks range from 240 million to more than 500 million years old.

The much younger Chugach terrane contains the towering Fairweathers and the 5,000-foot spine of Baranof Island with highest peaks in the Archipelago. Fairweather bedrock is largely gabbro, a dark granitic rock. Although gabbro erodes more readily than other kinds of granitics, the Chugach terrane is rising so vigorously that glacial grinding can't outrace the pace of uplift.

Hard, crystalline intrusive rocks resist erosion by glaciers and ocean waves. Spires rising from Coast Range Icefields near Juneau and Petersburg—Kate's Needle, for example—are mostly granitic. Resistant granitic headlands often protrude farthest into the sea as well as above it; an anvil of granodiorite armors the tip of Cape Addington.

Even where glaciers ground granitic landscapes into rolling hills, those monolithic and impermeable rock bodies host high densities of lakes and ponds. Margins are often steep, both above and below water line, lacking marshy shallows with deep, organic soils that form on gentler lakeshores. Granitic-basin lakes and ponds are therefore relatively sterile habitat for fish and waterfowl.

That's true on land as well. Scenic, Yosemite-like granitic landscapes such as Tracy Arm and Misty Fiords are tour ship and flight-seeing favorites, but rank among our least productive habitats for vegetation and wildlife. Soil weathered from granitic parent material contains few small clay-sized particles, important for retaining moisture and liberating nutrients. Granitics also have high concentrations of heavy metals toxic to plants.

At the other extreme from granitics are weak, fractured, or poorly cemented sedimentary rocks—often geologically recent—constituting today's lowlands and undulating hills. Examples are found near Angoon, Kake, and Petersburg.

The most productive mines—and our largest cities, Juneau and Ketchikan—occupy the Gravina and Behm terranes where the archipelago meets the mainland. Gold was emplaced in quartz veins here about 55 million years ago.

Geologic faults along convergent crustal plates explain much about the map of Southeast Alaska. In general, there's been a switch from subducting faults—when colliding oceanic plates were consumed beneath the continental plate—to transform, or strike-slip faults that glide laterally against each other. Differential weathering and deep glacial scour along these faults created Southeast's valleys and fiords including the world's longest: the Lynn Canal-Chatham Strait system. There's been 120 miles of separation along this transform fault. If you slid Chichagof Island south 120 miles, its Alexander terrane rocks would rejoin those of Kuiu Island.

The Fairweather-Queen Charlotte transform fault is a northerly extension of California's notorious San Andreas fault. Here, the Pacific plate slips northwestward against the continent. Passing the Southeast Panhandle, it drives head-on into Southcentral Alaska. Volcanic activity is uncommon in this zone, but earthquakes are frequent.

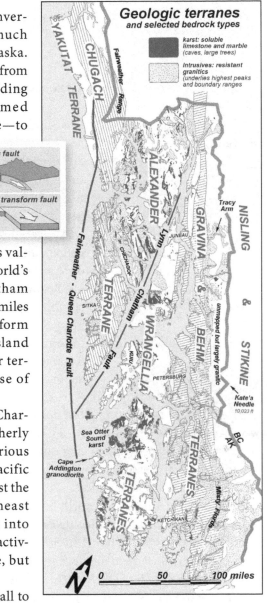

Hundreds of faults too small to show on this map explain landforms at island and watershed scales—fundamental landscape features dictating mountain and stream alignments.

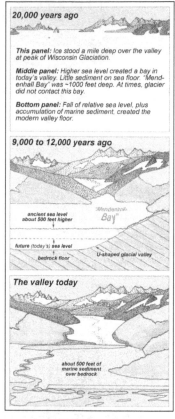

20,000 years ago

This panel: Ice stood a mile deep over the valley at peak of Wisconsin Glaciation.

Middle panel: Higher sea level created a bay in today's valley. Little sediment on sea floor. "Mendenhall Bay" was ~1000 feet deep. At times, glacier did not contact this bay.

Bottom panel: Fall of relative sea level, plus accumulation of marine sediment, created the modern valley floor.

9,000 to 12,000 years ago

ancient sea level about 500 feet higher

Mendenhall "Bay"

future (today's) sea level
bedrock floor
U-shaped glacial valley

The valley today

about 500 feet of marine sediment over bedrock

Glacial history of the Mendenhall Valley, near Juneau. A visualization of vegetation for the middle panel is in the sidebar *Paddle people* (p. 25).

Glacial history

Glaciers and their watery aftermath completely revised the topography of Southeast Alaska, and glacial landforms now dictate the distribution of upland, wetland, and aquatic habitats. About 20,000 years ago, at the height of the last great ice age, almost all of Southeast Alaska was covered by ice. Above its highest extent, jagged, angular nunataks remain, peaks that once stood like islands in the sea of snow and ice. Below them, hills now gently rounded were completely overridden. Examination of this boundary between angular and rounded topography shows that the ice was 4,000 to 5,000 feet thick over the mainland, declining to about 2,000 feet over the outermost islands.

Glacial landforms—Most of our large valleys were carved by glaciers into U-shapes, with steep walls and fairly level floors. In contrast are V-shaped valleys dug out since the end of the great ice age by streams, rivers, and associated minor landslides. These water-eroded drainages tend to occur on a smaller scale.

From Yakutat Bay at 60° north latitude to Portland Canal at 55° north, all of the straits and inlets of the Inside Passage are glacial fiords. A fiord is simply a submarine U-shaped valley. The enormous thickness and weight of Pleistocene glaciers enabled them to gouge into bedrock far below sea level. After glaciers receded, salt water flooded these valleys.

Minor tributary glaciers couldn't gouge as deeply as trunk glaciers. They created so-called hanging valleys, with floors high above sea level. Streams emerging from them cascade steeply to the ocean. The mere 12,000 years since ice retired hasn't been long enough for stream erosion to rework those glacial contours.

Surface deposits—In addition to tracks of glaciers on the bedrock of Southeast Alaska, the great ice age and its meltwaters were almost entirely responsible for present distributions of loose, overlying materials. To make sense of our present mosaic of forests and bogs, lakes and wetlands, it helps to subdivide these surface deposits into glacial till, outwash, and lake-bed materials.

Glacial till ranges from huge boulders to cobbles, gravel, sand, silt, and clay. Some till is let down from stagnating ice (ablation till), whereas most till left by the great ice age was plastered down by the moving ice foot (lodgement till). A moraine is a ridge of till pushed up by an advancing glacier, or built by till melting out of the ice as a glacier pauses in its recession. The mix of coarse and fine materials in till gives moderate drainage that often supports forest communities.

Outwash, unlike till, is composed of particles roughly the same size. Formed by high-velocity waters gushing from the ice face, an outwash fan may be composed mostly of cobbles or even boulders. A cobble or gravel flat is sorted; the fine materials are washed away. As water velocity decreases down-valley, progressively smaller particles are found in resulting outwash deposits. Coarse sorted outwash may also be buried under finer materials as the glacial source of meltwater recedes up the valley and water velocity slows. Yet glacial rivers are always on the move, migrating back and forth across their floodplains. Therefore a wide variety of dominant particle sizes can be found on the suddenly abandoned outwash surfaces of any glacial valley. Rainwater percolates faster through coarse outwash material than through unsorted glacial till, and these surfaces may even become excessively drained. Coarsely

Above: Rules of thumb for particle size. • **Right**: Surficial deposits are the veneer of loose debris atop solid bedrock. Here they're divided into unsorted material in a slide deposit, and water-laid alluvium, of more uniform size. Layers reflect changes in the energy of water delivery.

textured outwash flats (along with thin alpine soils) are among the few sites in Southeast Alaska where roots of plants must occasionally contend with summer drought. Plants such as Nootka lupine with deep taproots are common on outwash.

Fine suspended sediment settles in proglacial lakes. When these lakes fill in, or water level drops, a very different succession begins. Exposed pond and lake beds, unlike till and outwash, are usually poorly drained. Sorted silt and clay keep water continually at the ground surface. Trees fail to grow, and a freshwater wetland develops, after many centuries culminating in bog or fen.

Marine terraces and glacial rebound—During major ice ages, so much of the earth's water was locked up in ice that sea levels dropped as much as three hundred feet worldwide. But opposing forces operated near centers of glaciation.

Over mainland Southeast, the prodigious weight of glacial ice depressed the land twice as far as global decline in sea level. For several thousand years after the great ice sheet retired from the Alexander Archipelago, until land rose again, ocean waves lapped against shorelines that today stand hundreds of feet above present sea level. Marine deposits can be found on the mainland up to seven hundred feet above sea level.

In contrast, on the outer coast, thinner ice cover meant less depression. In fact, earth's crust bulged upward there in compensation for depression under mile-deep mainland ice to the northeast. Broad swaths of continental shelf were exposed, home to arctic fox and caribou that no longer inhabit the archipelago.

In addition to glacial rebound, mountain-building (tectonic) forces have raised some parts of Southeast as much as eight vertical miles over millions of years. Separating postglacial from tectonic uplift, both of which vary in time and space, is a complex problem and a long-standing challenge for researchers with the US Geological Survey.

Succession, habitats

The term "succession," fundamental to the study of natural history, means the change in plant and animal communities over time. Rate of change is greatest after a major disturbance. In addition to the glacial obliteration of Southeast Alaska, other disturbances punctuating successional cycles are windstorms,

Visualization for 'Mendenhall Bay' as first paddlers probably saw it. Sea level about 200 feet higher than today. Features cloned from other photos: glaciers, bergs, and unforested slopes from upper Glacier Bay; dry Denali tundra in foreground.

Paddle people—*Richard Carstensen*

In 1996, in a limestone cave on Prince of Wales Island, remains were found of a young man who died about 10,300 years ago. His diet was mollusks, sea mammals, and fish such as cod. His people traded widely, as shown by nonlocal obsidian in the cave. DNA from his teeth was compared with that of other Native groups throughout the Americas. So far, the closest matches are from southern California, Ecuador, and Tierra del Fuego.

That young man did not live in a rain forest, or travel in a Haida-style redcedar canoe. His landscape—paleobotanists tell us—was covered with *Artemisia* (probably mountain sagewort), and the largest tree was apparently scrub alder.

Human cultures and technologies are shaped by geology, climate, vegetation, and in our region, availability of marine invertebrates, fish, seals, and land mammals. As foods and environments changed, cultures and technologies followed suit. In the Southeast archipelago, one of the few constants until outboard motors appeared in the

Archaeology is challenging in dense, wet, rain forest, where artifacts of wood, skin, bone and fiber quickly melt into acidic soils. This speculative timeline is founded on only a few cultural snapshots—a fascinating work in progress.

date	event (BP = years before present)
10,000 BP	End of great ice age. Glaciers retracted but sea level higher. First humans arrive. Obsidian tools indicate long-distance trading.
10,000- 6,000 BP	Paleomarine tradition: microblades, deep ash middens with mollusks, fish bones, sea mammals.
6,000- 5,000 BP	Thermal optimum, warmer and drier than today. Tool diversification. Cultural identities undetermined.
5,000- 3,000 BP	Early stages of Northwest Coast culture. Microblades replaced by ground stone points, barbed harpoons, labrets, and wooden weir stakes for mass salmon harvest.
3000 BP	Cooler, wetter climate, episodic glacial advances, fluctuating sea level, more stressful conditions for wildlife and humans.
1500 BP	Fort proliferation, escalating warfare. Settlements shift from best resources to more defensible sites with good views
700 BP	Woven baskets and fish traps preserved in anaerobic mud.
1741 AD	Chirikov shore party lost off Chichagof. First Tlingit-European contact?

1920s—was stout shoulders wielding wooden paddles.

Archaeologists have documented stone tools, diets, and trade networks of ancient Southeast inhabitants. But artifacts and middens don't reveal genetic or linguistic relations. The question, When did the Tlingit arrive in the archipelago? is currently unanswerable.

What we *can* say is that for most of the 10,000 or so years since first human arrivals, Southeast had no carved canoes, split-plank longhouses, or bark-fiber clothing. Trees suitable to these technologies—western redcedar, yellow-cedar, and Sitka spruce—were laggard colonists.

Earliest Southeast cultures crafted microblade tools of obsidian and argillite. Although conifers and salmon were in short supply, skin-boat seal hunters of the Paleomarine tradition and subsequent transitional cultures enjoyed climates warmer and drier than today's. When the thermal optimum began to collapse, three to four millennia ago, lifestyles shifted toward what archaeologists call the Northwest Coast Culture.

The Late Phase of that tradition—resembling the cedar-based cultures later described by first European explorers—began around 1,300 years ago. Archaeologists report larger living quarters, more complex social organization, copper and salvaged-iron tools, new harpoon types, stone bowls, and lamps.

This is an exciting time for students of cultural heritage. Geneticists are tracing maternal and paternal lineages of living inhabitants, and of ancient human remains. Every year, these clues, plus insights from natural and cultural history, deepen our understanding of ancestral origins and travels.

Natural history of names

Tlingit place-names are poetic tributes to this bountiful archipelago. The 2012 Tlingit place-names atlas, *Haa Léelk'w Hás Aaní Saax'ú: Our Grandparents' Names on the Land,* represents decades of collaboration with fluent Tlingit speakers, preserving names of bays, streams, reefs, mountains, and villages. Edited by Oxford anthropologist Tom Thornton, *Haa Léelk'w Hás Aaní Saax'ú* is a wonderful resource for Southeast naturalists seeking stories of their favorite lands and waters.

Unfortunately, all maps before Thornton's are dominated by Important White Guy Names (IWGNs). Places named by explorers typically honored dignitaries back home, and tell us more about faraway politics than about the land we inhabit. IWGNs designating who once scratched who's back actually disconnect us from places. IWGNs cover stories of home like tasteless paint on fine hardwood: Prince of Wales Island, Shelikof Bay, Bucareli Bay.

Other Euro-names are worse than tasteless. Favorite and Saginaw Bays were named for steamships that destroyed Xootsnoowú and Kéex' Kwáan villages. These insults top the list of names we now can restore to Tlingit: Wankageey, *bay on the edge*; and Shanáx Aaní, *noisy beach country,* respectively.

Native Alaskans almost never named places for people. The place-grounded

Tlingit language can tell a story in five syllables: Sít' Eetí Geeyí means *bay taking the place of a glacier*. Other names reference Raven tales, fishing attributes, historic battles, shamanic deeds, or tidal patterns.

To know Southeast Alaska is to know her real names. Thanks to the generosity of the elders and Tom Thornton's monumental archiving effort we've shared some of them with you in this book. Our convention in most cases is to give the Tlingit name first, followed by its translation *in italics*, and the English, Russian, or Spanish IWGN in parentheses. For example: Kadigooni X'áat', *island with spring water* (Spuhn Island). To Tom and all his teachers: Gunalchéesh!

floods, earthquakes, landslides, logging, insect infestation, and disease epidemics.

To study nature is to study change. Today's salt marsh may be forest in a century; today's forest may be bog in a millennium. To understand the present or to predict the future, we look into the past. Succession is important to gardeners, archeologists, forest managers, road maintenance crews, and beaver trappers. To unravel mysteries of succession, ecologists start at raw beginnings, searching out examples of disturbances so catastrophic that community recovery or 'primary succession' must proceed almost from scratch. Virtually no living things or even organic soils are available on these sites; seeds, spores, and colonizing animals must move in from elsewhere. The world's best examples are in such places as the suddenly emerged island of Surtsey off Iceland, and in Southeast Alaska, where retreating glaciers are still uncovering lifeless landscapes of till and outwash materials.

Each habitat has its own unique disturbance regime. For example, an avalanche may snap the trunks of spruce and hemlock but pass harmlessly over more flexible alders. Where avalanches happen every few decades, alder thickets may be maintained indefinitely. In old-growth forest throughout Southeast Alaska, the major disturbance is wind. Every few years a storm topples some of the dominant trees, but sub-canopy hemlocks grow up to fill the gap. Disturbance can be

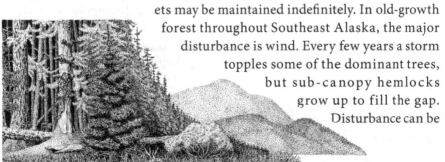

old-growth forest   freshwater pond   salt marsh
high-country parkland   freshwater marsh   rocky intertidal
flood-plain stream   sphagnum bog   saltwater archipelago

Habitat diversity
From the deck of a ferry, the shore is a solid wall of forest. These raven's-eye perspectives peer over that wall at the region's habitat diversity. What are the geologic and climatic underpinnings of this diversity, and how does each habitat change over time?

beneficial: uprooted trees expose fresh mineral soil; more light reaches through the gap in the canopy; and understory plants are given new lease on life.

Forests—For thousands of years after the great ice sheet receded, an initially cooler and drier climate resulted in alternating colonization by tundra plants, or alder and shore pine. Not until about 7,000 years ago did hemlock-spruce forests dominate moderately drained surfaces. Even then, forest fire was widespread, judging from ash layers in ancient soil. Today we find it hard to imagine Southeast Alaska without soggy coniferous rain forest. Most of our unforested natural communities are either too wet (peatland) or too high (alpine/subalpine). Others are simply too young; that is, if given enough time without disturbance, a forest would develop there.

High country—Moving upslope, precipitation increases. More rain falls in summer, and more snow accumulates in winter. At the upper limit of tree growth—usually at about 2,500 feet around Juneau—winter snowpack often remains until midsummer. Trees can't establish, resulting in a zone of lush subalpine meadow. High bowls on Admiralty Island, for example, are filled with this meadow vegetation.

Proceeding upward from subalpine elevations, precipitation tapers off. Less snow falls in winter, and it's drier and lighter, often blown away by ferocious alpine wind. Here begins the true alpine tundra, a slow-growing community enduring unforgiving extremes of temperature and moisture. Tundra survives even on nunataks at the head of Glacier Bay

*From field sketches
of heron catching
staghorn sculpin,
May, 1980: 8 strikes;
1 miss; 7 fish.*

Traffic

The great blue heron stands frozen in a river-mouth tidal slough, eyeing a marine sculpin that, swallowed, it will carry to roost in an old-growth spruce. Cutbanks reveal gray glacial silt, carried down from a grumbling ice face and trapped in leaves of salt-marsh sedges. In the main channel, a hook-jawed salmon muscles into cloudy currents, bound for a clear headwater spawning stream overhung with willow and alder. Bucking estuary traffic, it passes mallards and dragonflies born on margins of upper-valley kettle ponds.

As bonds between species create communities, so bonds between communities animate watersheds and bioregions, all of them shifting allegiances and melting at the edges, to the frustration and delight of naturalists looking on.

Streams, rivers, lakes, and ponds—Because of their critical importance to sport and commercial fisheries, Southeast Alaskan streams and rivers are perhaps our most intensively studied natural habitats. Although they occupy only a small fraction of our total landmass, they could be viewed as a kind of circulatory system binding together the productivity of land and sea, mostly in the form of salmon and other fish living in both fresh and salt water. Lakes and ponds boost diversity and productivity of any watershed.

Freshwater marshes and wet meadows—On terrain with good to moderate soil drainage, upland succession leads eventually to old-growth coniferous forest. But on poorly drained substrates, usually with fine sorted particles, a parallel successional process leads to freshwater wetlands and culminates after many centuries in peatland. Dewatered pond and lake beds, uplifted salt marshes, and annually flooded margins of streams and rivers are typical birthplaces of freshwater wetlands.

Peatlands—A youthful freshwater wetland has only a shallow depth of organic material overlying mineral substrate. Over time, undecomposed remains of mosses and sedges build deep peat deposits. A peat bog has at least several feet of this peat, often representing millennia of wetland succession. Bogs also replace some old-growth forests.

Salt marshes—At mouths of streams, and near heads of protected bays and indentations in the coastline, fine sediments collect in the intertidal. Salt-tolerant species such as Lyngbye sedge and goose-tongue grow here. Salt marshes are coastal wetlands, of mid- to upper- intertidal elevations.

Rocky intertidal—Most Southeast Alaska shoreline is steep. Forested slopes plunge into ocean depths, and horizontal extent of the intertidal zone is limited. On these wave-pounded shores the substrate is either bedrock or boulders. Vascular plants of the salt marsh find no foothold. Dominant organisms are seaweeds (marine algae) and invertebrates such as mussels and barnacles.

Salt water—This book emphasizes terrestrial and intertidal communities and species, but this is not to understate the importance of ocean environments to terrestrial and freshwater aquatic communities of Southeast. Sea rain bathes our forests. Salmon battling up rivers feed bears. Nearly every terrestrial mammal, even an occasional mountain goat, at some point feeds on the beach. No one considers robins or yellow-rumped warblers to be seabirds, but even these species scavenge sea-goodies in spring when terrestrial pickings are buried in lingering winter snow.

Muir Glacier, in the upper East Arm of Glacier Bay, calved into tidewater in this 1991 view (photo-point on inset map). By 1996, it completely grounded. In 2011, it had detached from Morse Glacier. Pioneering land plants grow on the outwash flats now exposed here. While the half mile of recession since 1991 is notable, the rate actually slowed with grounding by more than an order of magnitude! In 1960, the merged Muir and Morse Glaciers extended seven miles down Muir Inlet, and covered the entire inset map to a depth of 2,000 feet.

Succession on glacial till

Glacial landforms left by the great ice age dictate arrangements of natural and human communities from Seattle to Manhattan. These tame cities haven't seen glaciers for 10,000 years. But in some wet coastal bioregions, cooling temperatures about 2,000 years ago brought on another advance—the Neoglacial. This episode was exuberant in northern Southeast Alaska, where advancing glaciers reached maximum downvalley positions as recently as the mid-1700s—the Little Ice Age. Since that time most glaciers have receded. In places such as Glacier Bay we can see in action the forces that once excavated Lake Superior, deposited the moraines of New England, and then slowly healed the devastated land.

Plumed seed of dwarf fireweed (*Chamerion latifolium*).

Onto the raw surface creeps a procession of living things.

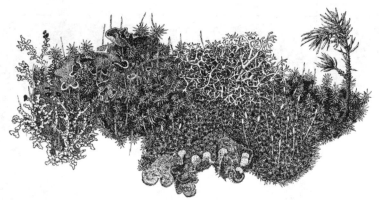

Pioneering plants on outwash or recently ice-covered sites. Left to right: foam and pelt lichens (*Stereocaulon, Peltigera*), reindeer lichen (*Cladonia*), frayed-cap and haircap mosses (*Racomitrium, Polytrichum*), and seedling of Sitka spruce (*Picea sitchensis*).

From the first mosquito larvae, wriggling in puddles left by melting ice, to the woodpecker's nest in nearby old-growth forest, a story is written, perhaps the easiest reading in the world. In theory, by traveling from bare rubble at the ice face downvalley into mature forest, we witness the changes we'd see, sitting patiently on the rubble site for centuries. Ecologists have been coming to Southeast Alaska for just this purpose since 1914, when Professor William S. Cooper first visited Glacier Bay. Cooper's studies were continued and expanded by Professor Donald B. Lawrence, whose work, and support of further research,

Problems with space-for-time studies

Early studies of succession in Sít' Eetí Geeyí, *bay replacing the glacier* (Glacier Bay) employed a chronosequence approach. Researchers assumed that changes observed on a spatial transect from young to old sites were proxies for change over time on any one of those sites. In the 1990s, ecologist Chris Fastie applied other clues and methods to reconstruct histories of individual stands. He learned that successional trajectory had differed from site to site. Two key variables were seed source and substrate. Fastie proposed that presence or absence of alder in early succession has a huge influence on subsequent forest development. On sites far from upland slopes there was insufficient seed source to establish this nitrogen provider and soil builder.

As for substrate, we earlier described differences in glacial till, outwash, and former lake-bed or raised-marine landforms. The description of postglacial succession in this chapter comes mostly from our studies of glacial-till surfaces in Mendenhall Valley, where alder was plentiful throughout glacial recession.

Homesteaders. One-sided wintergreen (*Orthilia secunda*) in litter of Sitka alder (*Alnus viridis*). Groundcone on right (*Boschniakia rossica*) is parasitic on alder roots.

established northern Southeast as a mecca for students of succession.

Pioneers—A jumble of rock, sand, and ice lies at the glacier's snout. Even before embedded ice blocks finish melting, first plant colonists arrive, wafted on breezes bearing tiny spores of mosses and plumed seeds of dwarf fireweed and willows. These extremely mobile seeds can travel miles from the parent plant, an advantage in upper Glacier Bay, where ice retreated so rapidly that vast wastelands were uncloaked, distant from any seed source.

For a decade or more, only occasional sprouts and tufts of moss dot the gray till wreckage. Gradually, green patches expand and merge over the bare mineral substrate. The frayed-cap moss is common in these pioneering stages, binding loose rubble and providing a moist seedbed for later colonizers. Northern horsetails and yellow mountain avens move in, along with pelt and foam lichens. Also germinating are shrub and tree seedlings, not yet obvious, soon to completely alter the face of the land.

Succession involves animals as well as plants. The first adventurers into deglaciated places include wolf spiders, hover flies, Dolly Varden char, threespine sticklebacks, American pipits, black-legged kittiwakes, dusky shrews, and wolverines.

Homesteaders—Pioneering plants are adapted to stressful environments and are usually small, quick to reproduce, and shortlived. They're soon replaced by more durable species we might call homesteaders, such as willow and black cottonwood. These arrive in the first wave of colonization, but on sterile soils they grow slowly, yellow-leaved and prostrate.

The first homesteader to thrive is Sitka alder, a nitrogen-fixer like beans and clovers. This thicket-forming species has a winged seed, which flies shorter distances than plumed seeds and may reach the site a bit later. Leaf litter from alder adds nitrogen to the soil, so willow and cottonwood respond with rapid upright growth. Within about forty years from time of deglaciation, many cottonwoods stand well above the fifteen- to twenty-foot alders.

Thrashing through alder thicket, we find lots of prickly saplings of Sitka spruce, which, like alder, has a winged seed and usually arrives at about the same time. Spruce grows slowly in thick shade and remains suppressed for decades beneath alder. But like cottonwood, it benefits from soil enrichment by alder leaf litter. When it eventually emerges into direct sunlight, spruce grows rapidly.

Few low-growing plants survive the dense shade of alder thickets or the annual autumn burial under leaves. The bizarre ground-cone has solved both of these problems. Parasitic on alder roots, it produces no chlorophyll and needs no light. Its stiff, upright stem deflects falling leaves. Also common under alders are wintergreens, a genus of semisaprophytic plants. Saprophytes are plant counterparts of scavengers, subsisting on dead plant and animal matter. While semisaprophytes are capable of photosynthesis, they can endure deep shade. Wintergreens need rich humus and are aided by fungi in their breakdown of organic materials. Their tiny seeds are easily carried by breezes. They appear with the alder and persist into spruce-forest stages, when decline in soil nutrients starves them.

Mosses and lichens do poorly in the alder litter. Instead they take to the branches. There, as epiphytes (plants that grow on other plants), they escape smothering and find more light. They luxuriate as alders mature and lean over, until the last dying trunks are enveloped in greenery. The alder-willow thickets and mixed spruce-cottonwood forests, which mellow the harsh postglacial land, also support more animals. Black flies, fungus gnats, western toads, orange-crowned warblers, hermit thrushes, Keen's mice, snowshoe hares, beaver and moose all probably peak in population density during these successional stages.

Above: Yellow-rumped and Wilson's warblers abound in thickets and mixed spruce-cottonwood stages of succession.

Left: Moose skull found by elementary-school students in cottonwood-alder thicket on Stikine River sandbars.

Hermit thrushes are generalists who thrive across a broad successional range from mixed spruce-cottonwood to old growth.

Bourgeoisie—Barren terminal moraines abandoned
two centuries ago by Little Ice Age glaciers are now covered with even-aged spruce forests, the penultimate step in
succession toward old growth. Cottonwoods are on their last
legs, with a meager show of foliage high in the crowns, hemmed
in and overtopped by conifers. An occasional remnant of the earlier alder jungles leans rotting at the edge of an opening. Most settled into humus a century ago. At the risk of overcivilizing our colonization
metaphor, let's call this stage the bourgeoisie.

These forests lack that aura of rich decadence found in fully mature old-
growth stands. Spruce growth may have slowed, but few are dying. Western
hemlocks are just beginning to share the upper canopy; most are less than half
the diameter and age of the spruce. Hemlocks are more shade-tolerant than
spruce, and reach into canopy gaps wherever these appear. Few small, live spruce
remain. Within another century, dominance of these stands will shift from
spruce toward hemlock.

Two centuries is just a moment in terms of soil development. Digging
through duff on the forest floor we quickly come to glacial till.

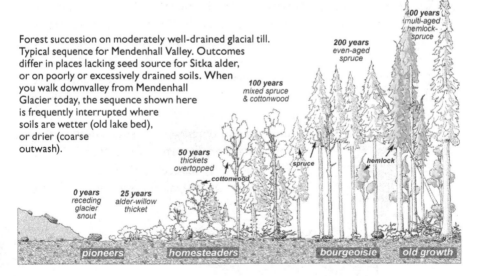

Forest succession on moderately well-drained glacial till.
Typical sequence for Mendenhall Valley. Outcomes
differ in places lacking seed source for Sitka alder,
or on poorly or excessively drained soils. When
you walk downvalley from Mendenhall
Glacier today, the sequence shown here
is frequently interrupted where
soils are wetter (old lake bed),
or drier (coarse
outwash).

400 years (multi-aged hemlock-spruce)

200 years even-aged spruce

100 years mixed spruce & cottonwood

50 years thickets overtopped

spruce

hemlock

cottonwood

0 years receding glacier snout

25 years alder-willow thicket

pioneers   homesteaders   bourgeoisie   old growth

Bark of Sitka spruce has shallow 'potato-chip' bark. Compare with more deeply furrowed hemlock bark on facing page. Tube lichens (*Hypogymnia*) festoon the bark.

The few down logs to be found are mostly in early phases of decay. Rotting wood, standing and down, is the signature of old growth. Mosses, now free of the smothering alder litter, can again cover the ground, but different species are involved. Step moss and lanky moss now blanket most of the forest floor. Overhead foliage interlocks, admitting little light. Bunchberry and blueberry make their first tentative appearance.

Lichens retain the epiphytic niche of the alder-thicket successional stage, but new species now bedeck spruce trunks and branches. The lilliputian lichen community, studied by naturalists on their bellies in pioneering stages of postglacial succession, is still best viewed from eight inches away. Conveniently, that's about the distance of a tree trunk from our noses, as we scramble into the high canopy.

Birds nesting in these young coniferous forests include Townsend's warbler, varied thrush, Pacific-slope flycatcher, and Pacific wren. Most probably fare somewhat better in older, more structurally diverse forest, but we find no lack of them on terminal moraines of Little Ice Age glaciers. Brown creeper, red-breasted nuthatch, and several woodpeckers, all dependent on snags for nesting and feeding, concentrate seasonally in old growth.

Population density of porcupine and red squirrel probably peaks in even-aged forests and declines slightly with transition to old growth. The reverse is expected for northern flying squirrel, which usually nests in snags. The most studied mammal in Southeast is Sitka black-tailed deer, scarce in recently deglaciated regions. Snows are deeper in these areas, and winter

a) Sitka spruce cone; **b)** pollen-producing strobilus appears in May; **c)** cone core with bracts chewed off by red squirrel; **d)** bract with adhering seed; **e)** enlargement of winged seed.

Red-breasted sapsucker drills holes in bark of western hemlock (*Tsuga heterophylla*) and other trees, returning later to feed on upwelling sap.

forage plants are slow to colonize in post-glacial succession. Red-backed vole is the most abundant small rodent in mainland conifer forest, using rotting down logs for cover.

***Succession on raised tidelands*—** Glacial recession since the end of the Little Ice Age has also driven successional development along our coastlines, miles away from areas actually covered by ice. Just as great ice sheets pressed the land down, raising relative sea levels throughout mainland Southeast, the Little Ice Age again depressed the land, but less profoundly. In northern Southeast, land is now rising relative to sea level. Near Glacier Bay, crustal uplift is occurring at about one and a third inches per year. On the Gustavus Forelands, scattered trees advance into uplifted tideflats. Near Skagway, rebound rate is almost an inch per year, and in Juneau about half that. Land is rising fastest where it was most depressed. Gravity studies indicate that in the Glacier Bay area tectonic (mountain-building) forces apply as well.

Whatever its cause, uplift leaves clear evidence on beaches and in the immediate forest fringe. Rotting drift logs may be found, now overgrown by meadow and pole timber. They were stranded there by high tides a few decades ago, when land was several feet lower. Pushing back into the forest, we often find abrupt escarpments, now held in place by tree roots, but originally shaped by waves.

In most watersheds north of Petersburg and Sitka, the amount of recently uplifted shoreline far exceeds that of land uncovered by Little Ice Age glaciers. Post-uplift succession affects our coastal habitats, such as salt marshes and rocky intertidal beaches, even more valuable to people and wildlife than

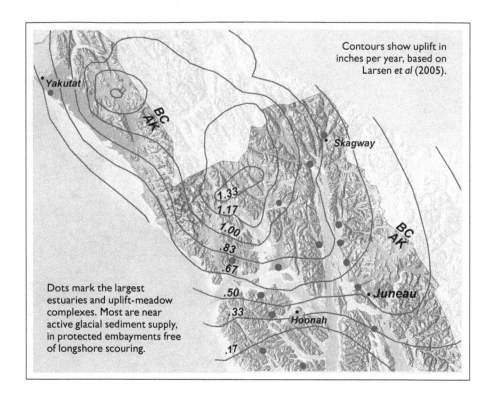

Contours show uplift in inches per year, based on Larsen *et al* (2005).

Dots mark the largest estuaries and uplift-meadow complexes. Most are near active glacial sediment supply, in protected embayments free of longshore scouring.

habitats developing in deglaciated valley headwaters. South of the area of active uplift, old-growth forests often come right down to high-tide mark, and transitional meadows and thickets are less extensive.

Will uplift continue to expose new land along our coast? Climate change may introduce yet another factor. Predictions for worldwide sea level rise, as a result of warming climates and melting polar ice, range from three to six feet over the next hundred years. It isn't known how much longer northern Southeast's rising shoreline will outpace global rise in sea level.

Other kinds of succession—Postglacial and post-uplift succession are only two varieties of community redevelopment on disturbed terrain. We have focused here on the postglacial story in part because studies in Glacier Bay and Mendenhall Valley contributed so heavily to scientists' understanding of succession—standard fare in *Ecology 101*.

But of greater relevance to the daily lives of Southeast Alaskans is

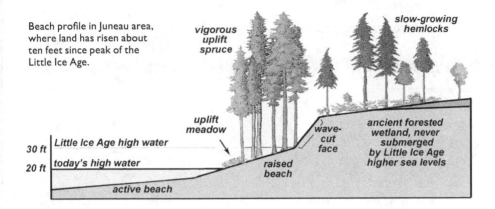

Beach profile in Juneau area, where land has risen about ten feet since peak of the Little Ice Age.

vigorous uplift spruce

slow-growing hemlocks

uplift meadow

wave-cut face

ancient forested wetland, never submerged by Little Ice Age higher sea levels

30 ft | Little Ice Age high water

20 ft | today's high water

raised beach

active beach

succession on nearly a million acres clear-cut since industrial-scale logging began in the 1950s. While glacial rubble supports 'primary succession,' most other examples of succession are 'secondary'; that is, community dominants may be killed, but abundant organic material, seeds, and even surviving tree saplings remain. Although forest recovery is thereby accelerated, that's not always a good thing.

After logging on upland surfaces, hemlocks and some spruces typically spring up at such high densities that canopies interlock. Deciduous stages with alder, cottonwood, and willow—described above for postglacial succession—are lacking or of shorter duration. The successional sequence on logged uplands usually provides little food for herbivores (deer, moose, beaver), carnivores (wolf, weasel), insectivores (warblers, bats), or omnivores (bear, mouse). Most Southeast Alaskans have had the gloomy experience of bushwacking through dark, fifty-year-old second-growth 'doghair' stands with only moss and dead wood on the forest floor.

Fortunately for species such as salmon and bears, prospects are somewhat brighter in logged forests on stream and river bottoms—places we call 'hammered gems.' More on this follows in the sidebar *Muddy boots and hammered gems* (p. 51).

Forest succession will be still different after avalanche, flooding, insect infestation, or storms that blow down trees. There are as many ways to rebuild a forest as there are to knock it down.

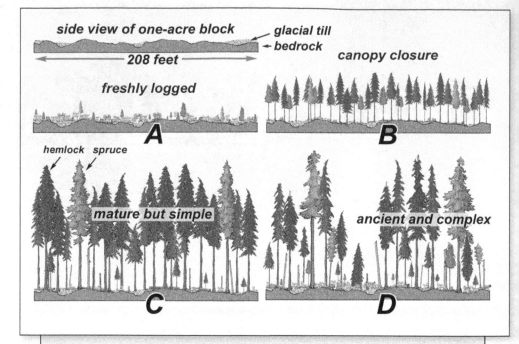

Post-logging succession on upland slopes. Sequence is very different on valley-bottom alluvium. Compare sidebar on Hammered gems (p. 51).

Post-logging succession

These cartoons show succession after logging on a moderately well-drained surface of till-mantled bedrock. Block diagrams represent one acre, about two hundred feet on a side; a one-hundred-foot tree is half as tall as the block is wide. Spruces are pale; hemlocks darker.

A) A few years after logging. Rapid growth of blueberry and strong release of preexisting hemlock saplings. Spruces seed-in on soil exposed by uprooted trees, or scarred by machinery.

B) Between twenty and seventy years, depending on drainage, brush capture, and site productivity, hemlocks and a few spruces close canopy, killing understory shrubs and forbs with deep shade and litter. During the subsequent century, most down wood will rot. Understory will remain shady and depauperate.

C) Shrub and forb layers return slowly. Subcanopy hemlocks still small. Spruces, though few in number, are tallest in the overstory. Clean, pointed crowns indicate a prime timber. But it's still pre-old growth, with low wildlife value due to sparse forage, structurally simple canopy, and minimal dead wood.

D) After three or four centuries mortality produces gappy old-growth mosaic. Abundant deer forage, standing and down dead wood for cavity nesters, rich fungal and invertebrate communities. Foliage in vigorous stage-C forests is top-weighted, concentrated in the crowns. By stage D, foliage is bottom-weighted, offering more habitat in the middle and lower levels.

Old friends: Seven-foot diameter Sitka spruce, with 250 rings just in the outermost eight inches; the rest too rotten to core. It could be a thousand years old! While most Sitka spruce have flakey, 'potato-chip' bark, a few very old, slow-growing trees develop deep furrows, almost resembling Douglas fir.

Above: Large spruces grow where streams deposit nutrient-rich, well-drained alluvium, seasonally refreshed by percolating ground water.

Left: Stink currant (*Ribes bracteosum*) grows beneath riparian spruce on flood-plains, and in aldery avalanche slopes. With very high fat content, it's probably the most important of all late-summer berries for brown and black bears.

Old growth

Throughout the world, temperate rain forest occurs only in coastal regions with cool summers (less than 60°F for warmest month) and abundant, year-round rain—generally at least fifty-five inches annually. Snow usually falls during the dormant season. Because of high timber values, intact, old-growth temperate rain forest has become one of the world's most endangered habitats. About a third of it lies within the Tongass National Forest.

Temperate rain forests host some of the world's largest and oldest tree species. In forests lacking a prolonged dry season, where fire is rare, wind is the dominant natural disturbance. On much of the Tongass, stand-replacing gales come from the southeast in fall and winter. Since 1950, however, logging has displaced wind as the principal forest disturbance on federal, state, and private timberlands.

Old-growth forests are multi-aged, with conifers from saplings to old-timers, in a cycle of decay and regeneration. Trees weakened by insects and fungi are toppled during storms, opening gaps in the forest canopy that eventually are filled by extension of tree branches and by young hemlocks, redcedars, and occasional spruces growing into the opening.

In general, upland forest plants could be considered winter forage species, remaining green in snow (or with leafless blueberry, at least *available* as woody browse). In contrast, riparian herbs typically wilt in fall, but in summer are more palatable than upland evergreens.

These are not strict habitat associations, but rather tendencies useful in conceptualizing seasonal trends and wildlife values of different forest types.

Understory plants—Patchy old-growth canopy is mirrored by an equally patchy growth of herbs and shrubs on the ground below. In that ground-cover mosaic, plants such as blueberry, bunchberry, five-leaved bramble, foamflower and fern-leaved goldthread offer critical winter forage for Sitka deer. Many low-growing understory plants are evergreen, an advantage in dim light. Rather than relying on seed reproduction, they spread by extending rhizomes or runners, quickly invading newly opened gaps when a tree falls.

Common forest plants

riparian shrubs

thimbleberry
Rubus parviflorus

salmonberry
Rubus spectabilis

stink currant
Ribes bracteosum

devil's club
Oplopanax
horridum

red elderberry
Sambucus racemosa

riparian herbs

deerberry
(false lily-of-the-valley)
Maianthemum
dilatatum

sweet cicely
Osmorhiza
purpurea

yellow violet
Viola glabella

rattlesnake-root
Prenanthes
alata

foamflower
Tiarella trifoliata

enchanter's
nightshade
Circaea
alpina

rosy
twisted
stalk
Streptopus
roseus

spring-beauty
Claytonia sibirica

upland shrubs

blueberry
Vaccinium spp

rusty menziesia
Menziesia
ferruginea

five-leaf bramble
Rubus pedatus

upland herbs

fern-leaved
goldthread
Coptis
asplenifolia

bunchberry
Cornus canadensis

single
delight
Moneses uniflora

Elaborate microcommunities of mosses and lichens live high above the ground on branches of conifers. These mosses and lichens are epiphytic—growing on, but not parasitizing the conifers. They subsist mainly on nutrient-containing dew, rainwater, and fog. Epiphytic lichens feed old-growth mammals such as northern flying squirrel, and when blown to the ground are eagerly consumed by Sitka deer. Many species are also nitrogen-fixers. Soil nitrogen benefits from litter-fall and even from rain leaching off epiphytic lichens.

Southeast Alaska and northern coastal British Columbia collectively constitute the moss capital of the temperate world. In old growth and in peatlands, moss serves as a sponge, moderating effects of rainstorms, protecting vascular associates from being swept away to sea.

Coralroot orchids, and the wintergreen relatives pinesap and Indian pipe, are well-suited to old growth. Assisted by soil fungi these saprophytes feed on organic material in the soil and, unlike most green plants, don't need sunlight

Left: Brown creepers typically nest behind delaminating bark flakes on large conifers, and are strongly associated with old-growth forest.

Below: Pacific-slope flycatchers—along with Townsend's warblers—are the most frequently heard singers from the old-growth canopy.

to make their own food. Some may be connected via fungi to roots of green plants, parasitizing them. Saprophytic plants tolerate dense shade.

Old-growth animals—Snags over twenty inches in diameter with well-decomposed centers are valuable to excavating woodpeckers. Later, holes carved out by hairy woodpeckers and red-breasted sapsuckers are renovated by so-called secondary cavity nesters—chestnut-backed chickadees, and small owls such as the northern saw-whet, western screech, and northern pygmy. The availability of such cavities may limit population size for some birds. Other characteristic old-growth breeders are Townsend's warbler, Pacific-slope flycatcher, brown creeper, Pacific wren, red-breasted nuthatch, and marbled murrelet. Sharp-shinned hawk and northern goshawk find breeding and hunting habitat in old growth. Bald eagles typically nest in the largest beach-fringe spruces.

Right: Logs diversify stream channels, creating plunge pools, overhangs, and hiding cover for rearing and resident fish.

Below: In November, black-tailed bucks associate with does, but may pretend uninterest.

Compared to birds, Southeast mammals use a wider range of habitats, and few spend all their time in old-growth forest. On the other hand, few mammals avoid old growth altogether. Mammals with especially strong ties to ancient forest are marten, Sitka black-tailed deer, and northern flying squirrel. For others, connections may be less clear but still critical. For example, some mountain goats descend into cliffy but forested habitat in winter, when their alpine range is buried in snow. River otters benefit from old forests because roots of big trees provide the best den sites, and indirectly because of the value of old growth to coho salmon.

Dead wood—Nature never wastes dead wood. From death until completely rotted, trees feed and shelter a complex succession of forest plants, animals, and fungi. A thirty-inch spruce log may require fifty

years or more to fully return to soil. Spruce heartwood, high in lignin, rots slowly, but large hemlocks usually have heart rot even when living—shattering and decomposing more rapidly. Wood-boring insects begin the breakdown, tunneling through sapwood, admitting oxygen, and transporting fungi and microbes. Bacteria in logs break down wood and fix nitrates usable by plants.

Fallen logs help prevent erosion of forest soils, especially on steep slopes. A rotting log stays moist inside, even in times of drought. Down logs provide nurseries for hemlock

Logging ancient trees—*Richard Carstensen*

Tongass logging became controversial in the 1970s, as annual cut topped half a billion board feet. Even Alaskans most directly dependent on timber dollars grew alarmed as their favorite hunting and fishing places were altered beyond recognition.

Let's back up to the beginning of logging on the Tongass, and trace the changing relationship between humans and trees. While tools for cutting, moving and milling wood evolved, basic tactics remained unchanged; take the best and leave the rest. Loggers call it common sense; biologists call it high-grading.

Although the Tongass National Forest covers 17 million acres, only about half is actually forested, and far less than half of *that* is interesting to a logger. In this silvicultural austerity lies the germ of high-grading. Unlike western Washington State, for example—once liberally endowed with massive conifers—desirable forests of the Tongass were never widespread.

When spruces and redcedars were felled with stone axe and stump-fire, it was physically impossible for thinly dispersed humans to exert pervasive influence on forest structure. Western redcedar has probably only grown on the Tongass for a millennium or two. It may even have been brought here by Tlingit or earlier cultures who revered cedar as the gift of transportation, lodging, and fiber. Large redcedars free of heart rot within dragging distance of the coast were quite unusual. So a search for prime canoe logs was the first example of Tongass high-grading. This organic industry inspired a market for better tools. Before European explorers "discovered" the Inside Passage, Tlingit and Haida woodworkers fashioned chopping adzes from iron, salvaged from Asian vessels washed up on Alaskan shores.

Beginning in 1799, Russians felled trees with razor-sharp broadaxes, converting Sitka's coastal forest to lumber, firewood, and charcoal. It was almost another century before eight-foot-long, two-handled crosscut saws came into widespread use. Skillfully-filed raker teeth could drop a five-foot spruce in half an hour.

Handloggers selectively felled giant spruces referred to as "pumpkins." Trees toppling directly into the ocean were "stumpers." Handloggers scoured the coast so thoroughly that by the late 1920s, one forester reported: "in almost any bay or good booming and rafting grounds we find that most of the handy spruce has been removed."

Above: *Marten probably have the strongest ties to old growth of the Southeast mustelids.* • **Left**: *Handloggers felling "pumpkin" on Long Island in 1941. No spruces this large remain on the Tongass.*

Chain-saws appeared in the 1940s—ponderous and cranky at first, but increasingly sophisticated. In the 1950s, due in part to tireless promotion by forester-turned-governor Frank Heintzleman, fifty-year contracts established state-of-the-art pulp and lumber mills at Ketchikan, Wrangell, and Sitka.

At that point, high-grading shifted from beach-fringe to road-based, and from single-tree selection to clear-cutting concentrations of Sitka spruce, our most valuable species. These forests grew on karst, and on alluvial fans and floodplains. Within three decades, by my estimate, 99 percent of the superlative karst forest was gone. Liquidating streamside forests took longer, but by the 1990s, our finest giant-tree salmon watersheds had been shaved from wall to wall.

Once again, high-grading strategy shifted. As stream buffer regulations removed alluvial stands from the timber base, logging roads snaked into upland large-tree hemlock forests, sold at a loss to American taxpayers, in order to honor the long-term contracts.

In the 1990s, just before their expiration dates, those contracts were cancelled. Intolerable environmental impacts, and exhaustion of valuable timber reduced annual cut on federal, state, and private lands tenfold between 1973 and 2003.

But high-grading continues. Today, most timber sales attractive to bidders feature pockets of western redcedar or Alaska yellow-cedar, now extremely valuable due to global rarity. Hemlock is often mere bycatch, cut at a loss to the operator, in order to pluck these fashionable, hollow-centered, often immeasurably old cedars. Although annual board-foot exports have slowed, the age and irreplaceability of wood leaving the Tongass may never again be equaled by any of the world's temperate forests. In the words of old-growth ecologist Jerry Franklin, most of the developed nations have *"taken their old forest off the table."*

Red-backed voles (Myodes rutilus and gapperi) are the most common small rodents in our mainland forest. On the archipelago, where redbacks are absent, marten researchers notice that long-tailed voles—elsewhere considered meadow inhabitants—occupy the redback's forest niche.

seedlings. Logs without bark, in advanced stages of decay, provide optimum rooting for trees that will dominate tomorrow's old growth. Birds and mammals use rotting logs too. Bears tear them apart in search of insects, and small mammals use logs as protected runways through the forest. Some mammals and birds build their nests within hollows of fallen logs and up-twisted root pads.

Logs falling across streams slow the current and create small pools, which dissipate the erosive energy of the stream, stabilize streambeds, and impound fine sediments, diversifying habitat. Stream logs also feed aquatic invertebrates.

Subadult sharp-shinned hawks sometimes entangle in nets set up to capture songbirds. Like their larger relatives, northern goshawks, 'sharpies' are *accipiters*, so agile in flight that birds comprise a large portion of their prey.

Abundant invertebrates, in turn, feed fish. Fish values of streams and rivers depend on forest quality.

Small forest streams are protected by the canopy. This insulating cover may keep small streams from freezing solid in early winter before snow bridges them. Small fish in streams need running water to stay alive. Dropped branches and leaves are the principal nutrient input to small forest streams. Old growth is better than young, even-aged forest at protecting streams from flooding during torrential rain-on-snow events.

Banks and groceries—In the 1970s and '80s, as "old growth" became a battle cry for conservationists throughout the logging heartland of the Pacific Northwest and Alaska, there was a tendency among advocates and scientists alike to paint old growth as rich in everything from berries to songbirds.

But in the northern temperate rain forest, the most fruitful and musical summer forage communities are those where frequent disturbance prevents or delays establishment of conifers! As measured by plant ecologists, productivity—annual vegetative yield per unit area—is higher in early successional communities such as salt marsh or lush subalpine meadow than in stable, mature forest. And young, unstable communities with strong annual pulses of boom and bust offer up more of their productivity to animals from neighboring communities than do old-growth forests, which tend to hoard their production. The problem with these 'generous' young communities—especially in severe northern climates—is they shut down in winter. Vegetation dies back, or is buried in snow. Old growth then becomes survival habitat, not as forage-rich as summer wetland or upland meadow, but at least available in hard times.

Even the salmon spawning streams of large-tree, old-growth forests that we think of as productive are perhaps better described as stable nurseries. Salmon fatten more at sea than in streams. Old-growth streams are *protectors* of fish, during spawning and early rearing phases of their life cycle.

On limestone-enriched soils of northern Prince of Wales Island, bucks grow larger, and develop wider, thicker antlers. Here on the bank of Thorne River, a weathered skull lies in a bed of mosses and five-leaved bramble (*Rubus pedatus*), probably most important of all foods for wintering deer.

If young communities are nature's grocery stores, old communities are banks, where productivity is hoarded and nurtured and carefully rationed out. Old growth is a stingy breadbasket. The real resource of old growth is in wintry havens, precious tree-ring archives, in the subtle, elderly way her pieces fit together, in longevity, and in the thousand lessons we've not yet learned.

Twenty years of learning—*Richard Carstensen*

When *The Nature of Southeast Alaska* was published in 1992, I had little direct experience on Tongass timberlands. My naïvety was rectified beginning in 1996, when Sam Skaggs asked me to lead the Landmark Trees Project—a search for Alaska's finest remaining one-acre patches of large-tree spruce forest. For the next ten years I ranged the Tongass, eventually measuring and describing seventy-six megastands. Although our targets were the surviving giants, it was impossible to miss those massive stumps of larger, unluckier trees. In 2005, driven by an increasing sense of urgency, I back-burnered Landmark Trees and, with naturalist Bob Christensen and conservationist Kenyon Fields, founded the Ground-truthing Project—the "eyes and ears in the woods for the Southeast conservation community." We surveyed past and proposed cutting units from Hydaburg to Hoonah.

Throughout that period, often-heated discussions about appropriate forestry were muddied by fundamental inadequacies in the way we mapped and talked about forest types. But in the mid-1990s the Forest Service drafted a brilliant young statistician named John Caouette, to address that problem. John joined us on the very first Landmark Trees expedition, and was henceforth our most trusted advisor on matters of forest metrics and rhetorical civility. At the Forest Service, John tirelessly fine-tuned an evolving depiction of forest structure that most people today call the Caouette map. John was about getting it right, even if that meant endless revisions.

Beyond volume

Before John, Alaskans described forests in terms of board-foot volume. Timber planners used volume classes in laying out sales. Deer biologists used them describing winter habitat. Conservationists spoke of "high volume" in lawsuits. The old-growth section in our first and second editions of *The Nature of Southeast Alaska* basically equated wood-per-acre with ecological value.

But a forest is obviously more than a potential stack of lumber. One of John's mantras was moving beyond volume in our forest conversation. This was easier stated than accomplished. It took years for John to gain trust on all sides. Fortunately he was good at that too.

The most useful forest metrics, Caouette concluded, were average tree diameter and stand density, or number of trees per acre. In combination, they describe a wide range of forest types, each a distinctive habitat for fish and wildlife. What we all had in mind when speaking of "high-volume" forest was very large trees at low density—extreme examples being our Landmark Tree stands. Only Caouette and a few foresters recognized that densely stocked stands of smaller trees, widespread on older clear-cuts and wind-felled sites, could have even higher volume. But volume of such closed-canopy forest is difficult to judge from air photos, so it's poorly mapped. For that reason the oft-repeated claim that most of our high-volume forest has been logged is not only irrelevant but probably false.

Muddy boots and hammered gems

Armed with John's more meaningful language and forest-type maps, Bob Christensen and I set about surveying the Southeast timberlands. In some regards, our experiences confirmed expectations. Logged upland hemlock forest, if not precommercially thinned, comes back thick and shady. On thinned sites, tree growth surges but not understory forage plants, which stay buried in shade and litter. It will take radical treatment such as chain-sawed openings in overly dense young growth to rescue and stimulate understory in these stands.

John Caouette, 1964-2010

Probably most unexpected was the story of 'hammered gems'—our most productive bottomland forests, most heavily logged. Due to a combination of high-disturbance yarding techniques and severe over-bank flooding, red alder (lover of exposed soils) inherits these gems. Unlike young upland conifer forest, alder woods have high values for fish, songbirds, mammals, and even soil arthropods, *throughout* the slow return toward gappy large-tree spruce forest. Because spruces come up widely spaced beneath alder, they never completely shade out the understory. Hammered gem watersheds never stop cranking out pink and chum salmon, feeding

Post-logging succession on alluvium. One-acre blocks. Unlike upland succession (block diagrams on p. 40) it features lush undersory and red alder, with spruces often suppressed and dispersed. Hammered-gem succession rarely enters conifer canopy closure.

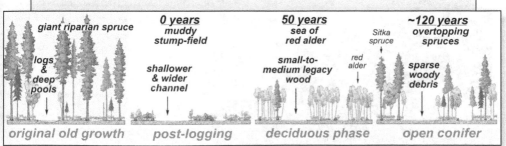

bears, and exporting precious nitrogen and phosphorus to surrounding terrestrial and marine habitats.

Ancient cedars

The previous sidebar, *Logging ancient trees*, explains that red- and yellow-cedars—once shoveled over road embankments as junk wood—are now principal targets of Southeast timber industries. Our Ground-truthing surveys revealed that stands of large western redcedar are only sparsely distributed across the southern Tongass. Most that we found were inside proposed cutting units, and many have since fallen to chain-saws. On top of these human impacts, yellow-cedar is experiencing a mysterious dieback that seems related to warming winters and reduced insulation under skimpier spring snowpack.

Today, we are high-grading the dwindling population of redcedar millennium-trees so fast that—like the great karst spruces—they could mostly be gone before we understand their distribution or wildlife value. Red- and yellow-cedar are short, slow-growing species, poor competitors with spruce and hemlock on productive land. I return to the dilemma of growth rate and sustainability in the sidebar *Harvesting longevity* (p. 211).

John Caouette's last big statistical challenge was analyzing ground-based timber inventories conducted since the 1970s, to develop forest-structure models. One goal of this modeling was to predict cedar distribution. Meanwhile, John purchased a load of red- and yellow-cedar from a small Hoonah mill, and began construction of a glorious canopied deck in his backyard. We shook our heads in amazement at the tightness of annual rings in his cedar lumber. He joked that the timber-data-processing work was "penance" for the ancient wood in his deck. But if anyone paid in full for that cedar, it was John Caouette.

Counting rings in hollow-centered redcedar—about 700 annual rings just in the outer rind. This tree may have been among the first generation to colonize Tàan, sea lion (Prince of Wales Island).

View across Chilkat River from Haines. Contact between jagged and rounded topography shows height of mile-thick ice during the great ice age. • **Inset**: Same scene about 20,000 years ago.

High country

In 2010, an interdisciplinary team of biogists began a multiyear survey of high-mountain habitats throughout Southeast Alaska—the first such study ever conducted in our region. Although our heather-clad, snow-crowned mountains have immense romantic appeal, research funding is typically less attached to romance than to commercial resources, so this inventory has been a long time coming. Traditionally, the most recognized Tongass commodities have been trees and salmon. Timber harvest is not feasible above tree limit, nor do salmon run that high.

Even mountain recreation is limited in Southeast Alaska. Except for Juneau, few communities offer extensive networks of trails into the high country, so a stroll along an alpine ridgetop requires helicopters, or 3,000 vertical feet of off-trail bushwacking through forest and thicket.

Subalpine forests—At about 1,500 feet above sea level, mountain hemlock replaces western hemlock as the dominant forest tree. Conifers become smaller and gnarlier, and forest is broken by ferny glades, seeps, and brushy slide areas. Plants such as false hellebore hint that we're nearing forest limit. Invaders from

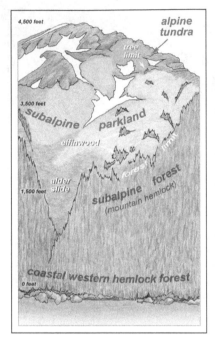

4,500 feet

alpine
tundra

tree
limit

3,500 feet

subalpine parkland

elfinwood

tree limit

alder
slide

1,500 feet

forest

subalpine forest
(mountain hemlock)

coastal western hemlock forest

0 feet

Mountain belts. Elevations vary with aspect, snow depth, soil moisture, parent material, latitude, and disturbance regime.

higher communities, such as deer-cabbage and Alaska moss heather, appear in the understory. Scrubby high-elevation forests with plentiful openings and edges have luxuriant herbs and shrubs, seasonally important to deer. During severe winter weather, mountain goats seek refuge in cliffy forested areas. Weasels and marten hunt subalpine forest for red-backed and long-tailed voles.

Forest limit, tree limit—Alpine ecologists distinguish between forest limit (upper limit of closed forest) and tree limit (uppermost elevation of dwarfed and scattered trees). At tree limit, Sitka spruce and mountain hemlock may tolerate extremely harsh winter conditions, as long as the summer growing season offers enough warmth for reproduction. Throughout the northern hemisphere, in those places where mean July temperature runs colder than 50°F, trees cannot become established. This applies to both arctic tundra, north of the 50° mean summer isotherm, and to alpine tundra, which lies above it.

The 50° isotherm has not been mapped in Southeast Alaska, but we suspect that on many slopes it lies far above the highest trees. Other factors such as slope steepness and direction, wind, soil water, and snow accumulation can depress tree limit well below the 50° isotherm potential. In humid coastal mountains, depth, persistence and mobility of snow is especially important. Studies in southern British Columbian coast ranges found that depth of late-winter snowpack increased from sea level into the subalpine, where it peaked, and then declined at greater alpine elevations. Maritime mountains also have much wetter snow than interior ranges. In spring, this saturated snow begins to creep slowly downhill. Woody-stemmed plants at tree limit, such as blueberry, Sitka alder, copperbush, and saplings of mountain hemlock, are either temporarily flattened or snapped off. Mountain hemlocks that endure decades of this snowcreep may eventually grow upright, but their bases bear evidence of the power of moving snow.

Subalpine parklands—In some places one can step directly from closed subalpine forest into alpine tundra, but in Southeast Alaska this is quite unusual. More commonly, islands of meadow within otherwise-closed subalpine forest enlarge as we climb, morphing into islands of shrunken forest on mini-convexities with reduced snowcreep—the subalpine parkland. Interspersion of rich herbaceous forage with elfinwood cover makes subalpine parkland superb habitat, albeit only briefly snow-free.

Outside those elfinwood patches, annual snowcreep and an occasional avalanche exclude most woody-stemmed plants. Instead, tall perennial meadow herbs spring up after snowmelt and wilt back in fall, thereby avoiding confrontation with a nine-month-long winter. Plant assemblages of subalpine parkland remind us of lowland coastal meadow, including many of the same robust species—cow parsnip, lady fern, fireweed. Signature flowers of subalpine meadows are deer-cabbage, Sitka valerian, monkshood, and broad-petalled gentian. Even these are not unique to mountains; they occasionally appear in lowland fens or proglacial habitats. That species overlap is not coincidental; both coastal and

Above: Snowcrook in mountain hemlock (*Tsuga mertensiana*), developed in sapling stages by pressure from the downward-creeping spring snowpack.

Right: Blacktail bucks in meadow of almost pure deer-cabbage (*Fauria crista-galli*).

subalpine meadows are early successional communities. However the latter are typically arrested in this productive condition by repeated disturbance, whereas coastal uplift meadows slowly succeed toward forest.

At high elevation, the growing season is short. Many herbs don't melt out of the snow until July, and must flower and set seed before snow flies again in mid-September. While that might seem to reduce value of mountain habitats to wildlife, it results in a flush of plant production that actually makes this zone a mid- to late-summer mecca for grazers, insectivores, and their predators. Compensating for brief growing season is nearly twenty-four-hour sunlight near the time of summer solstice. Short-fuse, low-toxin plant growth translates into fast-fattening herbivores.

Deer nibble through the meadows in a slow upward movement we might characterize as following spring up the mountain. Where lush forage grows close to cliffy escape habitat, mountain goats may venture (they're slower than deer and more vulnerable to predators on moderate terrain). Bears sometimes just belly-slide downhill through the subalpine salad bowl, raking herbs into their mouths as they go. Marmots grow so bulgy and wide they could be run down by a fit human, and must remain close to their burrow entries.

A pulse of leaf-eating insects erupts in subalpine meadows, as in any habitat where vegetation races to fruition. Those insects attract female sooty grouse, clucking warnings to hunkered broods. Naïve and clumsy grouse chicks—and equally delectable teenaged ptarmigan higher on the slopes—in turn draw predators such as northern goshawk to subalpine parkland. Two ground-nesting songbirds common in coastal meadows are also found in the subalpine—savannah and Lincoln's sparrows. Where willow-lined creeks meander through subalpine bowls, plaintive *oh dear me* songs of golden-crowned sparrows may be heard.

Earlier, we noted that snowcreep and avalanche can arrest mountain meadow communities in early successional condition. But an

Sooty grouse broods (*Dendragapus fuliginosus*) abound in lush subalpine parkland, typically trading off with rock and willow ptarmigan at the transition to alpine tundra. Formerly called blue grouse ('hooters' locally), they were recently split from interior dusky grouse (*D. obscurus*).

Grazing selection

You'd think since deer-cabbage (*Fauria crista-galli*) is the presumptive favorite summer food of Sitka blacktails, then more deer would equal less deer-cabbage. But the reverse seems true. Deer cabbage appears to like the attention given it by these dainty-footed grazers. Mainland mountain meadows with fewer summering deer have higher plant diversity and less *Fauria* than do topographically similar habitats on islands of the archipelago where deer abound.

Deer are catholic grazers, eating almost every vascular plant species. Perhaps deer-cabbage is simply the subalpine herb most tolerant of steady foraging pressure. As other species are mowed down, *Fauria* inherits the space they vacate. Like the primary lowland winter deer foods—five-leaved bramble, bunchberry, fern-leafed goldthread—deer-cabbage spreads clonally. Hundreds of kidney-shaped leaves may belong to a single, tenacious plant that surrenders a portion of its growth in return for weeding out of taller competitors, and the compensatory nutrient-injections of semi-liquid August deer droppings.

Large grazers such as cattle and horses have a similar relationship to grasses. More trample-resistant than tender herbs, grass replaces them under heavy grazing pressure. Grasses also grow from the base and endure repeated clipping. Although *Fauria* grows at the tip, a clipped leaf of deer-cabbage leaves the below-ground runner unharmed. As for trample-resistance, deer-cabbage seems rather fragile. Cattle would quickly turn deer-cabbage pastures into mud-slicks. Narrow hooves of deer are friendlier to deer cabbage, brushing harmlessly and quietly through the leaves.

---

exception should be noted. During the Little Ice Age, alpine cirque glaciers swelled, and even unglaciated slopes endured deeper, longer-lasting snow. Particularly in mid-elevation bowls, subalpine forest was erased by never-melting snow fields. With the warming climate of recent decades, conifers and alder are recovering lost ground. Succession takes longer at high elevation, but in some locations, thickets of Sitka alder, and scattered young conifers may represent successional stages in return of subalpine forest to pre-Little Ice Age elevations.

Alpine tundra—Alaskans commonly apply the misleading term "alpine" to any open slope above forest limit. But moist fields of ferns and umbellifers just above subalpine forest bear little resemblance to genuine alpine tundra, which is often hundreds of feet higher, with drier, thinner snow cover, often blown away by violent wind. Alpine plants are more tolerant of desiccation than those of subalpine meadows, sheltered under deep snow throughout the winter.

The ability of wind to redistribute snow makes microtopography important in the alpine zone, creating a vivid mosaic of tiny communities with crisp boundaries. In a small hollow where snowdrifts persist throughout winter, plants such as mountain marsh-marigold may be tender and succulent. Immediately next to this late-snowbed community, on ridges or prominences, winter conditions can be so harsh that ground is quite barren of plants except in lee of boulders. This drier alpine habitat is referred to as fellfield. Creeping leathery-leaved plants such as alpine azalea, and cushion plants such as moss campion, are the only rooted survivors. Lichens such as rock tripe, yellow map lichen, and whiteworm lichen cling to rock and gravel.

But the classic alpine tundra of Southeast Alaska is the heath community of low woody-stemmed plants such as white and Alaska moss heathers, yellow mountain-heather, crowberry, arctic willow, dwarf blueberry, and bog blueberry. Tough plants such as partridgefoot, Alaska saxifrage, sibbaldia, and mountain sagewort are also found among the heathers. Almost all large mammals of Southeast Alaska travel the high alpine ridges at times, but most forage elsewhere. Lower subalpine meadows are more productive habitats for such creatures as Sitka deer, or brown and black bears.

The ultimate mountaineers are mountain goats, so bound to craggy refuges that they languish and die in captivity. Wolverines and wolves are also tundra travelers, tracing alpine ridges. Our most successful alpine nester is American pipit. Like the less common gray-crowned rosy-finch, it often feeds on sluggish

Above: American pipit is the most successful songbird nesting on the ground in the rainy Southeast alpine. • **Left**: *Oreamnos americanus* should probably not be called the mountain "goat." It's more closely related to the European chamois and even the bighorn sheep than to the familiar domestic goat.

Clockwise: Alpine ridges are highways for wide-ranging predators such as wolves and wolverines. • In winter plumage, rock ptarmigan can be distinguished from willow and white-tailed ptarmigan by a dark bar through the eye. • Common plants of the alpine tundra include broad-petalled gentian (*Gentiana platypetala*), yellow mountain-heather (*Phyllodoce glanduliflora*), and Alaska moss heather (*Harrimanella stelleriana*).

insects lying on summer snow patches. Male rock ptarmigan often sit atop prominences, entertaining us with display flights and strange nasal cackles. At times the alpine ridgetops become fair-weather hangouts for large collections of eagles and rowdy ravens ascending on thermals. We can't explain their presence in terms of food. Perhaps like us, they just enjoy the freedom of the hills.

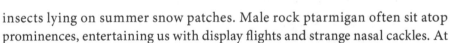

Streams, rivers, and lakes

A subalpine snowpatch melts in the heat of June. Along its downslope margin, trickles merge and drop into a tiny ravine, carrying water at high speed toward the ocean 3,000 feet below. This headwater stream, which hydrologists call "first order," is abrupt and businesslike, with none of the lazy meanders of its final lowland reaches. A mountain stream, it contains many aquatic insects crawling about the pebbles and stones, but lacks fish.

A very different first-order stream emerges from a spring on lower forested slopes. Fed by groundwater, this forest stream supports plentiful aquatic liverworts, a sign that water temperatures remain just above freezing in all but the harshest winters. This type of stream also has a relatively stable water flow, unlike those more directly tied to whims of rainfall and snowmelt. Adult coho salmon and Dolly Varden char struggle almost to its spring-fed source to spawn in the most stable environment our streams have to offer. Here their eggs and yolk-sac young can incubate and grow, protected from extremes of temperature and gully-washer floods.

Where the mountain snow-melt stream and the forest spring-fed stream merge, a "second-order" stream is created. Where two second-order streams meet, a third-order stream begins, and so on. At each graduation in stream order, physical and biological properties change.

Forest streams—Small first- and second-order streams are heavily influenced by their forest surroundings. Uppermost headwater reaches usually don't have the brushy, deciduous margins of more powerful channels downstream. The shade of overarching conifer branches may prevent strong sunlight from reaching the stream, keeping the water cool. Mosses and liverworts are the only common plants within the channel.

The food base in these small streams derives largely from tree and shrub litter, rather than from plants that grow in the water. Invertebrates make their living by devouring wood, bark, and needles. Trees lie where they fall, since the stream

Two mosses found in rain-forest streams. Common water moss (*Fontinalis antipyretica*, left) grows in beds of slow-moving streams. Streamside moss (*Scouleria aquatica*, right) blankets boulders on margins of fast, sediment-laden streams and rivers.

is too small to move them. Down logs reach from bank to bank, forming small pools where organic and fine mineral sediments collect.

Pools and riffles—Between the pools are riffles, where faster currents scour beds of cobbles and gravel. The frequent pool-riffle alternation in first- and second-order streams results in a stepped downstream profile, which detains organic matter long enough to be efficiently used by invertebrate residents. For spawning and rearing fish, channel stability is just as important as high productivity. And in some situations, small old-growth streams offer fish the best of both worlds.

When first- and second-order streams pass over slopes of gentle gradient, beaver may find opportunities to dam short reaches. Here water surface area is vastly increased, sunlight warms the water, and a fringe of brush develops. By dragging streamside brush into the pools, beaver provide cover for fry and fingerlings. Beaver ponds scattered along an otherwise shady old-growth stream can enhance both stability and productivity for rearing fish.

Deposition—Downslope, as stream order increases, the creek exerts more influence on its surroundings. Instead of being confined to a narrow channel eroded into till or bedrock, it spreads out. During extreme high flows, sediments are deposited over neighboring floodplains, which widen to include more and more terrestrial habitats as streams become rivers. This alluvium, or water-sorted material, actually dictates the type of forest growing there. In Southeast Alaska our largest spruce forests are found on river-bottom floodplains and on steeper alluvial fans. Closer to the channel on regularly flooded sites, a deciduous fringe develops with red and Sitka alder, willows, black cottonwood, and berry bushes such as

Above: Two first-order streams combine to form a second-order channel. Two second-orders form a third-order, and so forth.

Near right: Mayfly with nymph.

Far right: Stonefly with nymph.

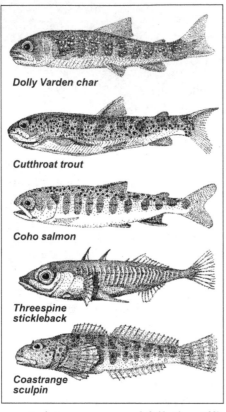

Dolly Varden char

Cutthroat trout

Coho salmon

Threespine
stickleback

Coastrange
sculpin

Left: Fish that rear in Southeast streams. (All use saltwater as well.)

Below: Marsh-marigold *(Caltha palustris)* occupies a range of aquatic habitats, from still-water ponds to banks of gently moving streams.

devil's club, salmonberry, and stink currant. Exposed to the sun, these streamside communities bustle with insects and songbirds and annually dump a nutritious load of leaves into the stream.

In third- and fourth-order streams, fallen logs may still span the channel, but here the greater volume of water is capable of dislodging them during storms, sweeping them down into debris jams. Pools become scarcer, and riffles dominate. These medium-sized channels are less stable than small first- and second-order streams, where logs may lie in place for many decades.

In late summer and fall, the riffle areas are hotbeds of biological turmoil. Pink and chum salmon, often in the thousands, compete with one another for a piece of stream substrate in which to excavate their nests and deposit their eggs. Male salmon fight over spawning rights. Wave upon wave of new salmon enter the riffle areas, only to dig up previously buried eggs with their nest-building activities. Dolly Varden char and sculpins dart about gorging themselves on these dug-up eggs. Gulls and bald eagles squawk and scream over the right to share in the bounty of the dead and dying salmon. Mergansers swim quietly through the turmoil, picking up eggs and small fish attracted to the eggs. On occasion the scene may be disrupted by a brown bear plunging after a salmon, or augmented by a mink, river otter, American dipper, belted kingfisher, or great blue heron.

Yellow warblers captured at a stream-side banding station. Male on left; female on right. In Southeast, this species seems to prefer riparian willow.

Stream plants—In larger, sunnier channels, algae make greater photosynthetic contributions. Cobbles of fast mountain streams are optimum sediment size for diatoms and green algae, which can quickly form a slippery coating over the rocks. As strands lengthen, they're constantly trimmed by current and washed downstream. In gentler reaches downstream, finer sediments accumulate in eddies and quiet backwaters. Vascular plants such as speedwell, yellow marsh-marigold, forget-me-not, and yellow monkey-flower spread leaves and flowers over shallow margins. On the bottom in center channel, white water crowfoot and common water moss provide excellent fish cover and support microcommunities of aquatic insects and epiphytic algae. Along the slowest and most sedate streams, plants characteristic of freshwater marshes and wet meadows may be found.

Meanders—Larger streams have more room to move. A deflected current cuts into the bank, steepening it and even undermining roots of trees. Continuing downstream, the water is thrown onto the opposite bank, eroding there too, eventually creating a series of meanders in the channel. Sediments mined from steep outer bends are deposited on the inner bends where the current slows. Meanders offer a range of conditions for stream inhabitants: fast and slow currents, shady

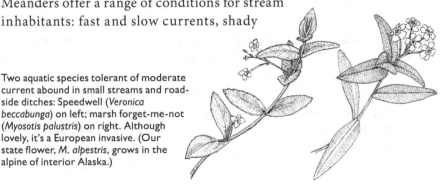

Two aquatic species tolerant of moderate current abound in small streams and roadside ditches: Speedwell (*Veronica beccabunga*) on left; marsh forget-me-not (*Myosotis palustris*) on right. Although lovely, it's a European invasive. (Our state flower, *M. alpestris*, grows in the alpine of interior Alaska.)

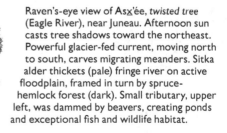

Raven's-eye view of Asx̱'ée, *twisted tree* (Eagle River), near Juneau. Afternoon sun casts tree shadows toward the northeast. Powerful glacier-fed current, moving north to south, carves migrating meanders. Sitka alder thickets (pale) fringe river on active floodplain, framed in turn by spruce-hemlock forest (dark). Small tributary, upper left, was dammed by beavers, creating ponds and exceptional fish and wildlife habitat.

undercuts and sunny shallows, warm and cold waters, gravel and silt bottoms. On larger meandering streams, steepened outer bends are overhung by spruce and hemlock, while bars on inner bends are colonized by younger deciduous shrub thickets.

On fifth-order and larger rivers, logs no longer span the channel and are piled on banks during high flows. This is a further step in liberation of the stream from the surrounding forest. Gradient typically decreases, and current slows except during high flows. The bed is now largely composed of sand and silt.

Estuaries—Where rivers meet the sea, their sediments create rich intertidal marshlands in the heads of bays, or delta formations protruding from more exposed shorelines. These estuarine salt marshes are focal points for many residents of the watershed.

Glacial watersheds—At first glance, turbid glacial lakes and rivers appear to be rather sterile environments. Since we can't see into the water, we assume that not much lives there. However, with nets and traps, biologists discover that these murky waters abound with fish and insects. Numerous Dolly Varden and some cutthroat trout were found in Juneau's Mendenhall Lake during a study in the 1980s by the Alaska Department of Fish and Game. Most were caught near shore at depths less than fifteen feet. The fish began entering the lake in early August and left between March and May the following year.

We believe that most glacial lakes with access to the sea are used by Dolly Varden char for overwintering. The high water turbidity and many months of ice cover make them sanctuaries offering a nearly predator-free environment. The low water temperature means the fish need little food to maintain themselves. We have generally noted that Dolly Varden obtained from Mendenhall Lake in March appear about as plump as when they entered the previous summer.

Glacial rivers are used by fish for spawning, rearing of young, overwintering, and as a highway to clearwater tributaries. Usually when salmon spawn in the main channels of glacial rivers, it is near sources of groundwater or springs. For instance, up to 500,000 chum salmon spawn in spring-fed upwellings where Gathéeni, *sockeye stream* (Tsirku River) meets Jilkáat, *cache* (Chilkat River) near Tlákw.aan, *eternal village* (Klukwan). In silty glacial rivers, as in clearwater rivers and streams, undercut banks, log jams, and backwaters abound with young coho salmon and Dolly Varden char. Most king salmon young rear for one year among log jams and side channels of mainland river systems fed mostly by glacial waters.

Eulachon usually choose lower portions of glacial rivers for spawning. Their eggs are adhesive and lie exposed, usually on a substrate of coarse sand and pea-sized gravel. Perhaps potential predators may have difficulty seeing the tiny eggs in the silty water.

Lake systems—Lake-dominated systems are essential for certain species of fish. Sockeye salmon and cutthroat, rainbow trout, and steelhead are almost always associated with lakes. Most sockeye young live for one or two years in lakes or beaver ponds, fattening on abundant zooplankton before heading out to sea. Resident cutthroat trout live year-round in lakes, and sea-run cutthroat overwinter in them. Outlets of lakes provide a more stable environment, as lakes buffer periods of heavy rainfall, gradually releasing the accumulations. This seems to be important for steelhead, which usually choose lake outlets for spawning and rearing of young. Kokanee, a nonmigratory form of sockeye salmon, are found only in lakes. These small fish, in turn, provide excellent forage for the larger cutthroat trout. Many of the lake-dominated systems in Southeast provide some of our finest and most diverse sportfishing. Near Ketchikan, for instance, the watershed of Nàa.áa, *distant lake* (Naha River) contains high mountain lakes with stocked Arctic grayling, landlocked lakes with

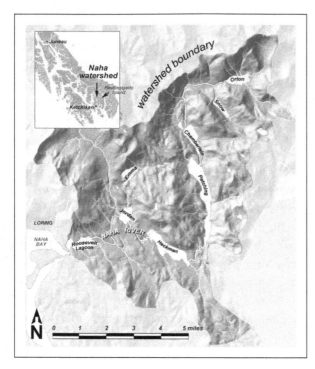

Naha watershed has seven valley-bottom lakes, a saltwater lagoon, and high mountain lakes in cirque basins. Bedrock is productive phyllite and schist. Alaska's tallest known Sitka spruce (250 ft) was measured here by the Landmark Trees Project.

large trophy-sized cutthroat trout, lakes and associated streams with sockeye, coho, chum, and pink salmon, both sea-run cutthroat trout and Dolly Varden, and a large river with an excellent run of steelhead. In the late 1970s the Alaska Department of Fish and Game's Division of Sport Fish submitted to the Forest Service a list of quality fishing waters that should be preserved from logging and other types of development. Almost all of these quality watersheds were lake-dominated systems.

Transboundary rivers—Southeast Alaska's largest rivers originate on interior plateaus of British Columbia and the Yukon Territory. The Stikine, Taku, and Alsek Rivers drain vast areas and form major biological pathways from Canada

The border-busters

Shouldering through the AK-BC border ranges southeast of Yakutat, the Tatshenshini-Alsek River is one of our great transboundary corridors. Quaking aspen (drawing, river-edge) are found only in the driest corners of Southeast, but abound just across our borders, where clones resprout from surviving roots after fire. The ubiquity of fire and flood throughout the Tat/Alsek bottomland creates a mosaic of young distur-

bance forests. White spruces (*Picea glauca*) in mid-distance indicate longer fire-return interval.

Aalséi<u>x</u> means *resting*. T'áchán shahéeni means *stinking king salmon at headwaters*, originally applied only to Blanchard River, tributary to the Tatshenshini.

Center: Western tanager.

Right: Warbling vireo. These song-birds are uncommon in Southeast Alaska, except along trans-boundary rivers.

Above: Rough-skinned newt. Recent observations suggest a connection to river corridors.

through the coastal mountains to Southeast Alaska. For example, the Stikine River drains an area of 20,000 square miles and snakes its way seaward for about four hundred miles from headwaters in northern British Columbia. Shtax'héen has conflicting translations, all fascinating. One is *water biting itself*, as in a dog chasing its tail.

Many species use these great rivers as migratory highways. The most obvious mammal to enter Southeast from Canada by way of rivers is the moose. Moose populations are now established in lower valleys of the Alsek, Chilkat, Taku, Stikine, and Unuk Rivers.

Several species of birds regularly make their way to Southeast through these major river valleys, among them the pied-billed grebe, American bittern, warbling vireo, and western tanager. Others new (exotic) to Alaska no doubt arrive here in the same way. The green heron, Virginia rail, orchard oriole, rose-breasted grosbeak, swamp sparrow, and house sparrow probably came from Canada, where they commonly breed.

Records of some species of freshwater fish in Southeast come mostly from major river systems: pygmy whitefish, round whitefish, longnose sucker, burbot, and slimy sculpin, for example. With just a few exceptions, all king salmon that spawn in Southeast utilize mainland rivers. Our best-producing king salmon rivers are the Stikine, Taku, and Alsek.

Most amphibians found in Southeast occur within or near the major river valleys (spotted frog, wood frog, long-toed salamander). Even the widespread western toad and rough-skinned newt may have entered Southeast via transboundary rivers. Except for a few presumed transplants, Alaska's sole reptile, the garter snake, has been sighted only along banks of the Taku and Stikine Rivers.

Marshes and wet meadows

A nondescript rodent swims through puddled marsh water and hauls out on a sedge hummock near the runway at the Haines Airport. The meadow vole (*Microtus pennsylvanicus*) is the most widespread vole in North America, but in Southeast Alaska, it's restricted mostly to large mainland river valleys. Its claim to fame is its staggering reproductive ability, and this soaked individual is one of a legion, at the peak of their three- to four-year cycle. As it kicks the water from its gray pelage, the vole is pinned to the sedges by a short-eared owl. Migrating birds of prey are quick to notice dense populations of voles, and linger for days, refueling. These freshwater wetlands bordering the Chilkat River host other mousers such as northern harriers, American kestrels, and northern shrikes. Larger hunters such as northern goshawks may even snatch a muskrat from the banks of meandering creeks. Chest-deep in the marsh, a cow moose calmly raises a snout full of pondweed as the roar of a climbing plane overwhelms the songs of warblers.

Classifying wetlands—Wetlands are edge communities, neither wholly aquatic nor upland. Aquatic habitats, according to the US Fish and Wildlife Service, are covered by water more than six feet deep. Upland sites, at the other extreme, are characterized by well-drained soils. Wetlands are in between, in areas of poor drainage. Because permits for development often hinge on wetland delineation, the vocabulary of wetland types has become rather precise.

Southeast Alaska's freshwater wetlands may be subdivided into wet meadows, marshes, swamps, peatlands, and forested wetlands. Wet meadows and marshes are relatively young communities dominated by soft-stemmed herbaceous plants. Marshes have at least several inches of standing water, while wet meadows simply have waterlogged soils through much of the year. Swamps are wetlands with trees. In Southeast Alaska the term "swamp" is usually reserved for beaver-flooded wetlands with snags of drowned spruces, which typically stand for several decades before toppling.

Sphagnum bogs and sedge fens (together called peatlands,

Small-fruit bulrush (*Scirpus microcarpus*).

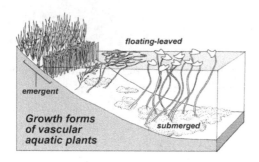

Growth forms of vascular aquatic plants

Aquatic plants can be classified by rooting position relative to the often-fluctuating water level, and whether stems are stiff and freestanding (emergents). Submerged and floating-leaved plants have limp, usually hollow stems and rely on water to float them.

or, colloquially, muskeg) are ancient freshwater wetlands with deep peat accumulating during thousands of years of wetland succession. Peatlands are very different from more frequently disturbed marshes and wet meadows, and are discussed in the following section. Forested wetlands comprise a substantial portion of the vast Southeast conifer forest. To distinguish them from upland forest according to specifications of the US Corps of Engineers, delineators study soil pits and map indicator species such as skunk cabbage.

Aquatic plants—Water depth determines plant growth form. This is best illustrated on gently shoaling margins of muddy-bottomed lakes and ponds. With increasing depth, species grade from stiff, upright emergents, to limp but buoyant floating-leaved plants, to those entirely submerged.

Emergent plants are rooted in mud and partially covered by shallow water. Stems, leaves, and flowers project above the water. Some are tall and grasslike with narrow leaves, such as the tussock-forming water sedge and small-fruit bulrush. Like swamp horsetail and common mare's-tail, these emergents may form almost pure stands. Water hemlock is scattered through many young wetlands. Buckbean is an emergent in both young marshes and ancient peatlands.

Floating-leaved plants may either be rooted in the bottom or supported freely without anchorage. Yellow pond-lily is a frequent community dominant. Narrow-leaved bur-reed may also blanket the surface of small shallow ponds. Pondweed, a cross between floating and submerged plant structure, is excellent waterfowl food.

Submerged plants have little need of the stiff supporting fibers found in upright terrestrial plants. Their stems and leaves are succulent and pliable, which increases palatability to waterfowl. The plants are often hollow-stemmed, which buoys them up in water and circulates oxygen. They lack the hard protective outer skin (cuticle), which in terrestrial plants prevents water loss, absorbing dissolved gases through their entire surface. Leaves tend to be small and

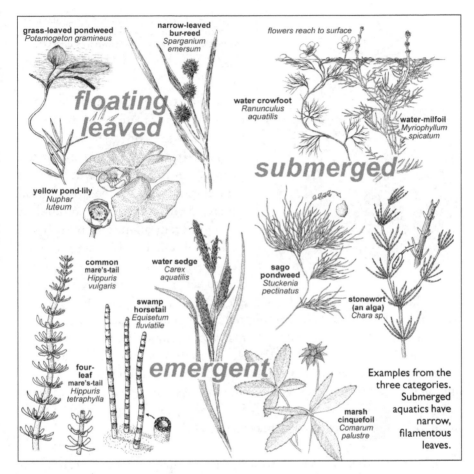

grass-leaved pondweed
Potamogeton gramineus

narrow-leaved
bur-reed
*Sparganium
emersum*

flowers reach to surface

water crowfoot
*Ranunculus
aquatilis*

water-milfoil
*Myriophyllum
spicatum*

**floating
leaved**

submerged

yellow pond-lily
*Nuphar
luteum*

common
mare's-tail
*Hippuris
vulgaris*

water sedge
*Carex
aquatilis*

sago
pondweed
*Stuckenia
pectinatus*

stonewort
(an alga)
Chara sp.

swamp
horsetail
*Equisetum
fluviatile*

four-
leaf
mare's-tail
*Hippuris
tetraphylla*

emergent

marsh
cinquefoil
*Comarum
palustre*

Examples from the
three categories.
Submerged
aquatics have
narrow,
filamentous
leaves.

finely divided, increasing surface area available for absorption. Water-milfoil is probably the most common submerged aquatic plant in Southeast. It grows in vast patches in muddy lake shallows. Stoneworts are nonflowering algae, submerged in kettle ponds and brackish sloughs. Crusty textured, stoneworts are easily recognized by their meaty odor.

Origin of marshes and wet meadows—In Southeast Alaska, these younger types of wetland are most common on flat, poorly drained surfaces near dynamic, frequently flooding rivers and receding glaciers. Alongside large transboundary rivers such as the Taku and Stikine, beaver swamps and marshes may cover more than half of the floodplain.

Bog buckbean (*Menyanthes trifoliata*) is an abundant emergent in a wide range of Southeast ponds and wetlands. It's a favored spawning substrate for western toad, and a forage plant for black-tailed deer.

Retreating glaciers and the waters draining them create many damp surfaces of fine sand or silt, which precipitates in fairly still waters such as lakes, ponds, and quiet backwater areas adjoining outwash channels. The transitional nature of freshwater wetlands is most apparent on quieter margins of these lakes and ponds, where wetland belts expand or shrink with the vagaries of associated water bodies. Kettle ponds form where ice blocks detach from the receding ice and slowly melt, leaving a water-filled depression. While kettles tend to be round or oval in shape, more linear, cross-valley ponds and wetlands form in swales between recessional moraines. Larger lakes such as the Mendenhall become cloudy with 'rock flour'—particles ground from rock by the glacier. Accumulation of fine sand and silt is rapid in these lakes. When infilling or lowered water levels eventually remove shorelines from the reach of floods and grounding icebergs, a sedge hummock marsh or wet meadow may be the result.

Uplifted salt marshes—When formerly marine surfaces are raised above the tides by glacial rebound, sediment size determines the course of succession. On coarse sand and gravel of storm beaches, drainage is good, and a spruce forest develops. On fine sand and silt typical of protected salt marshes, drainage may be poor. Intertidal sedge flats commonly have compacted and nearly impermeable beds of glacial silt, bound by intertwined roots. Recently uplifted salt marshes of this kind in lower Mendenhall Valley near Juneau now support

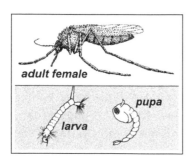

adult female

pupa

larva

Mosquitoes (*Aedes* and *Culiseta*) breed in still waters.

freshwater sedge hummock marshes and wet meadows. Sphagnum moss is beginning to colonize, but deep peat has not yet accumulated. The most extensive freshwater wetlands in Southeast Alaska are found on the Yakutat Forelands, a vast marshy plain of willow and sweet gale on shallow peat over marine sands and silts, much of it uplifted only within the past millennium.

Common yellowthroat nests in marshes and shrub wetlands.

Fish—Wetlands adjoining rivers, lakes, and ponds provide habitat when accessible to immature salmonids and adults of some other fish species. Channels of streams meandering through wetlands are termed "palustrine." These are often deep, with overhangs and excellent hiding cover. Even when inaccessible, wetland plants support a food chain that nourishes fish downstream.

Wildlife—Our salt marshes are famous for waterfowl, but young freshwater wetlands of Southeast Alaska can be equally important to them in summer and fall. Mallards, green-winged teal, and other dabbling ducks that stay to breed in Southeast prefer to nest in freshwater wetlands where high tides can't reach their eggs. In the fall, when hunting pressure is heavy on tidal marshes, many ducks and geese retreat to freshwater wetlands in quiet valley headwaters.

Freshwater wetlands are feeding sites for large flocks of migrating birds. Because the visit may be brief and the site remote, many of these stopover marshes have not been documented. One well-known resting area for migrating sandhill cranes is the Dude Creek flats near Gustavus.

Birds with the strongest ties to our freshwater marshes and wet meadows are great blue herons, belted kingfishers, Wilson's snipe, and several small breeding songbirds such as common yellowthroat and northern waterthrush (both actually warblers), and alder flycatcher. Formerly rare in Southeast Alaska, red-winged blackbirds are expanding their range, and their loud, clear *konk-la-ree* now enlivens some of our freshwater wetlands.

In addition to these wetland specialists, many songbirds from neighboring forests and thickets venture into wetlands to feed. Insect-eating swallows, warblers, thrushes, and flycatchers, which breed in upland habitats, all visit the wetlands, exporting the marsh's superproductivity back to nestlings hidden away in more sheltered locations.

Resident mammals of freshwater wetlands include beaver, muskrats, bog lemmings, and meadow, tundra, and long-tailed voles. Large mammals enter marshes to graze and hunt. Just as waterfowl do, moose appreciate the low-fiber succulence of floating and submerged vegetation.

Freshwater marshes are breeding grounds of the widespread western toad and rough-skinned newt. Spotted and wood frogs, although equally tied to wetlands, are more localized along transboundary rivers. Marshes and wet meadows are prolific producers of aquatic insects, such as mosquitoes, dragonflies, water striders, and whirligig and diving beetles. Our richest salmon streams are usually associated with extensive wetland systems. In a place where conservation concern is usually focused on old-growth forest and coastal wetland, it would be unwise to neglect our freshwater marshes and wet meadows.

Peatlands

The merlin comes barreling out of nowhere, its swift and lethal swoop across the bog punctuated by a soft *whump!* and an explosion of feathers. Later, those scattered brown and white feathers will be all that remains of a greater yellowlegs—a shorebird that nests on the ground in Southeast peatlands.

Peatlands are ancient wetlands. They can be distinguished from younger wetlands by their greater depth of organic peat (at least a foot), which may represent millennia of accumulation of dead mosses and sedges. The colloquial term "muskeg" refers to a complex mosaic of ponded peatlands, streams, and open, scrubby forest on poorly drained land. Peatlands are called bogs when dominated by sphagnum mosses, or fens when dominated by sedges. Because the term "muskeg" lumps these very different habitats, we prefer the more nuanced vocabulary of wetland ecologists. In both bogs and fens, trees are few and stunted, restricted to the drier hummocks. Peatlands have diverse and specialized flora and fauna.

Those who travel mainly by water in Southeast Alaska may be unaware of the many acres of peatlands hidden by the front ranks of tall evergreens, but even a short excursion by plane reveals how widespread they are—a far cry from the situation in the northeastern United States, for example, where botanists sometimes drive a hundred miles to visit a bog.

Bog history—Much of what we know about the last 14,000 years of vegetation change in Southeast Alaska derives from the study of peatlands and associated lakes. Wetland ecologists extract peat cores from bogs. Organic materials from these cores are radiocarbon dated, and unoxidized pollen grains and leaf fragments are identified to determine the species composition of the bog and its surrounding communities. Samples from varying depths in the peat document long-term successional changes.

The question of bog origin and climax is controversial, centering around postglacial successional research conducted since the 1920s in Glacier Bay. There, some researchers suggested that peatlands appeared to eventually overcome old-growth forests, a process called paludification, and that the eventual climax community on many forested surfaces might be bog. Other workers have insisted the opposite—that many bogs are being invaded by forests. The dispute is unresolved.

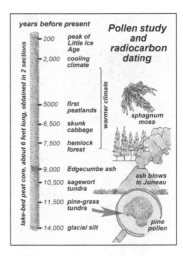

The story in peat. Dated record of changing plant communities.

Peatlands originate in areas of poor drainage. As with hemlock-spruce forests, it took thousands of years after the great ice age before bogs as we know them appeared in Southeast Alaska. In some cases bogs replaced open wetlands with shallow peat, similar to those described in the preceding section. This occurred roughly 7,000 to 9,000 years ago.

Peatlands also replaced forests. Rainwater percolating downward through forest soil carries minerals that accumulate in deeper layers, forming hardpan impervious to drainage. In forest where frequent windstorms uproot trees, soil may be churned and rejuvenated, drainage improved, and paludification resisted. Otherwise, over the course of centuries and millennia, waterlogged soils restrict rooting environment for forest trees, which decline in vigor. Wetland plants such as peat mosses invade the understory. Some researchers even suggest *Sphagnum* is a causal agent of forest decline, rather than just a beneficiary of increased soil moisture.

In coniferous forest, a succession of sphagnum species occurs. *Sphagnum girgensohnii* is the first of its genus to colonize, usually becoming established on

Reddish tussocks of *Sphagnum magellanicum*, slightly drier and warmer than surrounding 'lawn' *Sphagna*, often harbor ants.

bare mineral soil of windthrow mounds, and from there spreading into wetter depressions. In standing water, *S. mendocinum* and *S. squarrosum* may grow. Much later, in open bog conditions, these early colonists are replaced by others such as *S. imbricatum* (one of several green species), *S. magellanicum* (reddish), and *S. fuscum* (brown). These peat mosses not only hold tremendous quantities of water in their tissues, thus maintaining a high water table, but also release acids and phenolic compounds such as sphagnol, which further discourage organic decomposition.

Since organic material is not being decomposed, water of the developing peatland is low in nutrients. Phosphates and nitrates, especially, become critically short in supply. Meanwhile, at the bog periphery, trees may die when roots become waterlogged, and the bog expands. But perhaps it's best to describe forest-bog dynamics as a ceaselessly shifting equilibrium, responding to both long-term climatic changes and to changes wrought by the plants themselves, rather than attempting to label either forest or bog as the ultimate climax.

Xeromorphy—Paradoxically, many plants in soaking wet bogs share features with plants adapted to dry conditions. Bog biologists refer to these plants as xeromorphs, but differ in their attempts to explain them. Acidic bog waters are so inhospitable that many plants growing there can't use them, instead subsisting on whatever rainwater they can trap. Dry-adapted plants should have a competitive edge over those requiring groundwater supplies. Alternatively, the hardened, evergreen leaves may not be responsive to drought stress, but rather to a cold substrate, a short growing season, winter desiccation, or scarcity of soil nutrients.

Among the xeromorphs found in our bogs are bog kalmia, bog rosemary, Labrador tea, bog cranberry, and lingonberry—all members of the heather family. Xeromorphic features found among these shrubs, and also in the closely related crowberry, include thick, waxy evergreen leaves with undercurled margins. Such leaves resist desiccation because their thickness and waxy cuticle

Labrador, or bog tea (*Rhododendron groenlandicum*) has xeromorphic leaves.

decrease water loss from their upper surfaces, while in-rolled margins help prevent water loss from the delicate holes for gas exchange (stomata) on lower surfaces. Stomata of Labrador tea are further protected by a layer of rusty brown hairs on the leaf undersides. In addition, heather family plants have symbiotic fungi whose mycelia live on the plant roots. This association is called mycorrhiza; the mycelia pick up minute quantities of nutrients released into the waters of the bog from what little decomposition does occur and transfer these to the host shrub. Mycorrhizae are also important to the orchid family, including the white and slender bog-orchids.

Another xeromorphic bog plant is cloudberry. Fuzzy leaves of this rose-family plant have short hairs that reduce wind speed across the leaf surface, decreasing desiccation. Such sedges as the water sedge, few-flowered sedge, many-flowered sedge, spike rush, and tall cotton-grass all have exceptionally narrow grasslike leaves with reduced surface area, another xeromorphic feature.

Peat mosses (*Sphagnum spp.*) may have blue-green bacteria, such as species of *Nostoc*, associated with their tissues. These blue-green bacteria are able to manufacture nitrates from atmospheric nitrogen, and these nitrates nourish not only the peat mosses but probably other bog plants as well.

Lichens get their nutrients from rainwater, and they luxuriate in well-lit bogs. Some species such as the reindeer "mosses" form thick mats on the surface of the bog. Others form heavy encrustations on tree branches, while beard lichens and several species of *Bryoria* hang in long strands.

Peatland plants lacking the specializations discussed above may barely make a living. The bunchberry, for example, has deciduous leaves relatively

Foliage of bog laurel (*Kalmia polifolia*) is confusable with bog tea (*Rhododendron*) when pink flowers are absent. It's toxic, however, and those who gather bog tea should learn to distinguish the leaves. Undersides are similarly in-rolled but lack the fine red hairs of *Rhododendron*.

poor in nutrients when growing in peatland, but in nearby forests the leaves are higher in nutrients and are evergreen. Similarly, the stiff clubmoss appears yellowish and sickly in bogs, but a rich, dark green when growing in the forest. Shore pine, western hemlock, and mountain hemlock grow very slowly in bogs, taking bonsai forms. These conifers often have yellowish needles and are susceptible to many fungal diseases. Shore pines, for example, are sometimes parasitized by the western gall rust, which attacks the branches, forming swellings that may girdle and kill the branch. In June the galls crack, releasing clouds of orange spores, which can settle and germinate on other nearby shore pines, thus spreading the infection directly without the alternate host needed by most other rust fungi. Pines might not survive in our bogs at all, were it not for *Suillus* and other mushrooms mycorrhizal on their roots.

Pit ponds support buckbean and yellow pond-lily. Buckbean prefers shallow pools and edges of deeper ponds, while long stems of pond-lily enable it to colonize deeper waters.

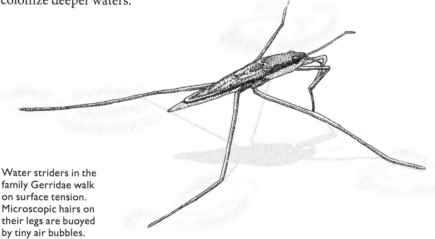

Water striders in the family Gerridae walk on surface tension. Microscopic hairs on their legs are buoyed by tiny air bubbles.

Predaceous diving beetles—family Dytiscidae—propelled by stiff hairs on swimming legs. Adult female.

Insects—Among the aquatic insects found in acidic bog ponds are predaceous diving beetles. These beetles have paddle-shaped hind legs and must come to the surface to obtain air. Their larvae, called water tigers, are predators that often tackle prey much larger than themselves. Water striders skate over pond surfaces, feeding on myriads of mosquito larvae and other insects. Above these ponds, the zigzag darner and other dragonflies form baskets with their hairy legs and strain small flying insects from the air. The Sitka darner lays its eggs in wet peat moss, while its carnivorous larval stages develop in bog pools.

Vertebrates—The peatlands of Southeast Alaska have few truly characteristic birds or mammals. Plant growth in sterile bogs is so hard-won that most species can't afford to be chewed on, and protect themselves with antiherbivore compounds such as ledol, a narcotic in Labrador tea. Relatively low herbivore use of bogs also means fewer predators, although wide-ranging mammals thread the peatlands, as humans do, simply for ease of travel. Bogs do produce delicious fruits—cloudberries, bog cranberries—that compensate for relative sparseness with distinctive flavor. Sedge fens, in comparison to sphagnum bogs, offer faster-growing and less toxic forage for grazing mammals.

In addition to the greater yellowlegs, other birds using peatlands include three-toed and other woodpeckers, who search in rotting wood of dead snags for insects, and such ground-feeding birds as Steller's jay and dark-eyed juncos. Sooty grouse, especially females with young, forage in bogs for berries and insects. At forested bog edges, raptors such as great horned owl, sharp-shinned hawk, merlin, and American kestrel may sit quietly, waiting for an unsuspecting vole to venture into the open. We've seen kestrels and olive-sided flycatchers capturing dragonflies in flight over the peatlands.

Among mammals found in Southeast peatlands are masked shrews and herbivorous northern bog lemmings. These species neither migrate nor hibernate, but remain active all year. In the November deer-rutting season, we find freshly thrashed shore pines, about three feet high and a few inches in diameter, with skinned bark and needles knocked off by argumentative bucks. Perhaps little pines offer just the right amount of resistance to simulate a sturdy rival. These beleaguered shore pines may be a century old. Their slow growth is mostly a result of wet, nutrient-poor soils, but certainly cannot be improved by generations of black-tailed deer using them for punching bags.

Salt marshes

Salt marshes are intertidal wetlands vegetated locally with sedges, goose-tongue, and other salt-tolerant plants. They usually develop on sand and mud deposits at river mouths and in bay-heads protected from wave action and longshore currents. Although salt marshes account for less than 1 percent of our total landmass, there are few Southeast Alaskan birds, mammals, or fish that do not benefit, directly or indirectly, from our astonishing salt-marsh productivity.

In summer 1987, with hydrologist Dan Bishop, we conducted a salt-marsh study on Juneau's Mendenhall Wetlands, to assess impacts of a planned airport expansion. From early morning bird counts, to stream mapping, to soil pits, to seining of brackish ponds and sloughs, we were immersed in the fascinating life of the intertidal marsh. Perhaps the most lasting impression left by this work was a sense of interconnectedness. A salt marsh is a giveaway system; it continually sends the fruits of its seething productivity to

Above: Olive-sided flycatcher hawks from peatland tree-tops for large insects such as dragonflies. This is one of our farthest-flying neotropical migrants, and unfortunately, one of the fastest declining landbirds of the continent.

Right: Greater yellowlegs nest in peatlands but often commute to nearby salt marshes to feed.

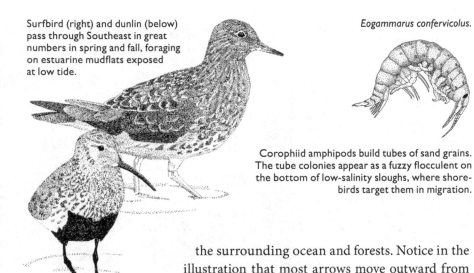

Surfbird (right) and dunlin (below) pass through Southeast in great numbers in spring and fall, foraging on estuarine mudflats exposed at low tide.

Eogammarus confervicolus.

Corophiid amphipods build tubes of sand grains. The tube colonies appear as a fuzzy flocculent on the bottom of low-salinity sloughs, where shorebirds target them in migration.

the surrounding ocean and forests. Notice in the illustration that most arrows move outward from the salt marsh to other systems.

For example, consider the life history of the Pacific staghorn sculpin. This medium-sized marine bottomfish of our shallow coastal waters lays its eggs in February, often under a clamshell, at moderate subtidal depths. By late March, Pacific staghorn sculpin fry begin to appear in brackish sloughs and lagoons of Southeast Alaskan salt marshes.

Until ice drives them out in the fall, these two- to six-inch juveniles fatten in warm, fertile waters. When you see a great blue heron stalking in the marsh puddles, chances are good that staghorns are its quarry. Kingfishers and terns plummeting into shallows carry other staghorns to their nestlings. Mergansers and mink cash in too. In some of our study area sloughs we captured dozens of baby sculpin in a single seine haul. The staghorn fry is a converter of salt marsh productivity into forms attractive to terrestrial predators.

This productivity is then removed. The work of sculpin fry doesn't end up in salt-marsh soil. In fact, salt marsh hardly even *has* a soil. Tides sweep decomposing organic material out to sea. And what about fry that survive? They return to subtidal zones at season's end, eventually to nourish marine animals such as seals and halibut. Salt marsh is forbidding in winter and has few year-round residents bigger than a clam.

Vegetation—Intertidal plants are also an elite group. Only a dozen or so have learned to tolerate periodic submersion in salt water. But the relative lack of

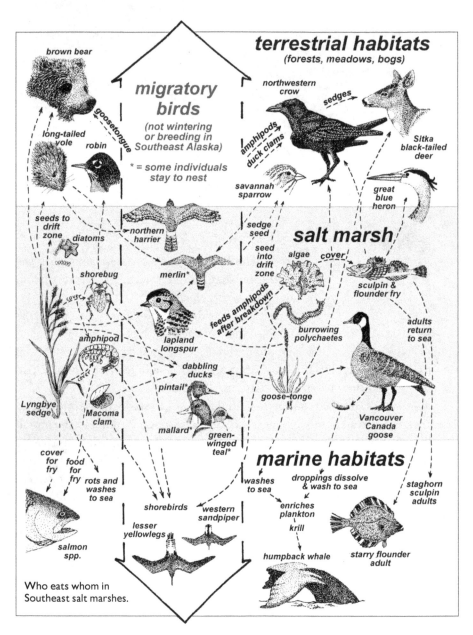

terrestrial habitats
(forests, meadows, bogs)

migratory birds
(not wintering or breeding in Southeast Alaska)

*= some individuals stay to nest

salt marsh

marine habitats

Who eats whom in Southeast salt marshes.

shading and root competition results in annual growth matched by few other natural communities or agricultural lands. Where the marsh is blanketed by fine river-carried silt, Lyngbye sedge dominates. On coarser sand and gravel, lower-growing species such as goose-tongue, Pacific alkaligrass, and sea milk-wort are found.

The basis of salt-marsh production is plant photosynthesis. Salt marsh is like forest in this respect, but with the difference that almost all annual green production is either eaten by invading herbivores or dies back in fall to rot and wash to sea. This annual cycle draws hordes of visitors—Pacific flyway migrants from Mexico to the North Slope, and closer neighbors from our rainy woods and sea. Compared to terrestrial plants of meadows and forests and bogs, salt-marsh plants are tender and mild-tasting. Many can even be eaten raw by humans, with our relatively unsophisticated digestive apparatus. For grazers such as geese, deer, and bear, salt marsh is a giant salad bowl devoid of thorns and woodiness.

Zonation—As in the rocky intertidal, elevation determines duration of submergence and exposure. Few vascular plants can survive below the upper limit of neap tides (the time of the month with least tidal range). In the Juneau area this elevation is about thirteen feet above mean lower low water, or 'sea level' (zero feet in tide books). Vegetated marsh is therefore confined to the mid- to upper-intertidal, bounded by sand or mudflats below, and supratidal forest or meadows above.

The salt marsh itself is sometimes divided into low and high marsh. Low marsh is dominated by sedges, goose-tongue, and Pacific alkaligrass, whereas high marsh is usually dominated by taller grasses such as tufted hairgrass, beach rye, and foxtail barley. For most birds, mammalian grazers, and fish, the low marsh provides far more valuable habi-tat. Throughout both low and high marsh,

Left: Goose-tongue (*Plantago maritima*) is grass-like but succulent. Probably Southeast's best-known edible potherb, it remains tender into late summer, when other plants have grown too fibrous to eat. • **Right**: Blue-winged teal are the farthest migrating of our dabbling ducks, and among the latest to return to the salt marshes in spring.

Above: In gently graded estuaries
of northern Southeast Alaska, glacial rebound is
lifting former tidelands above extreme high water. Mudflat becomes
low marsh, which becomes high marsh, which becomes uplift meadow, and eventually conifer forest. • **Below**: Chocolate lily (*Fritillaria camschatcensis*) or rice-root, is one of Southeast's few
easily collected wild edible roots—once an important carbohydrate in Tlingit diet. It needs open
sunlight and good drainage, so grows best in sandy uplift meadows.

two-way sloughs carry plankton as well as silt and detritus, bathing the flats in nutrients.

At the upper limits of the salt marsh, above highest tides but
below the forest edge, supratidal beach meadows are often found,
especially in northern Southeast, where coastlines are rising relative to sea level. Former salt marsh becomes lush uplift meadow,
an early successional community, eventually replaced by spruce
forest.

Rearing fish—Salt marshes are extremely important as nursery
areas for salmon. Young coho salmon grow faster in the intertidal
portions of streams, where the water is warmer and food more
abundant than farther upstream. Fry of chum and chinook are also
particularly abundant within the marshy areas of estuaries. The young
salmon prey easily on swarms of invertebrates such as amphipods. The invertebrates in turn feed upon algae trapped in the sedges as the tide advances and
recedes. Aside from sculpins and salmon fry, other fish drawn to our salt
marshes include Pacific sand lance, capelin, Pacific herring, threespine stickleback, and starry flounder.

Salt-marsh values sometimes surprise us. By the end of our 1987 Mendenhall Wetlands study, we came to regard what we called "Impact Pond"—a
brackish, unsightly, rectangular dredge pit—as a nearly priceless wetland asset.
Yet it had been created accidentally by gravel extraction! The bottom of this

Right: Lincoln's sparrows usually nest in deciduous scrub, including both coastal-uplift and subalpine parkland.

Below: Ditchgrass (*Ruppia maritima*).

shallow pond was covered with ditchgrass, a five-star aquatic forage plant for geese and dabbling ducks. The ditchgrass beds sheltered breeding sticklebacks and isopods that turned the pond into a nourishing soup.

Impact Pond was mostly filled for a taxiway extension. In mountainous country like Southeast Alaska, flat expanses of salt marshes are often the only level sites for airports, roads, and other human activities. On coastal wetlands we can destroy wildlife habitat or we can improve it—even accidentally, as with Impact Pond. Since our 1987 taxiway assessment, we've conducted dozens of estuarine surveys throughout Southeast, and each one has raised our estimation of the importance of these habitats. Coastal wetlands offer more than building sites and pleasant relief from rain-forest claustrophobia. The muck of the marsh is a gift.

Rocky intertidal

A kayaker, returned from a long journey through the Alexander Archipelago, said that he felt like an intertidal creature. He'd slept in the splash zone at extreme high water, gathered his dinner at low tide, and paddled hundreds of miles with his rear end below waterline and his head above it. He was not alone; most Southeast Alaskan terrestrial mammals and birds are happy to wet themselves in salt water in search of a meal. And their marine counterparts—seals and cormorants and ocean fishes—also dine on intertidal bounty, whether they actually come up from the subtidal to forage, or simply wait for it to drift or swim out to sea. Rocky intertidal habitats compose the vast majority of about 15,500 miles of marine shoreline. In Southeast Alaska, beachcombing isn't a diversion; it's a way of life.

Tides—The seashores of Southeast Alaska are subject to mixed semidiurnal tides; that is, there are two high tides and two low tides per day, and all four differ in amplitude. The tides are caused primarily by the gravitational pull of the moon and sun on the earth's seas. Tidal heights and times are modified by the shapes of shorelines and offshore basins, and by weather. Atmospheric highs can depress low tides below predicted levels, while onshore winds can drive

Nuttall cockle, littleneck clam, and mussel shells in the drift line.

waves above the predicted high. The lowest low tides and highest high tides of each month and the strongest shallow-water currents are associated with the full and new moons; such tides occur in the daytime in spring and summer and at night during the fall and winter. The highest high tides range from about 12.6 feet at Sitka to 20 feet at Juneau.

Marine waters of Southeast Alaska range the full spectrum from about thirty-three parts per thousand to sheltered inland bays with waters diluted by freshwater runoff. River runoff is highest in summer and fall due to snowmelt and heavy rains, and salinity of inland waters is lowest in those seasons, dropping to nineteen ppt or less. Only those intertidal and subtidal species tolerant of such lowered salinities occupy inland waters. Invertebrates living only on the outer coast, such as pinto abalone, purple sea star, red sea urchin, and purple sea urchin, may be intolerant either of lowered salinities of inland waters or of more fluctuating temperatures there. In addition, rivers carrying glacial runoff spew plumes of silt for miles offshore, restricting penetration of sunlight into water, fouling filter-feeding mechanisms, and inhibiting growth of marine algae. Bull kelp beds are more common on the outer coast than inside waters. Decreased plant growth in turn lowers productivity of all other trophic levels.

There are hundreds of macroscopic (easily visible with the unaided eye) invertebrates in the intertidal zone of Southeast Alaska. Here we will mention just a few of the more abundant forms, according to their favored elevational zones.

Upper intertidal zones—Here we find several species of barnacles, limpets, and periwinkles (tiny snails). Barnacles filter plankton from water during high tides, while limpets and periwinkles scrape delicate algae off rocks using a belt of chitinous rasping teeth called a radula. The high intertidal zone often appears more barren and desolate than either mid intertidal or supratidal zones which enclose it. Some naturalists consider it a no-man's-land, too infrequently flooded for most marine creatures, yet too salty for most terrestrial invaders.

Lichens colonize high intertidal and supratidal rocks in the spray zone where mosses and vascular plants fail to grow. Inconspicuous yet ubiquitous black seaside lichens (*Verrucaria*) may form continuous belts on rocks several feet below extreme high water. Above them are brighter splashes of white and orange lichens.

Mid intertidal zones—Extensive beds of rockweed occur in the mid -intertidal zone. Like the upper intertidal, this zone harbors barnacles, limpets, and periwinkles, but in addition has burrowing green anemones, several species of nemerteans or ribbon worms, chitons, snails, sea slugs, mussels, and various crustaceans. Anemones are predators, catching prey with stinging tentacles. Nemerteans are also predators, throwing a long muscular proboscis around their prey. In some species, the proboscis is armed with piercing stylets and associated poison sacs.

Chitons are mollusks with eight overlapping plates on their backs; they rasp primarily red and brown algae with toothed radulas. Some mid intertidal snails called whelks use radulas to drill holes in shells of mussels and barnacles. Sea slugs of the mid intertidal zone include the small barnacle-eating onchidoris, a specialist predator feeding on barnacles. The blue bay mussel often blankets the mid intertidal. It's a filter-feeder and frequently is contaminated with toxins from certain species of phytoplankton, which can result in paralytic shellfish poisoning if the mussel is eaten by vertebrates. Among the mid intertidal crustaceans are several species of isopods (flattened top to bottom), amphipods (flattened sideways), and hermit crabs living inside abandoned snail shells. Many of these crustaceans are scavengers.

Bald eagle nests in tall beachside conifers - crow in young conifers

Brush nesters: song sparrow, other edge-favoring songbirds

Beach nesters: oystercatcher, plover, spotted sandpiper, mew gull

highest tide

Intertidal foragers. When exposed: heron, sandpipers, gulls corvids, pipit, song sparrow

When submerged: scoters, goldeneye, bufflehead mergansers, kingfisher gulls, eagle

lowest tide

Low intertidal zones—These areas also support many species mentioned above, as well as invertebrates not common in mid- and upper levels: sponges, hydroids, other species of large anemones, chitons, limpets and snails, many bivalves, octopus, tiny colonies of encrusting animals called ectoprocts, many species of segmented worms (polychaetes), Alaska spoon

Beach profiles. Intertidal ecology texts commonly show invertebrate arrays. Here zonation is keyed to birds.

While most sandpiper species pass through Southeast to arctic breeding grounds, many spotted sandpipers remain here, nesting along marine beaches and lakeshores.

worms, shrimps, crabs, sea stars, brittle stars, sea cucumbers, and fish.

From one or two feet above sea level down into shallow subtidal zones, dense kelp jungles often completely obscure the rocky bottom. Ribbon kelp and sugar kelp dominate distinctive communities, feeding invertebrate grazers and offering cover for both residents and visitors from the deep. Not until these lowest intertidal reaches do plants regain the visual and ecological importance they held in most terrestrial environments. In upper and mid intertidal zones, organisms blanketing rock are animals, such as mussels and barnacles. Highly branched red algae are common in both low intertidal and subtidal areas, and encrusting species of coralline algae (calcified reds) often paint the lower intertidal rocks, especially where exposed to waves. Beds of eelgrass, actually in the pondweed family, grow on shallow sands of protected bays or river deltas.

The life of beach rocks and tide pools mesmerizes children and sourdoughs alike. Each spring during Sea Week, a statewide program of environmental field trips, grade-school classes throughout Southeast spill onto the

Alaska ShoreZone photos

High resolution oblique still photos and video segments—always taken at low tide—are now available for almost every foot of shoreline in Southeast Alaska. The Alaska ShoreZone Project is a collaboration of NOAA (National Oceanic and Atmospheric Administration), The Nature Conservancy, and John Harper of Coastal and Ocean Resources Inc. This example is Saint Lazaria Island, off Sitka. Download images and data from: *http://mapping.fakr.noaa.gov/szflex/*

Alaska Shorezone Project

beaches, noisy, wide-eyed, variably reverent, and invariably engaged. Maybe it's because intertidal animals can be almost extraterrestrially weird, or maybe because the tidy arrangement of elevational zones appeals to our sense of order, so often frustrated by nature's lively chaos. For many born-and-raised Southeasterners of the past few decades, it was a Sea Week field trip that first acquainted them with the grasped-yet-unfathomable wonders of the land's edge.

Outer coast bachelor club. Three bull sea lions posture and bellow on Graves Rocks, a storm-washed reef just north of Cross Sound. The Hoonah people, Xunaa Ḵáawu, who claim Cross Sound and the outer coast north to Lituya Bay, called these rocks Lakanaḵáa, *tell them by mouth.* This is where the hero X̲akúch' killed a giant octopus. In the northwest distance is Yéil Nées'kuxli Tashaa, *raven sea-urchin echo knife behind mountain* (Mount LaPerouse), 10,728 feet high and twenty miles away. Few places in the world have two-mile-high summits in the viewshed of marine mammal haulouts.

MAMMALS

Southeast Alaskans live among the last remaining healthy populations of 'deep-wild' mammals, such as wolf, brown bear, mountain goat, and wolverine. Because these animals fare poorly near civilization, in the Lower 48 states they're restricted to protected national parks and scattered wildlands. In much of Southeast, they still range freely. And any reader of travel brochures soon comes to associate Southeast Alaska with visibly thriving populations of marine mammals. Breaching humpback whales are close runners-up to bears and calving glaciers as attention-getters in the advertising trade, and seal-pup-with-mom-on-iceberg is another iconic theme.

Sitka black-tailed deer. Male yearling.

Great play; small cast—Our marine mammals and deep-wild land mammals are matchless attractions. Considering only these heavyweights, Southeast must be ranked as a top mammal-viewing destination. In one sense the reputation is deserved; Southeast Alaska—at least to our knowledge—retains its pre-contact complement of mammals, a claim made by few other regions of North America. (We did probably lose one marine mammal long before the first explorer-scribes arrived. See sidebar, p. 135, *A pre-contact extinction?*). While populations of some mammals are lower now than in the 1700s, we needn't wonder about the contents of—as Thoreau once described Massachusetts—a book from which the best pages have been torn.

On the other hand, the Southeast

Alaska mammal list is short by comparison with those of other states or Canadian provinces. Compare our fifty-seven known terrestrial mammals with the eighty-five mammals in Alberta or the sixty-seven mammals in Texas's Big Bend National Park alone. And of our fifty-seven terrestrial mammals, a third are rare or found only in scattered enclaves, perhaps introduced by people, or just sneaking over the borders of Southeast Alaska from interior regions.

Terrestrial mammals

Features of Southeast Alaska that limit distribution of terrestrial mammals include heavy rains, deep winter snows, geographical barriers such as the ice-draped coast ranges, dissecting rivers, and wide marine channels. Another feature is time. Except for the occupants of a few ice-free outer-coast refugia (bioregion map, p. 18), all mammals were evicted from Southeast during the great ice age. The intervening 12,000 years have not yet allowed recolonization by all those mammals that could live here. Subterranean homebodies like moles and ground squirrels and pocket gophers are conspicuously missing; our only true burrower is the hoary marmot, and it is found only on the mainland and nearly-connected Douglas Island.

Thanks to decades of work by Joseph Cook, Stephen MacDonald, and colleagues, we have pretty good range maps for Southeast Alaska's terrestrial mammals. How and when they reached specific islands, and which isolated forms represent distinct subspecies, are still under investigation. One approach is to categorize mammals geographically, in ways that provide clues to points of origin and means of dispersal (tables, p. 94-96).

Ubiquitous species—A first category might be called ubiquitous mammals, or species found throughout the mainland and on nearly all of the major islands of Southeast. This group includes only 10 species. Three of them—the little brown, California and Keen's myotis bats—are undaunted by saltwater crossings. These are currently the only bats for which we have sufficient records to demonstrate ubiquity. Three other species are listed in the following distribution tables. Acoustic monitoring by the Alaska Department of Fish and Game has rapidly expanded the known ranges since 2010, and ultimately all six species may merit 'ubiquitous' status. For now, however, we have not included silver-haired, long-legged or hoary bats in the tally.

Relationships between Southeast mammal groups. <u>Underlined</u> branches are mammal orders.

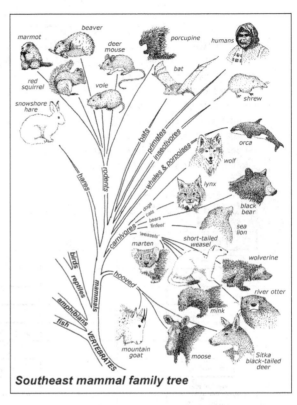

Southeast mammal family tree

Other mammals, such as beaver, Sitka deer, mink, and river otter are nearly as comfortable in water as on land (although sightings of beaver in salt water are rare). At unknown times in the past, these creatures negotiated ocean crossings that isolate our islands. Our most ubiquitous small mammals are the short-tailed weasel, long-tailed vole, and Keen's mouse. While all are good swimmers, their small bodies are challenged by lengthy crossings. Several hypotheses might explain their wide dispersal. Pregnant females could have hitched rides in seagoing Native kayaks or dugouts, as did a shrew we once uncovered while hauling crab pots from a modern fiberglass canoe. They could also have been swept into the water with landslide debris, floating to distant islands aboard resulting log rafts. Such slides were probably common following the great ice age, when destabilized mountainsides hadn't yet settled down.

Mainland and some islands—The largest geographic category of Southeast's mammals are those found widely throughout the mainland, but missing on one or more of the largest islands. This includes seventeen species: seven rodents, three shrews, five carnivores, and two hooved mammals. Most could probably survive quite well on the islands, given suitable amounts of their preferred habitat, as evidenced by successful introductions of marten and red squirrels to Shee, *volcano woman* (Baranof Island) in 1934. Others simply haven't made the crossings.

For some mammals, however, presence or absence on islands may depend

continued after sidebars

Distribution of Southeast mammals

Geographic categories in these tables are further explained in the text. **Ubiquitous**: Mainland and nearly all major islands. **Mainland & isles**: Widespread on mainland and many but not all of largest islands. **North & interior**: Interior species entering Southeast, especially in the north. **Southern**: Postglacial recolonization from the south. **Oddballs**: Distribution doesn't fit these other patterns (*subsp* are island subspecies, not tallied in total counts). **Intros**: Species introduced by people. More complete treatment of mammal biogeography is found in Cook and MacDonald's *Recent Mammals of Alaska* (University of Alaska Press, 2009).

Species	Ubiquitous	Mainland & isles	North & interior	Southern	Oddballs	Intros
RODENTS						
flying squirrel		◆				
hoary marmot		◆				
arctic ground squirrel			◆			
red squirrel		◆				
beaver	◆					
meadow jumping mouse			◆			
western jumping mouse				◆		
brown lemming			◆			
long-tailed vole	◆				ssp	
tundra vole					◆	
meadow vole		◆				
southern red-backed vole				◆		
northern red-backed vole			◆			
bushy-tailed woodrat			◆			
muskrat		◆				
Keen's (deer) mouse	◆				ssp	
western heather vole					◆	
bog lemming		◆				
house mouse						◆
brown rat						◆
porcupine		◆				
LAGOMORPHS						
collared pika			◆			
snowshoe hare			◆			

Species	Ubiquitous	Mainland & isles	North & interior	Southern	Oddballs	Intros
SHREWS						
Glacier Bay water shrew					?	
cinereus shrew		◆				
dusky shrew		◆				
water shrew		◆				
BATS						
silver-haired bat	?					
California myotis	◆					
Keen's myotis	◆					
little brown myotis	◆					
long-legged myotis	?					
hoary bat	?					
CARNIVORES						
lynx			◆			
mountain lion			◆			
house cat						
coyote			◆			
wolf		◆				
domestic dog						
red fox			◆			
black bear		◆				
brown bear		◆				
wolverine		◆				
river otter	◆					
American marten		◆				
Pacific marten					◆	
fisher			◆			
ermine	◆					
least weasel					◆	
mink	◆					
raccoon						?

Species	Ubiquitous	Mainland & isles	North & interior	Southern	Oddballs	Intros
HOOVED						
moose		◆				
elk						◆
Sitka black-tailed deer	◆					
caribou			◆			
mountain goat		◆				
Dall's sheep			◆			
57	**10**	**17**	**15**	**2**	**4**	**4**

less on colonizing ability (swimming or hitching rides) than on auspicious or inauspicious species combinations. Black and brown bears don't mix well on islands. While they often live together on the mainland, black bears are not found on the 'ABCs' (Admiralty, Baranof, and Chichagof Islands), and brownies are absent from most southern and central islands.

The assemblage of mammals on a particular island—reflecting interplay of time, chance, predation, wanderlust, food abundance, and resistance to drowning—has fascinating consequences. Admiralty Island lacks wolves. Without efficient predators, Sitka deer periodically reach high densities there. Certain deer forage plants are highly palatable but, unlike blueberry and bunchberry, are unable to survive repeated removal of their entire annual growth. Therefore, highbush cranberry, willow, black cottonwood, and beach strawberry are all uncommon on Admiralty. And the island's subalpine meadows, packed with deer all summer, lack the rich herb diversity of the

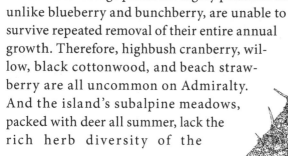

Native range of snowshoe hare is limited to the northern mainland. They do occur on Douglas Island, but because this was an introduction, we classified them as 'interior.'

mainland's wolf-patrolled high country with fewer deer. An island's fauna is not just icing on the ecological cake, but a pervading influence on its vegetative character.

Interior/northern species—A third geographical category is the fifteen mammals found only in northern mainland Southeast, or at the mouths of our largest rivers. These are interior species on the fringes of our bioregion, better adapted to drier climate or deciduous habitats of limited supply in rainy, coniferous Southeast. The Alsek, Chilkat, and Taku Rivers provide deciduous forage and cover on broad alluvial floodplains, and lowland corridors into Canada through otherwise impenetrable coast ranges and ice fields. Curiously, our more southerly transboundary rivers such as the Stikine and Unuk host fewer of these interior mammals.

The clearest example of a mammal unable to cope with Southeast's precipitation is collared pika, found only on the dry side of Chilkat and White Passes. Haymakers, instead of hibernating like hoary marmots, pikas collect herbs and grasses in the fall to sun-dry outside burrows, later caching them underground. Sun-drying green plants in the alpine in October in Southeast Alaska is a futile undertaking!

The interior group also includes tundra vole, heather vole, snowshoe hare, coyote, red fox, lynx, mountain lion, and fisher. Hoofed mammals are caribou and Dall's sheep, each with a smattering of records along the Canadian border north of Haines. In winter, Dall's sheep need dry slopes where strong wind blows snow off the vegetation. Such habitat is rare in Southeast.

Southern species—A botanist could assemble a long list of plants found in southern but not northern Southeast Alaska. These plants probably recolonized Southeast by working up the Pacific coast at the end of the great ice age. By contrast, only two mammals appear restricted to the southern part of Southeast Alaska. While seeds and spores of plants may blow (or fly inside birds) across miles of water, the countless fiords of coastal British Columbia must have been a formidable barrier to terrestrial mammals. It's easier to imagine

Above: Coyote is in the 'interior/northern' group. • **Right**: Least chipmunk (*Tamias minimus*) isn't documented in Alaska but could occur because it lives just upriver in the Tatshenshini-Alsek watershed.

them entering Southeast through the big river valleys than by moving north up the tortuous Pacific shoreline.

The southern red-backed vole reaches north only to Taalkú, *wide-mouthed basket* (Thomas Bay). Similarly, the western jumping mouse reaches the northern limit of its range in Southeast Alaska.

Sitka black-tailed deer could be classified 'southern,' since it hasn't quite colonized northernmost Lynn Canal. Our Alaskan subspecies (*Odocoileus hemionus sitchensis*) is more closely related to the Columbian black-tailed deer of coastal British Columbia and Washington than to the big mule deer of interior BC. This suggests our deer returned to Southeast via coastal BC during the last 10,000 years. Still, after seeing a Sitka blacktail on the Haines Highway in 1989, we decided it belongs in the 'ubiquitous' category.

Oddballs—After sorting native terrestrial Southeast mammals into the above categories, several remain—four full species and two subspecies—that are harder to pigeonhole. The subspecies are small rodents clinging solely to island outposts. The pudgy Coronation Island vole—larger cousin to our ubiquitous long-tailed vole—lives on a few small islands seaward of Tàan, *sea lion* (Prince of Wales Island). Similar isolation produced the Sitka mouse, an offshoot of the widespread Keen's mouse. Short generational turnover in these small animals accelerates response to selection for divergent characteristics.

Although few Alaskans have seen or heard of these 'oddball' mammals, their distributions shed light on Southeast biogeography. Even debatably mythical ones keep us on our toes. The alleged Glacier Bay water shrew verges on 'unicorn' status. Least weasel observations come from experienced naturalists in Gustavus and Juneau but it's so far evaded collectors. Other species are better documented but have puzzling distributions. Pacific marten is the only *Martes* on Admiralty and Haida Gwaii Islands. On Kuiu Island it overlaps with the more widespread American marten. Meadow jumping mouse is a northern *Zapus*, abundant at Yakutat and in Chilkat Valley. But an outlier population lives on Revillagigedo Island.

Are these oddball distributions postglacial phenomena, or do they hint at preglacial distributions, and survival in refugia? These mysteries are explored in the sidebar *Neo- versus paleoendemism*.

Introduced species—Several Southeast species native to the mainland have

Neo- versus paleoendemism

Endemics are geographically isolated taxa. Although Southeast Alaska has a rela- tively short mammal species list for an area of its size, the list of endemic *sub*species is substantial. Why?

Species typically develop through geographic isolation, and marine islands make good incubators. Compared to celebrated speciation on the Galapagos and Hawai- ian Islands, few would notice mammalian divergences on islands of the Alexander Archipelago. We're closer to the mainland, thus more easily colonized. And our fauna mostly arrived since the great ice age, within the past 10,000 years or so, whereas species had more time to evolve and diverge on remote Pacific islands.

Still, genetic studies and skull morphology show differences between Southeast islands at the subspecies level. Neighbor-joining diagrams (family trees) and other genetic tools allow estimates of how long these mammalian lineages have been isolated. As investigations proceed, it will be fascinating to ponder how and when each Tongass subspecies moved into its current range. Most mammals probably swam or floated (or crossed glaciers?) to islands since or just before the great ice sheets receded. The most unique among these recent colonists are considered 'neoendemic' subspecies.

In contrast, geneticists suggest our island brown bears, black bears, and one weasel subspecies could be 'paleoendemics'—mammals who diverged much longer ago than the last great ice age—who on further study might even be promoted to full species. How could this happen on a slate so recently wiped clean by glaciers? Although outer-coast refugia probably played a role, it's hard to picture bear or weasel populations surviving in small tundra enclaves throughout the depths of one or more great ice ages, sandwiched between seas crusted with pack ice and Green- land-style ice sheets.

But the sandwich may actually have been roomy, albeit volatile. Earlier, in *Glacial history*, we noted that Southeast's outer coast bulged upward, exposing parts of the continental shelf that today are submarine. Collaborating geologists and geneticists are slowly piecing together the implications of this fast-morphing coastal tundra plain for terrestrial and semiterrestrial mammals. We return to this deep history in *Brown and black bears: genetics*.

been spread to islands by people within historical times. And it seems probable that pre-European cultures conducted their own transplants, intentional and otherwise. But in addition to this shuffling-around of local species, six mam- mals entirely unknown in Southeast prior to European explorations were experimentally and accidentally released here. One—the arctic fox—has fortu- nately died out. In the early 1900s these foxes, called "blues" in the fur busi- ness, were placed on many small Alaskan islands. Although they persist in the Aleutians, no known wild populations remain in Southeast. Aleutian foxes

Arctic ("blue") foxes were introduced to many Southeast Islands in the early 1900s, but fortunately have not persisted.

continue to suppress nesting seabirds and waterfowl. Even in our area, they likely extirpated some birds and small mammals from fox-farm islands.

Persistence of another introduction is rumored but unconfirmed. Raccoons went feral near Sitka and off northwestern Prince of Wales Island in the 1940s and '50s. A few may linger. Like arctic foxes, raccoons can devastate nesting birds and intertidal fauna.

House mice and brown rats are the 'weeds' of the mammal world. Like their vegetative counterparts, common plantain and sheep sorrel, they've followed European colonists into nearly every pocket of civilization on the globe. So far they seem restricted to cities and villages.

Roosevelt and Rocky Mountain elk were introduced to Etolin Island in 1987. From there they swam to Zarembo and Wrangell Islands, up Stikine River, and onto Prince of Wales Island. Biologists fear that further spread is not containable, and that elk may outcompete and displace native Sitka black-tailed deer.

Although impacts of invasive species are increasingly acknowledged, we often overlook two of the most significant—domestic cats and dogs who go feral, or range unsupervised. Our tracking observations around Juneau show inverse correlation between abundance of dog and cat sign, and that of almost every native mammal.

Marine mammals—Salt water is habitat rather than a barrier for our marine mammals. The most common of them range throughout the inland waters of Southeast: humpback, minke, and killer whales, harbor and Dall's porpoises, harbor seals, and Steller sea lions. Most humpback whales migrate to Hawaii in winter, but a few remain in Southeast throughout the year. Also occasionally seen along the outer coast are gray, fin, and Pacific pilot whales, as well as the northern fur seal.

The sea otter, a seagoing member of the weasel family, was hunted to local extinction, finally protected in 1911, and reintroduced to Southeast Alaska in the late 1960s. Numbers have since risen dramatically.

Unlike humans, a bear's big toe is on the outside.
Left hind footprint of brown bear on Chilkat River.

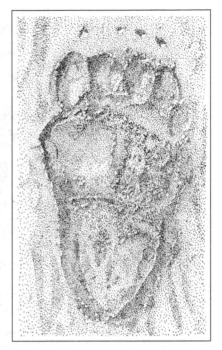

Brown and black bears

Most Southeast Alaskans are authorities on bears. Bears infest our imagination and quicken our love of the land. Comic, ominous, endearing, disgusting, bears are our own wilder selves. When conversation lags, we revive it with bears. There's no need for Sasquatch in Southeast Alaska; we have *Xóots*, brown bear.

Origins—Bears diverged from doglike ancestors about twenty million years ago. Originally carnivorous, they turned to eating plants. Today bears are neither honed killers, like the cats and weasels, nor sophisticated herbivores, like the cud-chewing deer. They have the canine teeth of wolves but the molars of pigs and people. Their carnivore's gut tolerates only the highest-quality vegetation, such as fresh sprouts, berries, and the more tender roots. Predators-turned-herbivores, bears met *Homo sapiens*—herbivores-turned-predators—coming the other way. Each of us straddles a dietary divide, and the position is often uncomfortable. As we do, bears survive by their wits and their penchant for experiment.

Also as we did, bears underwent physical and psychological revisions during the ice ages of the last two million years. Black and brown bears took different bites from the postglacial pie. The black bear is truer to standard bearlike behavior, an agile climber and furtive seeker of dense cover. The brown bear or grizzly has given up climbing except in cubhood, and often uses open tundra and preforest communities. The interior grizzly, once common throughout the continent, is the more typical *Ursus arctos*. Our coastal brownies are the same species, but rather atypical—larger because of salmon diet and a longer foraging season. Big males can exceed 1,000 pounds.

When brown bears moved into open country, females couldn't send cubs

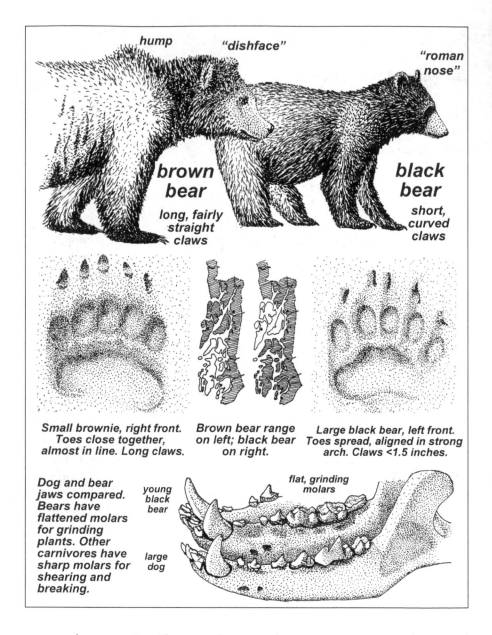

hump   **"dishface"**   **"roman nose"**

brown bear   **black bear**

long, fairly straight claws   short, curved claws

Small brownie, right front. Toes close together, almost in line. Long claws.

Brown bear range on left; black bear on right.

Large black bear, left front. Toes spread, aligned in strong arch. Claws <1.5 inches.

Dog and bear jaws compared. Bears have flattened molars for grinding plants. Other carnivores have sharp molars for shearing and breaking.

young black bear

large dog

flat, grinding molars

up trees for protection. They grew larger, and more aggressive toward potential predators, including wolves, people, and male brownies. A mother black bear, in contrast, will generally hide from danger once her cubs have treed. Most of

Bears and people

Visitors to Southeast usually ask one of two questions about bears: "How can I see them?" or "How can I *not* see them?" The best way to see bears is from a boat or unhunted observation area like Admiralty's Pack Creek, or with a knowledgeable guide. The best way not to see bears is to stay home.

In most of Southeast, bears are hunted in spring and fall. Typical response on seeing, scenting, or hearing a human is to flee. Where bears respond more casually, you may suspect either *habituation* or *food conditioning*. These terms are often misused. Habituation is gradual relaxation of flight-or-fight response, due to repeated nonthreatening encounters. Neutral habituation is what managers at observation facilities strive for. Food conditioning is more dangerous for the bear. Repeated food rewards bring it closer and closer to humans, until the bear is killed.

Unfenced garbage dumps are common near small Southeast communities. Even where dumps are secured, garbage-collection day in residential areas requires constant vigilance. It only takes a few careless humans to keep bears addicted.

Hollywood to the contrary, threatening bear encounters are rare. Still, it's wise to avoid active salmon streams and other high bear concentration areas. Bear spray and battery-powered electric fences surrounding tents have proven effective, if not foolproof. Bear-proof food canisters are required for kayak campers in Glacier Bay, where food conditioning *and* habituation have become unacceptable to managers.

Most outdoorspeople are less apt to kill a bear than they were a century ago—one reason we see many more bears per year than when we moved to Alaska in the 1960s and '70s. As with most ursine trends, that's a mixed blessing.

Clockwise: Standing is for information gathering, not an aggressive posture. • Head down, ears back, not good. However, few Alaskans have confronted a truly angry bear. • Canine marks of black bear, can-sampling in garbage dump. • Tracks in spring snow.

The brown bear's year
1) Emergence Late-March through May. Most dens are in the high country.
2) Spring Bears descend in search of sedges, skunk cabbage, and deer carcasses. Key habitats include south-facing avalanche slopes, fens, and especially tidal marshes.
3) Early summer Breeding season. Until midsummer, bears are dispersed from sea level to alpine ridges. Tidal sedge flats, subalpine meadows, upland forests, and avalanche slopes are the principal foraging habitats. **4) Salmon** By mid-July, most bears move into riparian forests and tidal estuaries for pink and chum salmon. Small, shallow reaches are easiest to fish, claimed by dominant individuals. Some sows with cubs never use the streams. **5) Berries** Beginning in mid-September, bears move into high forest and avalanche slopes for currants and devil's club berries. **6) Denning** Pregnant females are entering dens by mid-October, in roots of large trees or natural rock caves. Males are last to enter dens.

the field marks used by observers to distinguish brown from black bears can also be explained by the brownie's shift from forest into more open country. The brown bear's tree-climbing ancestors, like today's black bears, had more widely spaced, grasping toes, and shorter, more tightly curved claws. Brownies traded these clinging claws for longer, straighter digging claws, and their toes became almost bound together, probably to reduce damage to them when plowing up boulder fields. The brown bear's hump is actually an enormous set of shoulder-blade muscles, also a digging feature. Both black and brown bears will dig, but brownies seem to enjoy it. Shallow scrapes for angelica sprouts in a coastal meadow—the mosses delicately overturned—are usually black bear sign. Brownies collecting sweet vetch roots (*Hedysarum spp.*) leave signs more suggestive of rototillers.

In distinguishing black from brown bears, color may be misleading. Both can range from black to blond. Admiralty's brownies can be nearly black, and black bears are often brown. The elusive glacier bear, found mostly on the northern mainland, is a black bear with a bluish gray coat.

Black and brown bears differ behaviorally, but bears are opportunists and habitual rule-breakers. We've seen black bear tracks twenty miles from cover in the barrens of upper Glacier Bay, where only brownies typically go. And we've watched a two-hundred-pound brownie hitch rapidly up a branchless, thirty-inch-diameter hemlock.

Research—The Alaska Department of Fish and Game (ADF&G) began following radio-collared brown bears on Admiralty and Chichagof Islands in the early 1980s. More advanced GPS collars transmitting to satellites now allow more continuous monitoring of a wider range of data. Although Alaskan black bears are less well studied, tagging and telemetry of Juneau bears drawn to garbage has provided insight into home range and daily movements.

Researchers estimate 5,000 to 7,000 brown bears in Southeast Alaska, with highest density—about one per square mile—on Admiralty Island. About 8,000 black bears are thought to inhabit the Southeast mainland, and 9,000 on the southern islands. However, estimates for Kuiu Island based upon genetic sampling suggest these numbers could actually be much higher. Home ranges of coastal brown bears are about forty square miles for males and fourteen for females. Home ranges overlap wherever food is concentrated.

Telemetry paints vivid pictures of the bears' annual cycle. In spring, both brown and black bears venture onto beaches for fresh sedges, intertidal invertebrates, and umbel-family sprouts in uplift meadows. With the arrival of armed Europeans about two centuries ago, beaches became risky places to forage. Even today, Alaska has legal bear-hunting seasons in both spring and fall. Only where hunting is prohibited—Glacier Bay National Park, for example—can we fully appreciate bears' fondness for the coastline.

By midsummer, most brown bears move to salmon streams. A few females remain in the high country, avoiding the streams where their cubs are at risk of predation. By late summer when salmon abound but have depleted their fat stores in spawning, brown bears tend to eat only eggs and the fat-rich brains, leaving the rest for other scavengers. Black bears also target salmon streams, although brownies may displace them in mainland watersheds where the two species overlap.

Some brown bears dig dens under roots of large conifers; others den above tree line. Average elevation of eighty-six dens located by the ADF&G on Admiralty Island was 2,339 feet.

Mating season for both species is in early summer.

Individual bears rarely reuse dens in successive years. Bears den from about the end of October until the beginning of May, with time of emergence depending on spring snowmelt.

Some brown bears live twenty years or more. The age is determined by pulling a small premolar tooth from an immobilized or hunter-killed bear and sectioning to count annual growth rings. In Southeast, most female brown bears first breed between four-and-a-half and six-and-a-half years. Black bears probably reach sexual maturity at three to four years for females and a year later for males. Brown and black bear mating occurs between May and July, and one to four cubs weighing about a pound each are born in midwinter to sleeping mothers. Emerged females with cubs try to avoid cannibalistic males. Even females will kill cubs of rival sows. On Admiralty Island, brown bear cubs suffer 60 percent mortality in their first year. After reaching sexual maturity, brownie sows generally produce cubs only once every four years. Coupled with the high mortality of cubs, this gives brownies low reproductive potential and high sensitivity to overexploitation.

Genetics—In the 1990s, geneticists noticed that brown bears of Admiralty, Baranof, and Chichagof Islands (the ABCs) were strongly divergent from all other living populations of *Ursus arctos*, and—even more surprizingly—that they had polar bear mitochondrial DNA, inherited through the female lineage. Some hypothesized they were isolated in local glacial refugia throughout a series of Pleistocene ice ages. Other scientists even suggested the ABC brownies gave rise to modern polar bears. Further analysis in 2013 pointed to polar bears colonizing the ABCs, then hybridizing with brown bear males that swam out to the islands. Can we put a time frame on this colonization?

Ringed seals occurred in Southeast

throughout the last glacial maximum (25,000 to 14,000 years ago). Common prey of polar bears today, their former presence in the archipelago reminds us that for an ice-loving marine bear, the great ice age that evicted or created barriers to most terrestrial mammals may actually have enhanced connectivity throughout the entire Alaskan coastline. Did polar bears follow ringed seals to the outer coasts of Dall and Baranof Islands? This is a simpler story than the ABC bears somehow persisting *en situ* through multiple Pleistocene glaciations.

As for black bears, on a hemispheric scale they show genetic divergence into coastal and continental lineages, stemming from separation by the great Cordilleran ice sheet.   Today, those lineages are remingling in Southeast Alaska, but their ancestry can still be traced. The most distinctive populations are around Yakutat and on Kuiu Island.

The weasel family

From largest to smallest, the Southeast Alaskan members of the weasel family (Mustelidae) are sea otter (discussed with marine mammals), wolverine, river otter, marten, mink, short-tailed weasel or ermine, and least weasel. All have long bodies and stubby legs, with five toes on each foot. Fur is

Short-tailed weasel (ermine) with Keen's mouse in Sitka alder thicket.

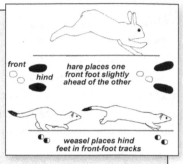

Rule of thumb and other handy references
Because most mammals shun humans, tracks and other signs are essential to students of mammal behavior. Some people even feel that bears leave droppings intentionally on our trails, to help prevent surprise encounters and let us know what and where they've been eating.

hare places one front foot slightly ahead of the other

weasel places hind feet in front-foot tracks

Tracks are equally engaging. When you've graduated from basic identification to story-telling through tracks, the land begins to speak. Naturalist Greg Streveler of Gustavus has invented a rule of thumb for identifying tracks of local members of the weasel family. Footprints the size of your thumbnail are probably the short-tailed weasel's. If the diameter matches the distance from your thumbtip to your first joint, the track probably belongs to the weasel's bigger cousin the mink. Marten are only slightly heavier than mink, but have larger feet for flotation on snow, measuring from your thumbtip to your second joint. Tracks larger than these are probably river otter or wolverine.

Of course there are other nonmustelid possibilities in all of these size classes. Other clues, such as the gait, or arrangement of tracks, must be studied. To teach yourself to track mammals, first learn what species could occur in your area (Carstensen, 2013), then read Mark Elbroch's *Mammal Tracks & Sign: A Guide to North American Species* (2003), a comprehensive and beautifully illustrated introduction to tracking and sign interpretation.

Wolf, trotting. Narrower hind foot overstepped the front.

dense, fine, and valuable. Anal scent glands emit a characteristic skunky odor that serves as a territorial marker and defense against larger predators.

No member of the dog or cat family is so widespread throughout Southeast as the short-tailed weasel, mink, marten, or river otter. Each mustelid species selects prey appropriate to its strength and dimensions. On a good day, a wolverine can drag down a mountain goat, whereas an ermine can squeeze into a mouse hole. Males of each mustelid species are larger than females and may concentrate on different prey, reducing competition between sexes when females are supporting families.

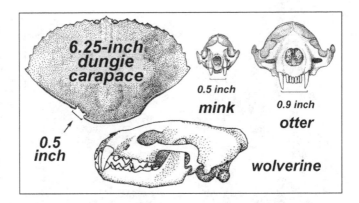

Mustelid skulls and feeding sign. To open a mature Dungeness crab, mink attack the weakest part of the carapace, along the relatively thin rear edge. On this shell from a beach-fringe midden, canine marks are half an inch apart, matching the inter-canine distance on the illustrated mink skull.

Habitats—Habitat specialization is also important. Wolverines are tireless wanderers, fondest of ridgetops and glacial barrens, seeking marmots, ptarmigan, and carrion. Sea otters are so aquatic they rarely come ashore, feasting on bottom-dwelling (benthic) invertebrates and fish. The river otter's diet overlaps somewhat with the sea otter's, but they are more tied to the land, working our coastlines, salmon streams, and lakeshores. And they apparently compete with mink; trappers notice that high river otter populations usually mean low mink numbers. Mink use the same marine and fresh waters as otters, but spend less time swimming. Their scats contain more mouse and vole hairs. The one habitat every Southeast mustelid eventually visits is the beach, so rich a food source that competition and encounters with larger predators are tolerated.

Marten probably evolved as tree-climbers and windfall-denners under pressure from dangerous midsized competitors such as fox and lynx. This pressure is mostly lacking in Southeast, and here marten often risk forays along the beach and into shrublands and subalpine habitats. But most of the year, marten remain in the forest, feeding on voles, mice, and berries in season.

The short-tailed weasel probably uses more habitats than any other Southeast predator including the wolf, since it penetrates into microsites the wolf can only sniff. Its paired line of dime-sized tracks meanders from rockweed to mountain heathers, through densest cover and widest openings.

Ancestry—The weasel family is one of the ancient lineages of the order Carnivora. Two of the North American subfamilies of weasels—the Lutrinae, including river and sea otters, and the Mustelinae, including weasels, mink, marten, and wolverine—went their separate ways thirty million years ago. This was

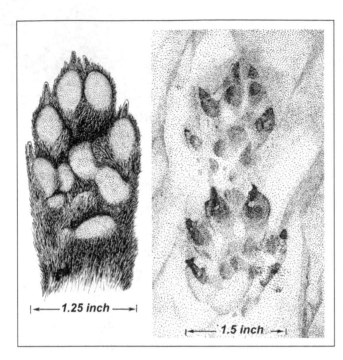

Left: Mink foot and tracks in fine sand. If you disregard the small fifth (inner) toe, mustelid tracks resemble those of dogs. Because this toe often fails to print, tracks should be studied carefully. Remember the palm print is more asymmetrical.

Below: Webbed track of river otter.

before seals or sea lions colonized the oceans, before early bears diverged from the canid line, and before the Hominidae (the family that eventually produced humans) split from the apes.

Still, examining skulls of Southeast mustelid species side-by-side, similarities overwhelm the differences. The ermine skull looks just like a scaled-down wolverine. Faces are snakelike in profile, with eyes far forward. Lower jaws move up and down like hinges, unable to grind sideways. The most unique skull is the sea otter's, which has flattened molars for pulverizing shell, a divergence parallel to that of bear molars from the standard carnivore type.

For their size, mustelids are startlingly powerful. One of the few safe ways to experience this strength is to tie a piece of meat firmly to a string and go 'fishing' for a short-tailed weasel. It takes a bit of teasing, but once frenzied, this five-ounce terror will brace itself against a chair leg and try to rip the string from your fingers. In its winter white, with never a disheveled hair, the ermine blends daintiness with applied fury. Wolverine fishing isn't recommended.

Especially around humans, mustelids prefer to hunt under cover of darkness. But in midsummer, night shrinks to a few hours, and every member of the family forages by daylight. And beach-cruising mustelids are more keyed to stage of tide than time of day. The most observable of our mustelids are mink and river otter, runners of beaches and salmon streams, happy to borrow a fish from your stringer or to scent-mark the deck of your boat.

Reproduction and abundance—Our mustelids give birth between late winter and early summer, so that the rapidly growing carnivore family places greatest demands on mom only at the peak of prey availability. The wolverine, slower to mature, gets a head start, as early as January. Most species mate in summer. As a result, gestation takes more time than the rapidly growing embryos actually need. Mustelids solve this problem by delayed implantation; the fertilized ova remain dormant, floating freely in the uterus until the last month or so of pregnancy. The mink has a relatively short gestation, mating in early spring and birthing in early summer. But delayed implantation occurs even in this species. Most mustelids are capable of breeding in their second summer. Only river and sea otters take longer. Life expectancy varies roughly with size. Few short-tailed weasels live more than a year or two, but wolverines may survive a decade. Litter size averages three or four in most species.

Mink, river otter, and ermine sustain fairly high population density as predators go, and removal of some by trappers may locally depress numbers but doesn't appear to affect regional density. Wolverines hunt beyond the range of most traplines, and are so thinly distributed that few are taken in Southeast. Marten glean most of their food from old growth, a less productive habitat than beach or streamside. But marten are easily trapped, especially where logging roads remain open to snowmachines. In the Lower 48 states, marten have repeatedly been overtrapped, and their current range is much reduced. The Alaska Department of Fish and Game has studied several mustelid species through radiotelemetry, especially where they're considered at risk from trapping or past and pending habitat changes. Studied populations include marten on northern Chichagof Island (introduced between 1949 and 1952), and native wolverine in Berners Bay.

Sitka black-tailed deer

For many, the Sitka black-tailed deer has come to symbolize the old-growth forests and subalpine meadows of Southeast Alaska. The deer distills our vast acres of coastal hemlocks and high-country parklands into one small package of flesh and blood. Deer have received more attention—scientific, romantic, and culinary—than any other local mammal.

Mule and black-tailed deer—Sitka blacktails are one of seven described subspecies of *Odocoileus hemionus*, a species that includes both black-tailed and mule deer. Black-tailed deer, in contrast to mule deer, have smaller bodies and antlers and less strikingly patterned coats, use denser cover, and are less gregarious. Sitka blacktails (*O. h. sitchensis*) have the thickest-diameter guard hairs of the species. The branches of their small antlers are thick relative to their length, and brow tines (points near the base of antlers) are larger and more common than in the closely related Columbian blacktails (*O. h. columbianus*), which occupy the coast ranges from northern Vancouver Island south to California. Sitkas tend to be stockier and shorter-faced than Columbians, but the two blacktail subspecies intergrade on mainland coastal British Columbia, raising questions about subspecies validity

Deer habitats—Ecologist Victor Shelford, in his classic 1963 treatise on geographical life zones of North America, described Southeast Alaska and coastal British Columbia as the "hemlock-Sitka deer-Sitka spruce association." In so doing, he recognized not only the wide range in habitat use by Sitka blacktails, but the major influence

O. h. sitchensis

O. h. hemionus

Compared to their interior relatives, Sitka blacktails are smaller, with proportionately smaller ears and antlers.

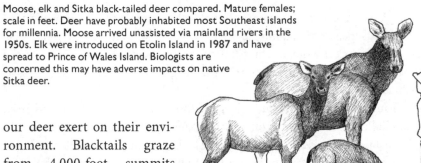

Moose, elk and Sitka black-tailed deer compared. Mature females; scale in feet. Deer have probably inhabited most Southeast islands for millennia. Moose arrived unassisted via mainland rivers in the 1950s. Elk were introduced on Etolin Island in 1987 and have spread to Prince of Wales Island. Biologists are concerned this may have adverse impacts on native Sitka deer.

our deer exert on their environment. Blacktails graze from 4,000-foot summits down to the intertidal. Their activities leave unmistakable evidence in forest, thicket, meadow, and beaches.

In most months, the bulk of our deer are at snow line, following its climatic whims up and down the mountainside. In spring, deer are selective feeders, preferring the first unfolding leaves and sprouts spread in the wake of receding snowpacks. Summer is devoted to replenishing fat stores, nursing young, and growing antlers, and the best place for this is fertile subalpine meadows, where high-protein herbs flourish in almost continual daylight. With the first high-country frosts, subalpine meadow herbs begin to wilt. Deer move down into mountain hemlock stands, beginning the shift from summer herbs to evergreen plants and stems of blueberry bushes. Especially where heavily hunted, deer linger near forest limit until deepening snow forces them down.

Deer and old growth—Logging is controversial on the Tongass National Forest, and since the onset of serious deforestation in the 1950s, deer have been at the heart of the contention. The debate centers on winter habitat needs of Southeast Alaskan deer and consequences of logging old-growth refuges.

In the Lower 48 states, it was long assumed that deer and other herbivores responded favorably to stimulation

Stunted early blueberry bush (*Vaccinium ovalifolium*) flowering in mid-April. Year after year, wintering deer have removed the annual growth, resulting in a stubbled, bonzai appearance. Amazingly, some of these ragged knee-high bushes still muster the resources to flower.

of forage plants in recent clear-cuts, and that "what's good for loggers is good for the game." This idea prevailed in places where winter snow accumulations rarely prevented deer or elk from moving into clear-cuts to feed. As recently as the 1970s, wildlife biologists considered mature old-growth forests almost useless as deer habitat.

As Tongass logging escalated, old-growth researchers in Juneau and Sitka began to challenge this assumption. Here, wintering deer make heavy use of old growth, sustained by evergreen forbs and blueberry shrubs. Multilayered old-growth canopy intercepts snow, yet admits light in summer for growth of forage species. In contrast, early growth after clear-cutting provides forage but accumulates snow, while older, closed second growth intercepts snow but has poor forage. This presents problems on northern Admiralty and Chichagof Islands, areas most accessible to early researchers. In most winters, snow lies deep in the clear-cuts here.

In 2009, a review of data from multiple studies throughout Southeast showed the relationship of deer to forest types is more complex than assumed from pioneering northern-Tongass work. One conclusion was that deer-habitat relations should be assessed at watershed- rather than stand-scale. Another was that habitat quality can't be evaluated independently of predation risk. Brushy, open-canopied old growth, for example, gives deer security from wolves (coursing hunters), but exposes them to black bears (ambush hunters). Predators can prevent deer from using otherwise optimal habitat. In some locations and seasons, aspect and slope steepness are more important than forest type.

Also, throughout the archipelago, and especially in the south, rain typically alternates with snow all winter. On Prince of Wales

Doe and her four-month-old fawn in mid-September. Nursing continues sporadically for another month or two.

Island (POW), snow infrequently piles deep enough to exclude deer from lowland openings, and there it's hard to convince residents that logging is a problem for deer. To motorists on logging roads, deer are highly visible in clear-cuts year-round. Studies consistently rank early successional clear-cuts highest in available forage biomass.

Another surprise is that logged forests are not recovering as rapidly as foresters or game biologists predicted. Few dispute that closed-canopy young growth with depauperate understory is lousy deer habitat in any season. But a 2007 survey of Prince of Wales Island young-growth more than forty years old revealed that only a few stands on ultra-productive karst were reforesting on schedule. On less productive sites, trees are still widely spaced, and forage remains abundant. That may be bad news to managers or conservationists envisioning transition from old-growth logging to an industrial-scale young-growth program (dubious anyway for market reasons) but it's good news for wildlife. It's even possible some of the scrubbier second growth will succeed all the way to old growth without passing through a closed-canopy, suppressed-forage, successional phase.

Throughout North America, deer of all kinds need 'edge,' the proximity of open foraging habitat and dense cover. In most states, where old growth was erased centuries ago, edge typically means the contact between a thick young forest (good cover, poor forage) and a meadow or farmer's field (good forage, poor cover). Edge takes on subtler meaning in Southeast Alaskan old growth. The patchwork understory offers *internal* edges—as one early ADF&G researcher described it—edge chopped up and scattered throughout the forest. A Chichagof-Island doe might rise from her December bed under a bushy subcanopy hemlock, take several steps, and find a nourishing evergreen clone of five-leaved bramble only lightly dusted by snow, while in nearby bogs and clear-cut openings, snow is up to her shoulders!

Wintering deer do best in a mosaic of large- and small-tree old-growth stands, each with a different balance of forage and snow-interception. As snow depth fluctuates, deer move. Large-tree hemlock stands are a relatively scarce element of this mosaic—periodic last-ditch survival habitat for Sitka black-tailed deer. In many watersheds, large-tree forest has been essentially extinguished. In such places, without expensive stand enhancements, it may take three hundred years to recover that particular component of winter deer habitat.

Beavers, porkies, marmots

In order of size, the three largest rodents of Southeast Alaska are beaver, porcupine, and hoary marmot. They represent three different families: Castoridae, Erethizontidae, and Sciuridae. Their habitats differ, but they use those habitats in ways befitting shared rodenthood. Physiques, personalities, and reproductive strategies are also alike.

Rodenthood—A rodent could be defined, with apologies to kangaroo rats and other racy exceptions, as a plump and visually unimpressive body designed to transport a formidable set of curved, chisel-tipped, ever-growing, self-sharpening incisors. The incisor has been for rodents what gunpowder and smallpox were for European invaders of the New World. Rodents followed these revolutionary front teeth into holes, up trees, and under water, thereby diversifying into about 1,700 species, more than that of any other mammalian order.

Reproduction—The incisor patent spawned staggering fecundity among smaller rodents. But beaver, porcupine, and marmot are not prolific. In fact the porcupine has one of the slowest reproductive rates of North American mammals. This may be hard for some dog owners to believe. A walk in the woods with a good porky hound quickly demonstrates the prevalence of this rodent; there must be some advantage to the porcupine's conservative reproductive effort! What are the pros and cons of speedy versus slow reproduction?

Beaver-gnawed cottonwood, left, was partially cut 10 years ago but survived. Bark is growing over the corner of the wound. Porcupine-girdled hemlock, right, was killed—the cambium mostly removed. Beaver and porky tend to target different trees, and for different purposes (construction versus sustenance in this example). But there's much overlap, and sometimes it helps to know how to distinguish chewing signs. Beaver incisor marks are almost twice as wide.

Speedy reproduction is a time-tested solution for species that are short-lived, promiscuous, have many offspring, often with multiple litters per year, and care only briefly for the young.

An often-cited rodent example is the meadow vole, who lives a year at most, and within a month of birth begins turning out litters of about six babies, up to three times per summer. This high turnover rate is appreciated and assisted by weasels.

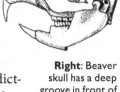

Right: Beaver skull has a deep groove in front of the eye socket, supporting the powerful jaw muscles.

Below: Hoary marmot.

Speedy reproducers immediately respond to unpredictable bonuses like bumper seed crops or beached whales. Slow reproduction is found in individuals that live for many years, are often monogamous, with prolonged child-rearing and few offspring. Classic examples are elephants and humans, but among rodents the extreme cases are the beaver, porcupine, and hoary marmot. These may all live for well over a decade, don't mate for at least two years, have four or fewer young per litter (only one for porkies!), and only one litter per year.

Populations of speedy reproducers wax and wane with environmental vacillation. Slow reproducers seek or even create more stable and predictable habitat.

Feeding behavior—Beaver, marmot, and porcupine have realized the full potential of the ever-growing incisor. Only a perpetually renewed and self-sharpening tooth could meet demands of bark removal or severing of gritty roots, let alone actual felling of trees by gnawing into undecayed heartwood. Wood chips at the base of a twelve-inch beaver-dropped cottonwood are as big as flakes from a razor-sharp axe. And though the work of beaver and porky teeth is seen everywhere in woods and streamsides of Southeast Alaska, marmot-incisor legacy is hardly less impressive—devouring tough willow rootstock and carrying rocks from burrows. As with all rodent incisors, those of beavers, marmots, and porcupines depend on constant heavy wear to prevent them from growing too long to use.

Although beaver and porcupine are considered tree eaters, consumption of inner bark and twigs is only a part of the annual foraging routine. Like most herbivores, beaver and porky shift in summer to juicy, fast-growing, nutritious sprouts. Beaver take sedge tips, pondweeds, and other aquatic vegetation, while porkies move out from forests into coastal wetlands to graze on seabeach sandwort and fireweed, or into subalpine meadows to share the marmot's fare of Arctic sweet coltsfoot and paintbrush.

Use of woody foods by beaver and porcupine is an answer to the same problem marmot solve by hibernating; there's nothing else to eat in winter. The porcupine's treetop escape habitat is also its winter larder. A frozen beaver pond has no such access to food, so the beaver puts down a cache of submerged willow and cottonwood branches in autumn to sustain it through the winter. Beaver and porcupine go into low-energy mode when the snow flies. Meantime, marmots are in almost zero-energy mode. Along with bats and jumping mice, they're the only true hibernators in Southeast Alaska (bears' body temperature stays high).

Large bellies, social life, and the cost of sedentary habits—Portly rodents are not swift. Only marmots can reach the feeble velocity of ten miles per hour. Partly as a result of this insecurity from predation, the beaver and marmot are sedentary, not wandering far from water or burrows. The porcupine, defended by quills, is freer to roam. But alarmed porcupines take to a well-known tree if possible, aware of their vulnerability to people, and to wolves which, when hunting cooperatively,

can kill porkies by biting repeatedly at their unquilled faces. And because its winter diet of spruce needles and inner bark of hemlock is unlimited, a porcupine, like a beaver or marmot, can live on a very few acres. Even in summer we see the same individuals week after week, grazing the same narrow strip of beach.

Porcupine in mountain ash. Falling results in broken bones. One study found their quills are antiseptic, possibly because they so often stab themselves.

The porcupine is normally solitary, except for mother-and-young pairs and brief but spectacular mating encounters. By contrast, marmot and beaver are extremely social. Marmots, also known as whistle pigs, live in noisy colonies for security against predators. The same holds for tail-slapping beavers, with added benefit of close teamwork in dam building and maintenance. Young marmot and beaver overwinter with their mothers. This is unusual among rodents, and allows for more learning and less dependence on hard-wired instinctual behavior. While most young marmot and beaver leave the parent homestead, a lucky few inherit valuable property, with generations of investment in tunnel-digging or dam construction.

But like human civilizations, marmot towns and beaver workings come and go with the rhythms of natural succession. Beaver exhaust supplies of streamside brush near their lodge, and may have to leave the site fallow for a time. And while gnawers and grazers rearrange the vegetation, predators rearrange the herbivores. In areas with few deer, most valley-bottom wolf scats we've examined contain bones and hair of beaver, while wolf scats on high ridges are often composed of the frosty-tipped guard hairs of hoary marmot. A family of wolves can extinguish a marmot colony in a summer, and brown bears excavating marmot burrows make some highland pastures uninhabitable, restricting marmots to bedrock outcroppings or fields of boulders too large to move.

Sedentary habits, combined with formidable appetites, means that our three large rodents leave unmistakable imprints on their environment. Marmots 'farm' the subalpine meadows, as if tethered like horses to their burrow entries, clipping, plowing, trampling, and fertilizing. Porcupines are the dominant herbivores in many Juneau forests, grazing and browsing herbs and shrubs in summer, but targeting the trees themselves in winter, occasionally killing hemlocks by girdling. And beavers are creators and modifiers of wetlands, factors as significant to the pageant of succession as landslides or wave erosion.

Red squirrels

Red squirrels are the most easily detected mammals in Southeast Alaska, due to diurnal, winter-long activity, and loud calls (in seven different patterns according to one study). They're usually most active in the morning and evening, but in winter they go about in the warmth of midday. In summer they have energy to spare, running up and down tree trunks headfirst and leaping ten feet between branches. They can also run along the underside of branches. They rarely fall, but when they do, usually escape injury.

Feeding habits—Red squirrels forage mostly in conifers. In early spring they consume tender buds, and in August they cut unopened green cones from the upper branches of Sitka spruce. To extract and eat the seeds, they hold each cone in the forepaws and rotate it rapidly while chewing; cone scales fly in all directions. In late summer and fall, most cones are not eaten but deliberately cached by each squirrel in its own midden—a large pile of cones on the forest floor—or in chambers connected to underground tunnels. The midden is usually located near the base of a large, productive spruce tree. These cones sustain the squirrel during lean winter months.

In some years spruce cone production is meager, while western hemlocks fruit copiously. Squirrels then shift to hemlock, but collect the tiny cones by carrying off entire twigsfuls at a time. Because of their ability to thrive on Sitka spruce seed, red squirrels fare better in early, impoverished-understory stages of forest succession than do most other local mammals.

In the interior of Alaska, red squirrels collect more than a hundred white spruce cones per day. A single midden may contain up to 16,000 cones. Up to 70 percent of the white spruce cone crop may be harvested. Peculiarly, some squirrels cache empty cones, while others remove a few scales from each cone, apparently checking to make sure it contains seeds. Juvenile squirrels cache fewer cones,

Compare elevated thumbs on front feet to following track illustration.

Right: Squirrel hopping gait. Among climbing rodents, front feet typically register side-by-side. Compare to snowshoe hare gait with diagonal front feet in *Rule of thumb* sidebar.

Below: Flying squirrel is common on the mainland but largely overlooked because of its nocturnal habits.

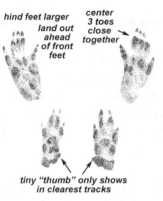

hind feet larger land out ahead of front feet

center 3 toes close together

tiny "thumb" only shows in clearest tracks

which helps explain their higher mortality rate. Red squirrels also cache alder cones.

Red squirrels are fond of sap and may drive red-breasted sapsuckers away from their carefully drilled holes in trees. They also cut mushrooms and 'squirrel' them away in branch crotches. Red squirrels consume even poisonous fly agaric with no apparent ill effects. They also eat small mammals such as shrews, and bird eggs and nestlings. In turn, squirrels are eaten by large birds of prey and by marten. But an adult red squirrel is a formidable creature, and predation (except perhaps by goshawk) seems to be less of a factor in population dynamics than territoriality and food supply.

Range and reproduction—The red squirrel's home-range size varies widely with food supply. It defends its territory against both sexes, striking a brief truce only at mating time. Each red squirrel typically constructs several nests. It builds arboreal nests of twigs and leaves, or grasses when available, on a limb not far from the trunk of the tree. The squirrel also may nest in tree hollows, carefully lined with plant material. Or it may construct a den underground. The squirrel sleeps in its nest at night and may spend several days there to wait out a severe storm.

Red squirrels reach sexual maturity at about one year of age, but not all females breed each year. Of seventeen squirrels we once live-trapped in June, only two were nursing females. Breeding occurs in March or April and is preceded by mating chases; the female scampers away, with the male in pursuit. After a gestation of thirty-six to forty days, three to four young are born in May or early June. They develop rapidly and are weaned at about five weeks of age, but they will usually remain with their mother until about eighteen weeks old, when almost adult size. Lifespan studies suggest only a quarter of all red squirrels survive a full year. Maximum age is about eight years.

Shrews, mice, and voles

Shrews, mice, and voles are the nickels and dimes of nature's currency, eaten by such diverse predators as great blue heron, northern shrike, house cat, and even red squirrel. Shrews belong to the order Soricomorpha and are only distantly related to mice and voles, which are members of the order Rodentia. We discuss them together here because they share a position at the base of the mammalian food pyramid.

Shrews—Shrews are among the world's smallest mammals; an adult of the smallest species weighs less than half a pat of butter. They lose heat rapidly, and to fuel a warm-blooded metabolism eat relatively enormous amounts of food. Shrews typically consume more than their own weight in meat every day. We've watched a two-inch shrew consume an entire earthworm in a sitting, devouring each segment as it was pulled out of the ground. Shrews' diet consists mainly of insects, but includes other small invertebrates such as snails and spiders, bird eggs, and occasionally plants and fungi. The pulse rate of frightened shrews may elevate to 1,200 beats per minute. If prevented from eating in a live-catch trap, they quickly die. This makes them difficult to study, and the biology of most species is poorly known.

Shrews twitter constantly at frequencies inaudible to us as they forage in leaf litter and under logs with their long, pointed, flexible snout. Like bats, they find their prey by echolocation, monitoring echoes of emitted squeaks in order to discern moving objects. Shrews attack and eat animals larger than themselves, such as mice and even small birds. In turn, shrews are eaten by hawks, owls, and mustelids, although a musk gland on each flank makes the shrew rather unpalatable.

The masked shrew is found throughout Southeast Alaska, except on Admiralty Island or Prince of Wales and neighboring islands. An adult masked shrew is about two inches long excluding tail, and weighs about a fifth of an ounce. Tiny eyes and ears are barely discernible.

The female masked shrew bears two or three litters per season. After a gestation of only seventeen or eighteen days, an average of five or six young are born in a nest of grass, concealed beneath a fallen log or rotting stump. The life span of the masked shrew is about a year.

Also common in Southeast Alaska is the dusky shrew (*Sorex monticolus*),

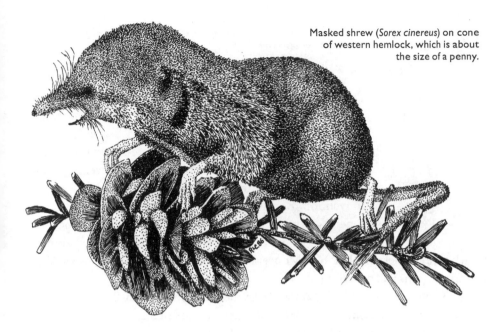

Masked shrew (*Sorex cinereus*) on cone of western hemlock, which is about the size of a penny.

found everywhere except on Baranof and Chichagof Islands. The water shrew (*S. palustris*) is less well known in Southeast, but has been found on mainland lakes and streams. This is a giant among shrews, reaching the size of a mouse.

Keen's mouse—Also called the northwestern deer mouse, *Peromyscus keeni* ranges throughout Southeast Alaska and adjacent Canadian mountains. Even in the hand, only a taxonomist could distinguish this species from the continent-spanning deer mouse (*P. maniculatus)*. Some biologists consider Keen's mouse more arboreal than deer mouse.

Keen's mice are larger than shrews, with blunter snouts, big eyes, and large bare ears. They're primarily nocturnal. Although Keen's mouse looks like a house mouse—an introduced Old World species—it's more closely related to voles and muskrats.

Keen's mice are found on almost every island of the Southeast archipelago. Optimum habitat appears to be edges of

Above: Masked shrew skull has pointed snout and large, hooked leading incisor. • **Below**: Keen's mouse. No canine teeth. Long gap (diastema) between flat-topped molars and chisel-like, deeply rooted incisors (arrow).

Above: Keen's mouse (*Peromyscus keeni*). • **Below**: Long-tailed vole (*Microtus longicaudus*).

streams, roads, and islands, and early- to midsuccessional stages of forest development. The most memorable mouse-density we've experienced was when camped in the middle of an avalanche fan covered in young Sitka alder. As soon as lanterns went off in the evening, our wall tent (which had no floor) hosted a Keen's mouse convention. Backwoods cabins also resound at night with scamperings and territorial scratchings of this lovely mouse.

The adult's coat color resembles a deer's—reddish brown above, with white underparts and feet. Mouse scats are somewhat less lovely, especially in frying pans and coffee cups.

Keen's mice are little dynamos. Their diet is catholic, consisting of seeds of grasses, herbs and conifers, fruits, berries, tender grass stems, insects, and other invertebrates. Like deer mice, they transport seeds to a cache near the nest, for consumption mostly in winter when other foods are scarce. In winter, Keen's mice remain active, tunneling beneath snow or dashing over it, so they're often caught by owls. Other important predators include weasels, mink, and marten. Mouse populations bottom out in spring after the rigors of winter, but after summer's fecundity, numbers are much higher. Few individuals survive an entire year.

Voles—Voles and Keen's mice are in the family Criticedae. Voles have fatter bodies and shorter legs than Keen's mice. Their noses are more rounded, and their eyes and ears are smaller, almost hidden in the fur. Most voles have relatively short tails, and seem less jumpy and hyperactive than Keen's mice.

The red-backed vole occupies the Southeast mainland but not the islands, according to current range maps. Its coat bears a broad reddish stripe down the center of the back, accounting for its common name. Like Keen's mice, red-backed voles are mainly nocturnal, but in summer the hours of darkness are so few that they're forced to forage in daylight. Red-backed voles are abundant in Southeast forests and thickets, consuming foliage, twigs, and fruit of shrubs as well as wintergreen and bunchberry plants. They produce two or three litters during the summer, with an average size of six.

We have at least two species of red-back voles, separated roughly along the

Right: Recently unfolded lupine sprout (*Lupinus nootkatensis*), nipped by long-tailed vole while still closed.

Below: Taxonomic relationships of Southeast shrews, mice, and voles.

Stikine River corridor. Northern redbacks (*Myodes rutilis*) appear to have colonized North America from Beringia, while southern redbacks (*M. gapperi*) expanded northward from ice-age refugia in the midwestern states. There are probably at least three cryptic species of southern red-backed vole.

Several other voles occur in Southeast. Most ubiquitous is the long-tailed vole (*Microtus longicaudis*), currently mapped throughout the mainland and on every large island except Baranof and Yakobi. Our observations suggest optimum long-tailed habitat is beach fringe. As its name implies, the tail is longer than that of other voles—nearly as long as that of the Keen's mouse. Every few years, long-tailed voles reach high population density. As winter snows melt back, vole clippings, shrub girdlings, root diggings, runways, and scat piles are highly visible in flattened mulch of coastal meadows. Ordinarily, though, it takes keener senses than ours to detect the presence of these voles. Harriers and hikers' dogs listen for their high-pitched squeaks and rustlings, while mink and weasel sniff them out. At low population levels, runways are less conspicuous.

Two close relatives of the longtail are the root or tundra vole (*M. oeconomus*) of early successional habitats on the northern mainland, Chichagof, and Baranof Islands, and the meadow vole (*M. pennsylvanicus*) of the mainland and Admiralty. Two species of jumping mouse are on the mainland and Revillagigedo Island. The northern bog lemming lives in fens and wet sedge meadows of the mainland and central islands.

Order Soricomorpha
Families:
  Soricidae shrews
    Sorex cinereus masked shrew
    Sorex monticolus dusky shrew
    Sorex palustris water shrew

Order Rodentia
Families:
  Cricetidae voles, deer and Keen's mice
    Peromyscus keeni Keen's mouse
    Microtus longicaudis long-tailed vole
    Microtus oeconomus root vole
    Microtus pennsylvanicus meadow vole
    Myodes gapperi Gapper's red-backed vole
    Myodes rutilus northern red-backed vole
    Synaptomys borealis bog lemming
  Dipodidae jumping mice
    Zapus hudsonius meadow jumping mouse
    Zapus princeps western jumping mouse
  Muridae old-world mice
    Mus musculus house mouse

Marine mammals

Sitka was a center for Tlingit sea otter trade long before Russians arrived in 1799. Marine mammals remained central to the Southeast economy, in ways we might prefer to forget. When otters were eradicated, facilities such as Port Armstrong whaling station appeared, converting leviathans to corsets and lamp oil from 1912 to 1922. Today, with most whales endangered, they're more valuable spouting for tour vessels than clamping waistlines or rendered into lubricant.

Our living marine mammals belong to two separate orders. The Cetacea include whales, dolphins, and porpoises. Carnivora include sea otters, seals, and sea lions. Some biologists place seals and sea lions in a third order—Pinnipedia or "fin-feet." Others suggest seals descended from the weasel family and sea lions are separately derived from early bearlike creatures that became aquatic. If this is correct, the order Pinnipedia is an artificial category.

Cetaceans—Whale ancestors appear suddenly in fossil records about 50 million years ago. Their closest contemporary relatives are even-toed ungulates such as pigs ("porpoise" is Latin for "pig-fish"). Cetaceans are now totally aquatic, even bearing young in water,

Above: Common Southeast marine mammals. *Locally or globally extinct species in pale grey. • **Below**: Pinniped family tree—times of divergence in millions of years ago. Based on Higdon *et al* (2007).

Order Carnivora
  Families:
    Mustelidae weasels
      Enhydra lutris sea otter
  Suborder Caniformia
  (unranked) **Pinnipedia** fin-feet
  (some rank Pinnipedia as its own order)
    Families:
      Phocidae true seals
        Phoca vitulina harbor seal
        Pusa hispida ringed seal*
      Otariidae eared seals
        Eumetopias jubatus Steller sea lion
        Callorhinus ursinus Fur seal

Order Cetacea
  Suborder Odontoceti toothed whales
    Families:
      Delphinidae dolphins
        Orcinus orca killer whale
        Lagenorhynchus obliquidens
          white-sided dolphin
      Phocoenidae porpoises
        Phocoena phocoena harbor porpoise
        Phocoenoides dalli Dall's porpoise
  Suborder Mysticeti baleen whales
    Families:
      Balaenopteridae rorquals
        Megaptera novaeangliae
          humpback whale
        Megaptera acutorostrata minke whale
    Families:
      Eschrichtiidae gray whales
        Eschrichtius robustus
          gray whale

Order Sirenia
  Families:
    Dugongidae dugongs and manatees
      Hydrodamalis gigas Steller s sea cow*

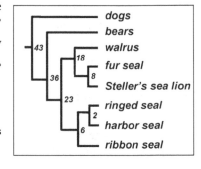

Southeast representatives of major marine mammal groups: baleen whales, dolphins, eared and earless seals, and the weasel family.

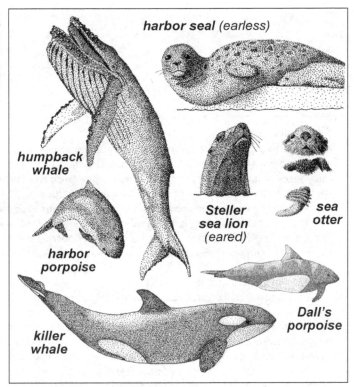

while other marine mammals give birth on beaches or icebergs. Cetaceans have no hind limbs, while other marine mammals retain four appendages, albeit highly modified in seals and sea lions.

Cetaceans include toothed whales—sperm whales, killer whales, and porpoises—and baleen whales, with fringed baleen plates of keratin suspended from upper jaws to trap small prey as water rushes through them. Since baleen whales have teeth before birth, it's believed they evolved from toothed ancestors.

Humpbacks belong to the rorqual family of baleen whales, whose pleats along throat and belly allow the body wall to expand when sieving huge quantities of water. They're often seen breaching and slapping the surface with tail or flippers. A small humped dorsal fin is set well back on the body, and many lumps cover the head and jaws. Much of their skin is encrusted with barnacles, a different species from those on intertidal rocks. These barnacles filter plankton and don't parasitize the whale, but do create drag, so humpbacks come into shallow waters to rub them off on the rocks. Humpbacks lunge feed, gliding open-mouthed through

Sea otters resting in kelp.

Sea otters and kelp

After reintroduction in the 1960s, recovering sea otter populations were closely monitored. Researchers from University of California-Santa Cruz have compiled forty years of data on otters and kelp stands, from Vancouver Island to the western Aleutians, documenting indirect effects of otters on kelp.

Sea otters are keystone predators, unwitting guardians of dense, productive kelp forests—habitat for myriad invertebrates that in turn feed more than twenty species of fish. Kelp forests are spawning habitat for herring and Atka mackerel and nurseries for salmon fry. Sea ducks rest and feed in kelp. Algal forests protect the shore from waves.

Principal grazers on kelp forests are sea urchins, which can decimate stands and prevent regrowth of fronds. Urchins graze freely when sea otters are absent, but in their presence must hide in crevices and eat just the plant scraps.

Sea otters rarely come ashore. They feed, mate and give birth in the kelp, wrapped in algal fronds when sleeping on their backs. At Sitka and Glacier Bay, hundreds can be seen, resting in the kelp and sometimes vocalizing to each other.

In addition to local impacts of sea otter recolonizations, the UC Santa Cruz review pointed to global implications. Otter-patrolled kelp forests can absorb twelve times more carbon dioxide than urchin-depleted stands, thus reducing global warming.

concentrations of krill (shrimp-like crustaceans) or schooling fish. Another method is bubble-net feeding, in which the whale spirals upward, blowing a curtain of bubbles concentrating prey. The whale then bursts through the surface inside the 'net,' trailing foam and fish. Sometimes several humpbacks blow bubble nets in a coordinated group. It's best not to float above a bubble net in a small boat!

Southeast humpbacks belong to the Central North Pacific population, which feeds from northern British Columbia through Prince William Sound between April and November, and winters mostly in Hawaii (although a few remain in Southeast). Southeast Alaskan whales comprise a distinct feeding aggregation within that greater population. Mating occurs on the wintering grounds and pregnancy lasts about eleven months, so calves are born there the following year. Since the calf is nursed for up to eleven months, babies are produced only every other

Whale-viewing opportunities are best in the northern half of the Archipelago. Data from Pacific Wildlife Foundation, and the Alaska State Geo-Spatial Clearinghouse.

Whale-viewing opportunities are best in the northern half of the Archipelago. Data from Pacific Wildlife Foundation, and the Alaska State Geo-Spatial Clearinghouse.

year. Over their life span females may bear up to fifteen calves.

Southeast whale biologists participated in the 2008 SPLASH study (Structure of Populations, Levels of Abundance and Status of Humpback Whales in the North Pacific), summarizing numbers and trends. At that time, the estimated Central North Pacific population was thought to number between 7,120 and 10,425 animals. The estimated annual increase was 7 percent between 1993 and 2000.

While humpback whale recovery is good news, it comes with cost and controversy, just as for crab-loving sea otters. Baleen whales compete with commercial fisheries for herring. Exceptionally long pectoral fins make humpbacks more manueverable in tight quarters than other rorquals. At several Southeast salmon hatcheries, humpbacks perform aquatic ballet between net pens as fry are being released.

Other baleen whales—Minke whales look much like small humpbacks and are the second most often-seen baleen whale in Southeast's inside waters. Unlike humpbacks, they surface snout first. Look for a weak, bushy blow, and no fluke display when diving. Minkes are the world's most abundant rorquals. Although stable in most of their range, they're still hunted by Japan and Norway.

Alaskan minkes are considered migratory—a population distinct from that of Washington's, where home ranges are established. Only selected portions of the Alaskan stock have been surveyed. For example, about 1,000 minkes were estimated between Kenai Fjords and the central Aleutians in shelf and nearshore waters, in water less than 650 feet deep.

Gray whales don't reside in Southeast, but large numbers move past the outer coast between summer arctic feeding grounds and winter calving grounds in the lagoons of Baja California. Once called devilfish for their propensity to attack whaling boats, they now approach tour vessels for chin-scratching. In addition to straining plankton with short baleen plates, gray whales scoop mud off the bottom and sift out marine worms and shellfish, a unique behavior among whales.

Killer whale—The killer whale, or orca, is the world's largest dolphin—at thirty feet, the ocean's pinnacle predator. Seen from a kayak, an orca's dorsal fin is memorable—two or three feet high on females, and six feet high on older males.

Biologists describe nonassociating resident and transient killer whale populations. Resident groups feed on fish and squid, while transients hunt mammals and occasionally seabirds. The term "resident" is somewhat misleading, as pods have ranged eight hundred miles. Resident pods are larger and more flamboyant—leaping and tail-slapping, active at the surface. Summer feeding studies suggest resident pods largely ignore pink salmon, selecting more fat-rich cohos. Some resident orcas are adept at stripping even fattier sablefish and halibut from longlines.

Southeast Alaska lies in an overlap zone of killer whale geographies. For both resident and transient behavioral types, northern and southern stocks meet in our waters. Among resident, fish-eating groups, the widespread Alaskan stock reaches as far southeastward as the Stikine River. Three pods, named AF, AG, and AZ, and totaling about one hundred whales, hunt within Southeast Alaska. The Northern Resident stock (actually southern from an Alaskan perspective) is centered in British Columbia but ranges as far north as Lynn Canal.

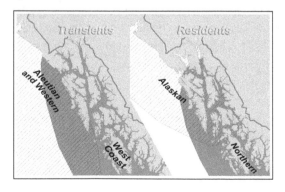

Unlike resident orcas, transients travel quietly, remaining below the surface for up to a mile, usually in groups of five or less. In this manner, the stealthy travelers

According to Allen and Angliss (2013), transient and resident killer whale stocks overlap in Southeast Alaska.

A puzzling entanglement—*Bob Armstrong*
Whenever I have been watching harbor seals and a
Steller sea lion approaches, the seals usually panic and
appear obviously afraid of the sea lion. There have
been several observations in Southeast of sea lions
attacking and killing seals, especially in Glacier Bay, so
their fear may be well justified.

Above: Steller sea lion
lunges after sea otter and
harbor seal. *Below:*
Otter holding seal. Rope
around seal's neck.

One of my most interesting observations involved
a sea otter. While on a whale-watching cruise in the
Juneau area the captain suddenly announced there was a sea
otter. Since sea otters are rarely seen around Juneau she
decided to move closer. Binoculars revealed the sea otter
was holding a seal on its belly and swimming rapidly away
from a sea lion. The sea lion had its mouth open and was
pursuing the pair.

I took several photos of the event. In one photo the seal appeared to have a
rope around its neck. Perhaps it had gotten tangled in a gill net. It appeared that the
sea otter was protecting the injured seal from the sea lion. We watched until the
sea lion eventually gave up its chase and swam away.

It is great to observe interactions like this in nature and wonder.

surprise porpoises and pinnipeds. Harbor seals scarcely react to resident orcas
but on hearing or sighting transients, they either hide or leave the water, sometimes even leaping into occupied boats. About five hundred transient orcas are in
the Aleutian and Western Stock, some of whom overlap with animals of the West
Coast Stock, which extends to California and totals about 350.

Harbor porpoises—Even without a close look, swimming styles immediately
distinguish harbor from Dall's porpoises. Harbor porpoises are usually seen
close to shore, backs and small dorsal fins rising and falling sedately. These
quiet, energy-conserving cetaceans feed mostly on bottom-schooling fish and
cephalopods (squid and octopus). The Southeast Alaskan population size is
estimated at about 17,000.

Dall's porpoises—Dall's are the porpoises seen sprinting, kicking up spray in
mid channel, or riding bow waves of larger boats. With their black-and-white
markings, Dall's resemble miniature orcas. They feed on mid- to deepwater
schooling fish and cephalopods, often at night when prey ascend toward the

surface. Dall's porpoises range from our inside waters out over the continental shelf, roaming oceanic waters nearly two miles deep. Population estimates are not available for Southeast Alaska, but the entire Alaskan stock numbers about 83,000. Boat-based surveys may be biased by Dall's attraction to vessels.

Pacific white-sided dolphins—In April 1993, pulling into Petersburg on the ferry, we witnessed the aftermath of an orca attack on a large school of white-sided dophins. Several of the victims had panicked and rushed up on shore. One large male was completely unscarred but had preferred death on dry land to the teeth of his larger delphinid relative. This is a mostly pelagic species that sometimes enters inside waters. There are estimated to be at least 26,000 white-sided dolphins in the Gulf of Alaska north of 45°.

Harbor seals—Like our two common porpoises, seals and sea lions are distinguishable by behavior. When a round head comes up quietly, turns 90° or so to take in the view, then slips gently under, it's a harbor seal. When you hear a vigorous *whoosh*, and see a bear-like head plowing purposefully through the waves, it's a Steller sea lion. Harbor seals play at the surface only on special occasions, but sea lions do it routinely, rolling, slapping, and sometimes leaping mostly out of the water.

Harbor seals eat squid, shrimp, and fish, especially pollock and capelin. Steller sea lions consume all these plus more cod and herring. Seals fish more often in estuaries and take more sand lance and eulachon than do sea lions. Seals stay down longer, hunting solitary or hidden prey such as octopus, while sea lions target mostly near-bottom schooling fish.

Many seals and all sea lions give birth on rocky islands mostly free of predation by wolves and bears. In northern Southeast, harbor seals also breed in icy waters near tidewater glaciers, where fast-weaned pups on icebergs are safe from all but winged or paddled harassment.

Although long-distance travel has recently been documented for Glacier Bay harbor seals, Southeast populations

5,042

8,870

8,586

Aerial harbor seal counts in 2003 and 2006, from six Southeast stocks. Based on Allen and Angliss (2013).

23,289

14,388

Sea lion rocks and sea otters are concentrated on the outer coast. Sea lion data from National Marine Fisheries Service.

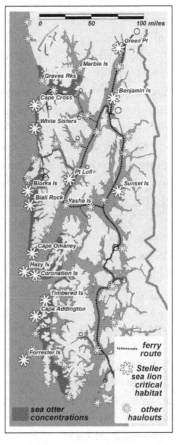

are considered mostly nonmigratory, with strong fidelity to haulout sites in breeding season. Six geographic stocks were defined for Southeast Alaska in 2010. Aerial surveys yielded an estimated 60,000 harbor seals, exclusive of the Yakutat unit. Largest populations are south of the Stikine River; the Clarence Strait stock has nearly five times more seals than the comparably sized Glacier Bay-Cross Sound unit.

Steller sea lions—Our cacophonous otariids breed principally on storm-denuded rocks off the outer coast (p. 90). The largest colonies are at Forrester, Hazy, and White Sisters Islands. Haulouts viewable from tour ships include Benjamin Island, near Juneau, and Marble Islands in Glacier Bay. Large males exceed a ton—more than three times the weight of females. Unlike harbor seals, sea lions can turn their hind flippers forward for walking. It's amazing to watch a ten-foot breaker crash harmlessly over a sea lion's back as it clambers determinedly up the precipitous haulout ramparts.

Northern fur seals don't reside in Southeast, but females and young pass by our outer coast in transit between pupping grounds in the Pribilofs and wintering waters as far south as California.

Sea otters—These eighty-pound marine weasels favor submerged reefs off rocky beaches. Diet reflects tenure of occupation: on first arrival, colonists enjoy large crabs, clams, octopi, and juicy urchins; later, as pickings diminish, otters make do with small mollusks, snails, and crustaceans. Recovery of sea otter populations and associated shellfish declines have brought them into competition with commercial and subsistence fishing. Sea otters give birth at any time of year. Unlike harbor seals, pups of sea otters enjoy prolonged maternal tutelage.

In the early 1700s, sea otters numbered 150,000 to 300,000 worldwide. When finally protected by international treaty in 1911, fewer than 2,000 remained in thirteen colonies—none in Southeast. In the mid-1960s, 412 otters were reintroduced to six sites along our outer coast. From those well-chosen nuclei, much of the sea otter's former range has been recovered; about 10,000 animals inhabited Southeast as of 2012. Glacier Bay—distant from any of the reintroduction sites—has been closely monitored. By 2006 the National Park hosted 2,785 sea otters—a growth rate too rapid for reproduction alone, suggesting substantial immigration.

Unlike other preceding marine-mammal range maps, our map of sea otter concentrations was assembled from unofficial sources and personal observations and should be considered incomplete. Although sea otters are occasionally sighted deep into the Archipelago (sidebar *A puzzling entanglement*), trend data suggest the rate of expansion into inner, protected waters has slowed notably.

Ups and downs—Although stewarded today by the Marine Mammal Protection Act of 1972, most Southeast species are recovering from numbers reduced nearly to vanishing. Those survivors were vestiges of prior opulence that geneticists are venturing to reconstruct statistically. Some estimate that preindustrial humpback whale populations, for example, were vastly larger than figures derived from whaling-ship logs. Imagine not dozens but hundreds of thirty-ton keystone krill-recylers, mowing and manuring the pastures of our sea.

Most marine trends are invisible, even to cutting-edge science. Cause-detection is a guessing game, as are recovery strategies. Meanwhile, global markets seek species progressively lower on food pyramids. Escalating herring seine and pollock trawl fisheries compete with baleen whales for food.

Although little bottom trawling currently occurs within Southeast Alaska, well over half the United States trawl catch comes from Steller sea lion range to the northwest of us—what is called the Western "distinct population segment" (DPS). While that Western DPS has plummeted, the Eastern DPS (our group) is rapidly increasing. Estimated Southeast Alaskan non-pup population increased 88 percent (from 6,376 to 11,965) between 1979 and 2009. In 2012, federal managers proposed to remove the eastern Steller sea lion, classified "threatened," from the list of endangered wildlife.

Glacier Bay harbor seals declined about 75 percent from 1992 to 2002, and more recent counts suggest the trend continues. Hunting is prohibited in the National Park, so why are numbers dropping faster here than almost anywhere in Alaska? 'Bottom-up' hypotheses include climate change and shifting prey abundance. In the East Arm, for example, grounding and cessation of glacial calving in 1993 eliminated floating ice resulting in the abandonment of upper Muir Inlet. 'Top-down' possibilities include tourism impacts, orca predation, and sea lion competition. And finally, telemetry studies show unexpected migrations from Glacier Bay breeding sites to wintering grounds as distant as Sitka and Prince William Sound. Three of those seals wandered more than a thousand miles. As with migratory birds, these travels hint that declines among Glacier Bay breeders could well be unrelated to changes within the Park.

Elsewhere, the world's oceans are in trouble. Vast dead zones bracket heavily developed shores, where jellyfish and toxic dinoflagellates dominate the fauna, and large vertebrates are functionally extinct. In coastal seas, large whales have declined 85 percent, sea cows 90 percent, pinnipeds and otters 55 percent, shorebirds 61 percent, sea turtles 87 percent, and oysters 91 percent. In deeper pelagic waters, large predatory fish fell 90 percent since 1950.

What a miracle then, to live where all nine of the commonest marine mammals—with only localized exceptions—are deemed stable or increasing overall! Certainly, the fate of other oceans abjures complacency. Even Southeast Alaska hosted centuries of slaughter, and only coastal resilence—little aided by human wisdom or restraint—fetched back our sea-fauna from the still-yawning brink.

But it slights Southeast not to celebrate her flippered denizens. For those who reside within daily earshot of huffing, submarine lungs, the fat of the land, often enough, is an emanation from the sea.

A pre-contact extinction?
Ancient hunting and fishing cultures of the northern Pacific Rim were thinly dispersed. Could they have extirpated any marine mammal species from the Alexander Archipelago before it was ever seen by European explorers? Bones of ringed seal (Pusa hispida) from 14,000 to 25,000 years old have been found in caves on Prince of Wales Island. Today, this ice-adapted arctic species no longer inhabits Southeast Alaska. Although it's likely Pusa fed the first humans to paddle into

berg-strewn bays in skin boats, no one has suggested people had a hand in its disappearance.

But another great beast—the dodo of northern marine mammals—did suffer from human over-consumption. The best documented extinction among north Pacific marine fauna was Steller's sea cow (*Hydrodamalis gigas*), wiped out within three decades of Bering's expedition to Alaska in 1741. Georg Wilhelm Steller, naturalist on that voyage, took meticulous notes on the huge sirenian's physiology and ecology based on observations in Russia's Commander Islands, 2,100 miles west of Southeast Alaska, at the tip of the Aleutian chain.

"These animals are fond of shallow sandy places along the seashore . . . especially . . . mouths of rivers and creeks . . . and they always live in herds. . . [They are] voracious and eat incessantly. . . so greedy they keep their heads always under water, without regard to life and safety. Hence a man in a boat, or swimming naked, can move among them without danger and select at ease the one of the herd he desires to strike." Steller described four giant kelp species eaten by the sea cow, and noted great heaps of stems cast ashore wherever they'd been feeding.

These cold-water manatees, up to thirty feet long and maybe incapable of diving, were so easily killed by humans that even in Steller's day only a few thousand survived, restricted to islands, such as the Commanders, uninhabited by Native peoples. But at one time, judging from fossils, *Hydrodamalis* spanned a 9,000-mile arc from Japan to California.

The sea cow was encased in a nine-inch-thick layer of fat. Steller reported the fat "can be kept a very long time, even in the hottest weather, without becoming rancid or strong. When tried out it is so sweet and fine flavored that we lost all desire for butter." It would be hard to design a more desirable (or more quickly extinguishable) prey for the first skin-boat colonists of the Pacific Rim. We don't know when this encounter took place in Southeast Alaska, or how long *Hydrodamalis* survived here.

Some think there was more to sea-cow decline than direct human predation. Wherever humans reduced otter populations, sea urchins decimated kelp beds the sea cows depended upon. Southeast witnessed the intersection of four colossal appetites—two grazers and two predators—each a keystone species in its own right: sea urchin and sea cow mowing kelp; sea otter preying on urchins, and sea-going humans enamored of the world's most valuable fur.

Sea otters today are 'boom and bust' species, and so, presumably were the cold-water sea cows. Did they graze kelp beds hit-and-run, consigned like bison to perpetual motion? Giant kelps are among the fastest-growing plants in the world. As bison and other great-plains grazers influenced evolution of hoof- and tooth-hardy grasses, are phantom sea cows one reason for today's explosive kelp growth rate?

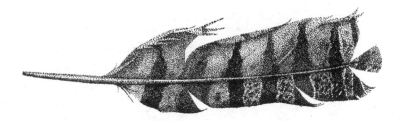

BIRDS

Over 350 species of birds have been documented in Southeast Alaska. This represents about 73 percent of the 487 or so species recorded for the entire state. Of these, 168 species are considered known or probable nesters in the region.

Nowhere else can you see black oystercatchers, harlequin ducks, varied thrushes, sooty grouse, and rock ptarmigan in just a few hours of birding. It's possible to cross several habitat zones by starting at a rocky seashore and moving inland through saltwater wetlands, bogs, deciduous woodlands, old-growth coniferous forests, and finally alpine areas, all in a relatively short distance.

The close proximity of habitats allows birds to nest in one and forage for a variety of foods in others. At least two-thirds of our species regularly visit more than one habitat. Bald eagles, for example, nest in old-growth forests yet survey saltwater beaches for dead fish or cruise alpine slopes for adolescent marmots.

Southeast Alaska's outer coastal islands are important nesting grounds for substantial numbers of seabirds, such as ancient murrelets, Cassin's and rhinoceros auklets, fork-tailed storm-petrels, and Leach's storm-petrels. Forrester, Hazy, and Saint Lazaria Islands have been set aside under the National Wildlife Refuge system especially for these nesting seabirds. From tour boats you can usually see tufted puffins, Kittlitz's murrelets, and occasionally horned puffins in Glacier Bay, where they nest.

Off Sitka, Kanasx̱'éey, *island of stunted spruce* (Saint Lazaria Island), is another fairly reliable place to see tufted puffins by boat, as well as pelagic cormorants, pigeon guillemots, and common and thick-billed murres. Some seabirds, such as Leach's and fork-tailed storm-petrels, are

Above: Secondary wing feather of great horned owl. •
Right: Cormorants on guano-draped island, outer coast.

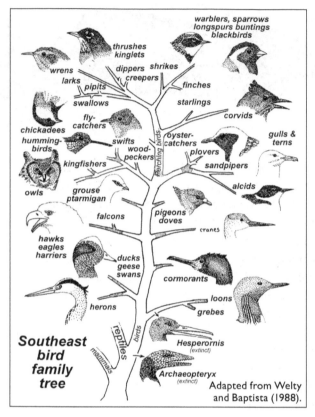

warblers, sparrows
longspurs buntings
blackbirds
thrushes
kinglets
dippers shrikes
wrens creepers
larks
pipits   finches
swallows   starlings
fly-   corvids
catchers
chickadees
humming-   swifts oyster-   gulls &
birds   wood-   catchers   terns
kingfishers peckers plovers
                     sandpipers
owls grouse   alcids
      ptarmigan
      falcons pigeons
               doves
hawks   cranes
eagles
harriers   ducks
              geese
              swans
              cormorants
herons   loons
              grebes

**Southeast
bird
family
tree**

Hesperornis
(extinct)

Archaeopteryx
(extinct)   Adapted from Welty
and Baptista (1988).

Perching birds

reptiles

birds

mammals

usually seen and heard only at night. Arriving and departing their nests under cover of darkness is an adaptation that certain seabirds have developed to avoid predators. Despite its small size, St. Lazaria is one of the more productive seabird colonies in Alaska. Half a million birds nest here—more than 7,000 birds per acre.

Other extremely small rocky islands provide nesting places for the unusual-looking black oystercatcher. In Glacier Bay, oystercatchers are less restricted to islands, and commonly nest at the high tide mark on rock or gravel beaches. From evidence of numerous pairs of marbled murrelets along coastal inlets and bays, the adjacent timber or mountains must provide ideal nesting sites for this elusive seabird.

Some nesting birds quite common or fairly common in Southeast Alaska are accidental in other regions of the state. You will see sooty grouse, red-breasted sapsucker, and Pacific-slope flycatcher on a regular basis only in this region.

Only about 16 percent of the birds seen here use Southeast Alaska as their permanent home. The Vancouver Canada goose, harlequin duck, bald eagle, rock ptarmigan, great horned owl, Steller's jay, common raven, northwestern crow, chestnut-backed chickadee, American dipper, and several others can be seen here any month of the year. Staying in Southeast year-round has several

Left: Steller's jay resides in Southeast.

Right: Gull foot resembles waterfowl's, but the latter toe inward, while gulls have more straight-ahead gait. • Bonaparte's (nonbreeding plumage) is a migratory gull that arrives in April. Many summer in Southeast.

advantages. Resident birds face none of the perils of long journeys. They can begin nesting before migrant birds arrive, often laying a larger number of eggs and sometimes having time to raise more than one brood per season. But in return they must survive the rigors of winter, with less food, shorter daylight in which to feed, and temperatures that require extra energy in order to keep warm.

Many birds normally do not enter western or northern Alaska because of natural barriers such as mountains or arctic climate but often move into Southeast Alaska by way of the valleys carved by major rivers originating in Canada. Usually such birds are more common in valleys and mouths of such rivers as the Unuk, Stikine, or Taku than elsewhere in the region. These include pied-billed grebe, American bittern, warbling vireo, and western tanager. Others, such as the western grebe, make their way up to Southeast Alaska by way of the seacoast from lower British Columbia and the Pacific Northwest.

Waterfowl and shorebirds often stop to rest and refuel in our numerous undeveloped estuaries, salt and freshwater wetlands, and lakes during their long migrations to and from their more westerly and northern breeding grounds. These include the tundra swan, northern pintail, American golden-plover, red-necked phalarope, long-billed dowitcher, pectoral sandpiper, and dunlin. Some, like the red-necked phalarope, occur in enormous numbers; over 15,000 have been observed on the waters of Glacier Bay in late summer.

Numerous land birds also use Southeast Alaska for a refueling and resting area on their way to and from nesting grounds. These birds include the northern harrier, American kestrel, short-eared owl, horned lark, northern shrike, Lapland longspur, and white-crowned sparrow. Many sea ducks find Southeast, with its relatively mild winters, protected inlets and bays, and abundant marine invertebrates, a suitable place to spend the winter. These include several species that usually nest farther north: common goldeneye, Barrow's goldeneye,

Sandhill cranes migrate through Southeast but few remain in summer. Footprints resemble those of herons, but have reduced rear toes.

bufflehead, long-tailed duck, and surf scoter. You can often see enormous flocks of these birds along the inside waters during winter.

Some land birds that nest farther north or east also find our climate and habitat suitable for overwintering: Bohemian waxwing, northern shrike, and dark-eyed junco (slate-colored subspecies). Some shorebirds that nest farther north spend the winter in Southeast, sometimes in flocks of several hundred: dunlin and rock sandpiper.

Important Bird Areas

The Important Bird Area (IBA) program is an international effort to identify, conserve, and monitor a network of sites that provide essential habitat for bird populations. BirdLife International began the IBA program in Europe in 1985. Since that time, BirdLife partners in more than one hundred countries have joined together to build the global IBA network. Audubon, the BirdLife partner in the United States, has been working since 1995 to identify and conserve hundreds of IBAs all across the country.

In order to qualify for a globally or continentally significant IBA, a site must support a significant portion of the flyway population of a particular species. In general, to qualify, the site must have supported over 1 percent of the North American population at one time, or more than 5 percent of the population for the season.

As of 2013, six sites in Southeast Alaska have been officially designated as Important Bird Areas. These include Icy Bay (Yakutat), Chilkat Bald Eagle Preserve (Haines), Berners Bay (Juneau), Mendenhall Wetlands (Juneau), Port Snettisham (Juneau), and Stikine River Delta (Wrangell). In addition, an

Establishing an IBA—*Bob Armstrong*

We were involved with helping to establish the Mendenhall Wetlands near Juneau as an Important Bird Area and eventually we helped write a book about the area.

In 2005, the Juneau Audubon Society applied to Audubon Alaska to have the Mendenhall Wetlands classified as an Important Bird Area (IBA). The application was reviewed by the Alaska Technical Committee and in 2006 the Wetlands were recognized as an IBA at the state level. The nomination was then sent to the National Technical Committee for their assessment of the site's continental and global significance. In 2007 the Mendenhall Wetlands was officially recognized as globally significant by the US IBA Committee.

At the time of application there were more than 10,000 records of bird numbers on the Wetlands. Several species fell within IBA qualifying criteria: greater white-fronted goose, Canada goose (Vancouver subspecies), surfbird, Thayer's gull, surf scoter, American golden-plover, lesser yellowlegs, ruddy turnstone, black turnstone, western sandpiper, pectoral sandpiper, rock sandpiper, dunlin, short-billed dowitcher, and Bonaparte's gull. The surfbird, plover, rock sandpiper, and dowitcher were also on the Audubon WatchList because of concerns about conservation status.

Mendenhall Wetlands provides food and/or resting space to thousands of birds. We know this because of more than forty years of records by birding enthusiasts, and two major studies documenting bird variety and abundance.

As of 2008, 256 species of birds were known on the Wetlands. That's 83 percent of 308 species seen between Taku Inlet and Berners Bay, and 73 percent of 352 bird species seen in all of Southeast Alaska (from Dixon Entrance to Yakutat).

Because of the variety and complexity of its habitats, Mendenhall Wetlands is one of the key stopover points for migratory waterfowl and shorebirds in coastal Alaska.

Map legend: *Icy Bay*, ○ **established IBAs**, ● **others under consideration**, *Chilkat*, *Berners*, *Mendenhall*, *Snettisham*, *St Lazaria*, *Stikine*, *Forrester*

the **Mendenhall** a globally recognized **Wetlands** Important Bird Area

extensive list of sites with potential to meet IBA criteria has been established for our area. About 30 percent are expected to be deemed significant at a global level. Nominations for many are in progress. Examples include Saint Lazaria and Forrester seabird islands.

DO YOU KNOW

BREEDING

Juneau

YEAR-ROUND

WHERE
YOUR
BIRDS ARE?

WINTERING

Tucson

***Frequent fliers, part I**—Richard Carstensen*
The western, Gambel's race of white-crowned sparrow migrates between Alaska and the southwestern US and northern Mexico, foraging in a huge variety of habitats. The bird above is shown in uplift parkland at Eagle River near Juneau. Below, a wintering Gambel's on ocotillo stem in cactus desert near Tucson, Arizona.

Bird habitats

Birds are far from randomly distributed among the marshes, peatland, tundra, shrub thickets, or young- and old-growth forests of Southeast Alaska. Each species has its own foraging and cover requirements. In time, the naturalist learns to identify these habitat needs. At that point, a cottonwood grove, for example, takes on a new dimension. It's more than tall, mossy poplars with lush understory on a predictable soil type with a given successional history. It's home—for Wilson's and yellow-rumped warblers, ruby-crowned kinglets, and hermit thrushes. It might even shelter one of the rarer songbirds of Southeast— a warbling vireo or a western tanager. The songs of these birds are as much the signature of the grove as the smell of young cottonwood leaves, or plumed seeds drifting in the summer breeze.

Birds of the beaches—"When the tide is out the table is set!" This saying applies not only to human clam-diggers and seaweed-gatherers, but to birds of many varieties. Sandpipers and plovers, geese and ducks, crows and ravens, eagles and gulls, all noisily collect the ocean's bounty. Some graze the low salt-marsh vegetation, some forage for intertidal invertebrates, some go fishing, and others scavenge tidal debris. The beach offers riches of both land and sea, often massed into convenient piles at the high-water line. In fall, the debris zone may look as though someone had dumped bags of bird seed, so concentrated are the seeds of sedge and goose-tongue. They draw flocks of American pipits and snow buntings, which, unlike most of their songbird relatives, dare to feed in open coastal spaces lacking vegetative cover.

Coniferous forests—This habitat offers forage for some birds and cover for many more. Although it is not really a prolific producer of bird food (except for seed-

Nesting bohemian waxwings can be found hawking insects over the Tatshenshini River in BC. In winter they converge on Juneau's mountain ash trees.

Lush uplift meadow on raised beach spit. Chilkat Range in background. Ground nesters here include savannah sparrow, and—with scattered spruce or deciduous scrub—Lincoln's sparrow.

eating siskins and crossbills), the great value of our hemlock-spruce forest to birds lies in its structural complexity. The multilayered canopy and abundance of standing and fallen dead wood provide cover for nesters and winter residents.

Woodpeckers are more important in forests than their numbers suggest. Digging nest cavities in rotten snags, they provide future homes for secondary cavity dwellers—chickadees, swallows, smaller owls, and even some diving ducks. Tiny insectivores like brown creepers and Pacific wrens use other elements of forest cover, such as upturned root wads or sheets of bark sloughing from dead logs. Townsend's warblers, Pacific-slope flycatchers, and golden-crowned kinglets sing from high in the canopies of old-growth forests. The male

Orange-crowned warbler (above) is a brush bird. Townsend's warbler (below) is a conifer-forest nester. Only side-by-side comparison shows subtle variations on the basic warbler body plan, such as the Townsend's slightly longer bill.

sooty grouse, or 'hooter,' is likewise best located by sound in the spring and early summer. Although he hoots near the treetops and may forage on fibrous needles in winter, his mate nests on the ground, and her young often feed on nutritious insects in lush meadow and shrub vegetation, as do the nestlings and fledglings of most other terrestrial birds.

Meadows and thickets—The importance of insects to baby birds (and many adults) brings us to meadows and shrublands. These early stages in vegetational succession green up suddenly each spring and die back as quickly each fall. Closely timed to the boom-and-bust of deciduous leaves is a corresponding flush of creeping, flying, and burrowing insects. Protein-rich insects of these young deciduous communities in turn feed most of our arriving songbirds, including almost all of our common warblers, flycatchers, and swallows, most nesting sparrows, and many thrushes.

Although we tend to group birds by where they nest or are most frequently seen—forest, beach, meadow—we should remember the dependence that most have upon more than one habitat. Many consider the varied thrush an iconic conifer-forest species. One May we examined the gizzard of a dead varied thrush. It was packed with wing covers of adult leaf beetles, which browsed the willow and cottonwood saplings where the thrush had been foraging. The varied thrush may nest in conifers, but often feeds in younger, deciduous habitats.

Bird sounds

From May to early July, our resident and summer nesting birds can easily be located by their songs. Territories have been staked out, and owners loudly and

Male American kestrel, common in open coastal habitats in migration.

enthusiastically proclaim their rights. The woods and meadows resound with hoots, twitters, squawks, and trills. Ornithologists think early calling reminds rivals of territory boundaries forgotten overnight. Silence ensues when hungry birds start feeding.

Most spring bird vocalizations are from males establishing boundaries of territories and attempting to attract a mate. Exceptions include the female red-necked phalarope, which breeds in Glacier Bay and the Yakutat Forelands. She engages in courtship displays and calls to attract a mate. After laying her eggs, she repeats her displays and calling and leads her mate to the nest, where he then incubates the eggs and cares for the young.

Some birds make sounds nonvocally. Probably most bizarre in Southeast is the courtship display of the Wilson's snipe. This bird displays by circling upward, then diving down toward earth. With tail well spread, air rushes over the extreme outer tail feathers, causing them to vibrate. The airstream over these feathers is broken about eleven times per second by quick wing beats, producing a loud winnowing or throbbing sound.

Woodpeckers also use nonvocal sounds. These birds establish territories by loud drumming, usually on resonant, hollow, drumming trees. In contrast, a feeding woodpecker may rather quietly chip away pieces of bark while looking for insects. We once nailed a wooden model of a black-backed woodpecker on a tree and played a recording of one drumming. The male in whose territory we did this

Many consider Swainson's thrush melody the loveliest of all Tongass bird songs.

***Sound recognition by birds**—Bob Armstrong*
Each species of bird has a unique song, call, or sound.
Birds can detect minute pitch differences, enabling
them to recognize different individuals of their own
kind. Studies of certain colonial nesting seabirds, for
example, have shown that while still in the egg, the
chicks learn to distinguish the voices of their parents
from others in the same colony. While photographing
Arctic terns at a nesting colony, I noticed that newly
hatched chicks would emerge from beneath one parent to prepare to accept fish
from the other parent before it landed! Apparently the chick could recognize its own
parent's voice among those of the many terns constantly circling and calling from
above the colony.

responded by enthusiastically pecking the model on the head until he knocked
it to the ground. He then appeared satisfied at having 'killed' the intruder and
flew off to feed quietly nearby.

Duetting occurs when a bird inserts notes with beautiful precision into the
songs or calls of its partner. Duetting is most common among birds of the tropical forests, where they employ it to keep in contact with each other as they forage in the thick foliage. In Southeast, duetting occurs in paired Vancouver Canada geese. The *a-honk-hink* call you often hear is actually produced by
two birds. The male gives the *a-honk* and the female follows
immediately with a higher *hink*. In species such as Canada
geese that may remain paired for life, mutual identification and maintaining contact between mates is very
important; duetting is one way they accomplish it.

Birds sing to stake out territories and attract
mates. It's safer to sing or make noise at an
intruder than to fight. Some ornithologists
even think that birds may also sing for
pure pleasure.

Male song sparrow singing
from broken spruce leader.

148 The Nature of Southeast Alaska

Winter adaptations

Many of the 487 or so species of birds documented in Alaska leave for the winter. Slightly more than one hundred species commonly remain year-round in Southeast Alaska, compared to just four species along the North Slope. In both areas, most overwintering species must contend with food shortage. Winter feeding is further complicated by less daylight in which to forage, less available habitat because of ice and snow cover, and the need to keep warm.

In general, birds are more resistant to cold than are mammals of comparable size. The coat of feathers on a bird's body serves as excellent insulation, and birds lack mammals' projecting fleshy ears and tails, which lose heat. Birds living in cooler latitudes typically have more feathers and more fat for insulation, and a faster metabolism.

Some birds, such as ptarmigan, ruffed grouse, and snow buntings, insulate themselves from winter cold by plunging under the snow, where the temperature may be many degrees warmer than at the surface. Some may even stay under snow both night and day in order to survive our occasional winter storm.

Many of our smaller birds conserve heat by roosting closely together in sheltered places. Chestnut-backed chickadees, for example, may pack together in holes in trees. Some birds, such as ptarmigan, possess a crop, a food-storage organ, that can be filled during a short winter day and the contents digested at night, allowing the bird to keep its metabolism and body temperature high during a cold winter night. Another example is the redpoll's enlarged esophagus, which acts like a crop. Redpolls quickly eat a large amount of food just before roosting for the night.

Other species, such as Steller's jays and chickadees, store food during times of plenty, retrieving it during lean periods. At feeders, chickadees seem to be constantly taking our offering of sunflower seeds to some secret hiding place. Chickadees practice what is called "scatter hoarding." Rather than eating food where they find it, they typically pick up one seed or insect at a time, and store them in a variety of places including a crack in the bark of a tree, beneath dead leaves, among lichens, and even in the snow. Scattering food this way hides it from squirrels and other birds that could quickly make off with a single large stash. It is amazing that chickadees can remember where they stored each food parcel. According to studies of the closely related black-capped chickadee, this memory lasts at least thirty days.

Small birds must feed every day in order to survive winter cold spells, and they must be able to find a sheltered area in which to spend the night. Feeding birds is one way to help them through the winter. However, once our resident birds become dependent on the food, it's a good idea to be a consistent provider throughout the winter. We find that a variety of food is needed: unsalted sunflower seeds attract chickadees; smaller commercial blends are good for juncos and redpolls, and suet for woodpeckers.

One of the joys of feeding birds in winter is the chance of attracting a rare bird, and many bird records for Alaska have been established at feeders. In Southeast a few of the rare birds that you might attract include the northern pygmy-owl (looking for small birds to prey upon), Clark's nutcracker, mountain chickadee, white-throated sparrow, Harris's sparrow, and purple finch.

Although most birds that commonly winter in Southeast do not, at first glance, appear to be as specialized for cold as the ptarmigan, they do have physical, physiological, and behavioral adaptations. More species winter in Southeast Alaska than in any other region of Alaska, owing to the moderating marine influence on temperature and greater food availability in coastal habitats. Still, winter conditions in Southeast can at times be very severe. It's remarkable that chickadees, nuthatches, and kinglets survive, and one can only wonder how an Anna's hummingbird in Juneau was able to tolerate several winter snowstorms.

Canada geese

Seven subspecies of Canada goose breed and winter in North America. Of these, three subspecies, Vancouver Canada goose, dusky Canada goose, and lesser Canada goose,

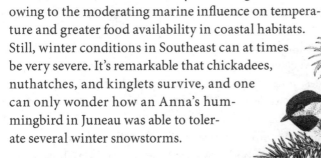

Chestnut-backed chickadees in Sitka spruce.

may be seen in Southeast. Only one, the Vancouver Canada goose, breeds in Southeast. The other two may be seen here during migration.

The Vancouver Canada goose lives and nests along coastal Southeast Alaska from northern Southeast southward to northern Vancouver Island, British Columbia. It is an essentially nonmigratory subspecies, and most live year-round within this area. Authorities believe that the numbers of Vancouver Canada geese have remained about the same over the years, probably because their nesting and wintering habitat remains mostly in pristine condition. Also, they are lightly hunted compared to other Canada goose subspecies, which migrate over major human population centers. In spring we briefly see some of these other migratory geese on our wetlands; most are smaller and paler than the Vancouver subspecies.

Studies of Vancouver nesting habits and distribution showed this to be a surprisingly unique subspecies. Most nests were found in forest among dense shrubs. Nests of other geese are usually associated with lakes, ponds, or bays. Most Vancouver nests were on the ground, but one was at the top of a spruce snag, and another was forty-eight feet above the ground on a moss-covered bough. Vancouver Canada geese have also been found nesting on bog fringes, along stream banks, and adjacent to lakes and estuaries throughout Southeast Alaska.

Around their nests, the geese were commonly seen perched in the upper portion of the nearby trees. When the pair returned to the nest site, they usually landed in trees before flying to their nest. While the female incubated, the male usually remained perched.

During nesting, the most common forage plant is yellow skunk cabbage. Geese are inefficient at digesting food; they must eat a lot in a short time. Huge green skunk cabbage leaves provide the necessary bulk food for rain-forest geese.

Although Vancouvers can be found throughout Southeast Alaska, the Mendenhall Wetlands near Juneau is probably the easiest place to observe them. In late winter and spring, the geese usually feed on the Wetlands right up to Egan Expressway, foraging for seeds, roots, and young shoots of sedges. About five- to seven hundred Vancouver Canada geese winter on the Mendenhall Wetlands. Although these intelligent birds vacate the Wetlands during hunting season, by mid-October they often come in to feed at night when hunters are elsewhere.

Soon after hunting ends in mid-December, geese return to the Wetlands,

Right: Mated pair of Vancouver Canada geese, our nonmigratory subspecies.

Below: Skunk cabbage (*Lysichiton americanum*) is an important goose food on the breeding grounds.

where they stay day
and night. By early
April, paired adults
move to their nesting
sites. Adolescents remain on
the Wetlands until late June, and
in July these nonbreeders fly to
secluded inlets in Glacier Bay or to other remote areas,
where they molt, shedding their worn flight feathers and
growing a new set. During this three- to four-week molting
period, the geese cannot fly and avoid people and other predators.
They seek open flats with abundant forage near expanses of water, to
which they can escape if disturbed. If approached by boaters, molting geese take
to the brush. In August the new families and these adolescents gather again on
Mendenhall Wetlands, where they spend the rest of the year, except when they are
chased out by an extreme freeze-up or by hunters or off-leash dogs.

Places like the Mendenhall Wetlands provide food necessary for our Canada geese to survive the winter and to build up energy reserves for nesting. Remote areas such as tidelands and adjacent forested parts of Seymour Canal are critical to nesting success. And finally, areas such as Adams Inlet in Glacier Bay, far from human disturbance and lacking predators found elsewhere in Southeast, improve survival during molting. Protection of these interconnected habitats and watersheds will help insure perpetuation of this subspecies of Canada goose.

Sea ducks

Southeast Alaska's protected, mostly ice-free bays, channels, and inlets, relatively unpolluted waters and abundant food offer ideal wintering habitat for all ten species of North American sea ducks: black, white-winged, and surf scoters, harlequin and long-tailed ducks, common and Barrow's goldeneyes, common

Family life of Canada geese

Once mated, Canada goose pairs usually stay together for life. Geese with families have higher status in the flock. Studies indicate that families of geese are dominant over mated pairs without families, and mated pairs are dominant over single adults and yearlings.

Geese stay together as a family unit after breeding. Migratory subspecies even travel south as a family, wintering together and returning together to northern breeding grounds. Only after arrival do the young of the previous season separate from their parents. These young join other subadults to form flocks, often at considerable distance from their nesting parents. Adolescents will not nest until they are two, three, or even four years old.

There are many advantages of staying together in family groups and flocks. Parents teach young about feeding areas, migration routes, and life-threatening dangers, enhancing their chances of survival.

and red-breasted mergansers, and buffleheads. Together they total more than 300,000 individuals. Aerial surveys by the US Fish and Wildlife Service have identified Southeast as a globally important region for sea ducks, hosting significant proportions of the world populations of Barrow's goldeneye and harlequins, and providing critical winter and molting habitat for surf and white-winged scoters.

Sea ducks obtain most of their food on or near the sea bottom and hence must dive to a variety of water depths. Long-tailed ducks are the champion divers and have been reported to reach depths of 240 feet. In general, long-tailed ducks feed farther offshore than the other species and so have little competition for food. Scoters often dive for food at water depths greater than twenty feet, but the goldeneyes, buffleheads, and harlequin ducks seem to prefer water depths of about ten feet or less.

Sea ducks eat a variety of food, with some species having obvious preferences. For example, scoters may gorge themselves almost exclusively on blue bay mussels in some seasons. A scoter commonly swallows several dozen mussels whole, shell and all, during one short feeding period. In fact, one surf scoter contained 1,100 small mussels in its gizzard! Many sea ducks also eat small crabs, clams, shrimp, amphipods, barnacles, sea urchins, sea stars, marine worms, small fish, and algae.

Harlequin ducks are specialists in prying limpets, mussels, and chitons off rocks and swallowing them whole; amazingly, they can do this while swimming underwater. Their gizzards can crush shells that we must open with a blow by rock or hammer. In streams we have observed harlequin ducks pushing up rocks with their upper bill, then grabbing the dislodged aquatic insects while swimming underwater against the swift current. Both harlequins and scoters eat herring eggs in spring.

Mergansers are fish-eating ducks with slender bills equipped with sharp projections especially adapted for catching and holding small fish. Common and red-breasted mergansers are similar in distribution and ecology, but the red-breasted more frequently occurs in salt water.

Birds and people can tolerate only up to 1 percent concentration of salt in their blood and other body fluids. This is less than a third of the salt concentration in open ocean water. If we were to drink sea water, our kidneys would excrete the excess salt by drawing additional fluids from our body, and dehydration would result. A bird's kidneys are even less efficient than ours at getting rid of excess salt. However, birds living on salt water have special glands in a depression just above each eye. Excess salt is picked up by the ducks' blood and transferred to these salt glands. The concentrated salt solution then flows via ducts to their nostrils, where it is excreted.

Harlequin pair. Male on left.

Sea ducks begin courtship antics while still on the wintering ground. Male goldeneyes court females by dipping bills in the water, raising their heads straight up, and then bending them clear over on their backs while uttering a peculiar whistle. Male buffleheads conduct a head-bobbing, chin-up display with their head feathers erected. Male long-tailed ducks become quite excited and spring into flight, dash madly about, and then abruptly splash back down into the water.

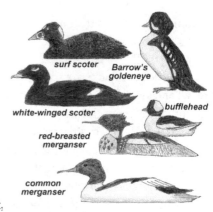

Males of Southeast sea duck species.

Despite all the courtship antics by sea ducks in Southeast, most species depart to breed in boreal and tundra habitats. Exceptions include both species of mergansers and common goldeneye. Many harlequins nest locally beside fast-flowing streams, but Canadian studies indicate that some travel great distances to feed on herring spawn.

Sea ducks do not nest until they are two years old, and the subadults, especially scoters, remain in Southeast and are joined in early summer by males returning from the northern nesting areas soon after their mates have finished laying eggs.

Most communities in Southeast have shoreline roads from which you can watch sea ducks. From January to May, look for their courtship antics. Also watch the feeding flocks of surf scoters. Often, for no apparent reason, they will form a long line, almost single file. First the leader will dive; then each one, like dominoes falling, will follow suit. With binoculars you can see them bringing mussels to the surface, which they will gulp down whole.

Listen for the unusual vocalizations of the long-tailed duck. Also look carefully for the beautiful male harlequin duck perched on the larger beach rocks, preening or sleeping. Despite their gaudy appearance, they blend in well with their surroundings.

Scoters from all along the Pacific coast migrate slowly to Southeast in April before heading inland for nesting. One can sometimes see flocks of 20,000 to 30,000 feeding in unison or flying. This is one of the grandest bird sights in our region.

Rock ptarmigan male in transitional plumage—well camouflaged against mottled granodiorite boulder-cobble field—feeding on tips of young alpine sedges.

Ptarmigan

Our most memorable encounter with ptarmigan was on a cross-country ski trip. We had skied up the icebound Herbert River near Juneau, almost to the Herbert Glacier, when our leader motioned us to stop. There, with the glacier as a backdrop, stood two white-tailed ptarmigan in about as beautiful a setting as can be imagined. The only disturbance of the freshly fallen snow was two sets of dainty ptarmigan tracks leading from some willows to the center of a small clearing. One ptarmigan had buried itself so that only its head and upper shoulders appeared above the snow. The other remained motionless, in full view, by its side. The skiers filed by about thirty feet away without causing the ptarmigan to flush.

This encounter was especially enjoyable because these were the first white-tailed ptarmigan we had seen in Southeast Alaska. Of the three ptarmigan species in the region, white-tails are the least abundant and the smallest, and tend to live at higher elevations than the other two. Rock ptarmigan are most numerous, with willow ptarmigan second. All three species are year-round residents and, aside from elevation movements, probably do not migrate long distances.

Ptarmigan are well designed for living in white, cold environments. White

---

Dirty little secrets—*Bob Armstrong*

In early summer, after most of the snow has gone, and the female rock ptarmigan have changed their plumage to a brownish, well-camouflaged coloration, the males  are still quite white. At this time I would occasionally see males with very dirty feathers, as if they had taken a mud bath. I wondered why.

Then I read a story titled *Dirty Little Secrets* about rock ptarmigan that appeared in an issue of *Natural History* magazine. It was not only fascinating but explained why I had been seeing rock ptarmigan with dirty feathers. The authors of the article thought that the males gained mating advantages with the conspicuous white plumage. However, they really stand out amongst the snow-free alpine boulders and vegetation and are probably quite vulnerable to predation. At this time the males would purposely bath themselves in dirt to take on a more camouflaged appearance. If a receptive female appeared they would clean themselves up to restore their immaculate white breeding plumage.

Through observations and experiments the authors gave a convincing theory for the male's dirty feathers. Whether completely true or not, I thought it was a great story.

---

winter plumage not only is excellent camouflage but also insulates better than colored feathers. White feathers are completely hollow, unoccupied by pigment, and this provides additional dead air space. Ptarmigan also are well designed for walking about in winter. In late fall they grow a dense mat of stiff feathers on their toes, which serves as snowshoes for walking on top of the lightest of snow. Long, sharp claws work like crampons for traction over icy slopes.

When temperatures drop, ptarmigan may spend as much as 80 percent of their time burrowed beneath the snow, where ambient temperatures are generally higher and wind is minimized. In early spring a hike into the alpine on the Mount Roberts Trail in Juneau usually reveals numerous depressions and pellets—winter beds in snow.

In winter, ptarmigan eat mainly willow twigs and buds. In summer, they feed on a variety of green plant shoots, buds, flowers, berries, and insects. To digest woody material of low caloric value, crops contain special bacteria.

As soon as the snow melts, female ptarmigan molt into a dark summer plumage and begin nesting. They nest on the ground and usually lay six to ten eggs. Around late June to early July, after an incubation period of about three weeks, the chicks hatch.

Males retain their white winter plumage longer for display purposes and possibly as a decoy for predators. Males, especially willow ptarmigan, are very territorial. They stand guard while females incubate eggs, and fearlessly attack any intruders. We once saw a male willow ptarmigan pounce on the back of a northern harrier and drive it away.

Male willow ptarmigan also help care for their chicks, a habit unique among North American grouse and ptarmigan. If the female is killed, the male will take over all family responsibilities. This habit, along with its beauty and widespread distribution, makes the willow ptarmigan a good choice as our official state bird.

Bald eagles

Bald eagles have been systematically surveyed in Southeast every few years by the US Fish and Wildlife Service. The surveys indicate that the number has stabilized at around 25,000 individuals. This represents over half of the total populations for Alaska, which has been estimated at around 44,000.

Bald eagles assemble wherever fish concentrate in shallow water to spawn. The largest number of eagles feeding on spawning fish occurs on the Chilkat River near Haines. Here over 3,500 eagles may gather during October and November to feed on the carcasses of spawned-out chum salmon. During April, from 500 to 1,500 eagles have been counted feeding on spawning eulachon in the Stikine River near Wrangell. Spring concentrations of spawning herring may also

While most raptors have pair-bonding displays, with female and male briefly touching talons in flight, bald eagles hang on, cartwheeling down. This maneuver sometimes ends alarmingly close to the ground.

Bald eagle bounties and legislation

A predator control program from 1917 to 1952 resulted in the killing of 101,000 bald eagles in Southeast Alaska. The bounty, established in 1917 by the Alaskan territorial government, was fifty cents per bird, increased to one dollar in 1923. A new bounty act was passed in 1949, paying two dollars per bird. The State continued paying bounties for Alaskan eagles, even after they were protected federally by the Bald and Golden Eagle Protection Act of 1940. Although Alaska was initially exempted from the Act, it was included in 1952, after studies showed that foraging by bald eagles did not affect salmon numbers.

This Act makes it illegal to kill or possess any part of an eagle without a permit issued by the Secretary of the Interior. A violation of the Act can result in a fine of $100,000 ($200,000 for organizations), imprisonment for one year, or both, for a first offense. A second violation of this Act is a felony. Up to half the fine can be paid to the person giving information leading to conviction. The act also makes it illegal to disturb eagle nesting sites.

On the Tongass National Forest bald eagle nests are further protected by a cooperative agreement between the US Fish and Wildlife Service and the US Forest Service. Under this agreement, a 330-foot buffer zone of uncut trees is to be left around each nest tree. In 1997, a thousand-foot-wide no-logging buffer was instituted along beach and estuary habitat on federal land, protecting eagle nest and perch sites.

Talons were once submitted to the state for bounty.

Additional protection was afforded to eagles in 1982 by state legislation creating the 48,000-acre Alaska Chilkat Bald Eagle Preserve and adjoining Haines State Forest Resource Management Area.

attract hundreds of eagles to other Southeast beaches.

As winter approaches, juvenile eagles tend to travel more widely than adults. Some travel as far south as British Columbia or Washington State in search of food. Adult eagles may travel to winter feeding grounds such as the Chilkat Valley near Haines. Those that have nesting territories, and that are likely to nest the next year, may remain near their territory or occasionally return to assert ownership throughout the winter.

Nesting eagles in Southeast Alaska typically choose a large old-growth spruce (most frequently) or hemlock within 220 yards of salt water. Of almost 3,000 bald eagle nests observed in Southeast, most were in old-growth stands, where trees had an average diameter in excess of three feet.

Northern harrier glides with wings in shallow 'V.' Short-eared owl glides with down-turned wingtips.

On average, about one eagle nest can be found per 1.24 mile of shoreline in Southeast. The highest density of nests (1.05 nests per mile of shoreline) was found on Admiralty Island. In Juneau, 130 eagle nests have been found between Berners Bay and Bishop Point (including Douglas Island).

According to the US Fish and Wildlife Service, the picture is not entirely rosy for Southeast eagles. Starvation (particularly in young birds), poisoning, and accidents kill many eagles. Eagles are shot and accidentally trapped each year in Southeast; the total number is unknown. Destruction and alteration of eagle habitat continues to occur on public and private lands through logging, road construction, community expansion, and other developments.

The Fish and Wildlife Service continues to monitor eagles in selected index areas within Southeast. In addition, it is analyzing eagle blood samples to detect accumulation of such heavy metals as lead, mercury, zinc, or copper. Lethal concentrations of lead have been found in numerous bald eagle carcasses in Alaska and mercury (in sublethal doses) is commonly found in tissue samples.

Harriers, short-eared owls

The most easily observed birds of prey that migrate through Southeast Alaska in spring and fall are the northern harrier (formerly "marsh hawk") and the short-eared owl. Both are prominent visitors to our coastal salt marshes and inland freshwater wetlands but only rarely have they nested here.

Hawks and owls are only distantly related, but we've chosen to describe these birds together because of their similar appearance and behavior. The

Above: Short-eared owl with ear-flaps erected.

Below: Regurgitated pellet of short-eared owl, with pelvis, leg, and rib bones of long-tailed vole at surface. Usually there are intact skulls within.

harrier has facial disks like an owl's, and both birds hunt for voles by day over our thick beach meadow vegetation. Flight patterns are subtly different. The harrier flies with several shallow wing strokes, punctuated by a glide, with wings held at an angle above the horizontal. The short-eared owl flies with deeper and faster strokes; observers liken it to a huge moth or butterfly, the resemblance heightened by a stubby, cigar-shaped body. The short-eared owl is such a lightweight bird that the wings' upstroke seems to drive the body down slightly, causing a wavier trajectory. A harrier's longer tail gives more stability.

To observe predation in the field is a rare experience. But northern harriers and short-eared owls often provide exceptions to this rule. With binoculars one can identify them almost a mile away, flapping languidly just above the tall coastal grasses. And to watch hawks and owls hunting nearby is an instant cure for spring fever.

Such closer views are fairly easy to come by. On occasion we have set out an old fish head in the marsh and then crawled into a blind and watched. Harriers often found the food within minutes. Large female harriers always displaced smaller males. Usually the male stood by until the food was nearly gone and the female had left. Perhaps this dominance by feeding females is why we see fewer males hunting in our salt marshes. Many of the males migrate through Southeast at higher elevations along mountain ridges, especially when southbound in fall.

Female harriers sometimes fought among themselves for the fish head. On one occasion, a larger red-tailed hawk came in and immediately displaced two female harriers. On another, a short-eared owl investigated the situation and gave its barking call, which seemed only a passing annoyance to the feeding harrier.

Throughout our observations, physical contact between rival birds of prey was rare. Usually the larger easily displaced the smaller bird. If both harriers were the same size, one would wait a few feet away while the other fed. Then a threatening spread-winged hop toward the feeding hawk would drive it away.

We once observed a harrier kill a green-winged teal. The harrier was gliding along close to the ground, and swooped in and landed on the teal. As it

Subadult saw-whet owl. Unlike migratory short-ears, these tiny owls are resident, favoring forested wetlands and edge habitats. They can be called in close at night by imitating their whistled calls.

began tearing into the teal, a bald eagle dived from its perch in a nearby spruce and stole the harrier's prey. The eagle flew off with the teal in its talons, and the harrier resumed hunting.

Aside from being easy to observe directly, northern harriers and short-eared owls are some of the easiest of all predators on which to perform feeding studies. This stems from their habit of regurgitating pellets, which consist of the undigested fur, feathers, bones, bills, and teeth of prey species. Often numerous pellets can be found near roosting areas. We have examined hundreds of pellets from short-eared owls, and a few from harriers, all found in the beach meadows around Juneau. In these marshes, owls seem to feed almost exclusively on long-tailed voles, as evidenced from molar patterns of skulls in pellets. The harrier seems only slightly less specialized.

Long-tailed voles in tidal wetlands are often forced to swim during extreme high tides. Although they are good swimmers, they become easy prey for short-eared owls. These owls have even been observed to completely dive under water and emerge with a vole in their talons.

Harriers and short-eared owls must be able to hear their prey. Voles scurrying about beneath thick grass cover cannot be spotted from a perch, or by soaring. Instead, these raptors hunt by cruising slowly and silently, almost brushing the vegetation, listening for ultra-high-pitched squeaks and inopportune rustlings. An owl's facial disks can be repositioned by erectile flaps in front of its ear openings. Perhaps these maneuverable disks serve not so much to pick up prey sounds as to muffle the unwanted sound of wind. For harriers and owls, silent flight may be more important in allowing the bird to listen than in sneaking up on prey.

While all of these shorebird species pass through Southeast in great numbers, breeding and wintering ranges differ. Western sandpipers and dunlin move on to northern breeding grounds. A few leasts and many spotted sandpipers, Wilson's snipe and semipalmated plovers nest here. In winter, some snipe and dunlin remain, but other species move south to warmer shores.

least

spotted

western

dunlin

snipe

semi-
palmated
plover

Shorebirds

Plovers, sandpipers, and oystercatchers are the shorebird families found in Southeast Alaska. Within these families forty-five species have visited our region, and ten of those species nest here. The abundant islands, lakes, marshes, rivers, and tidal flats of Southeast Alaska provide extensive shorelines and ideal habitat for shorebirds. Our region is important to these birds during three phases of their life cycle. First, Southeast Alaska provides necessary resting and feeding areas for shorebirds during their long migrations to and from their more northerly breeding grounds in Alaska. Second, many species use the region for nesting—the most abundant nesters are semipalmated plover, black oystercatcher, greater yellowlegs, spotted sandpiper, least sandpiper, and Wilson's snipe. Third, a few species overwinter here. Most abundant is rock sandpiper; others are dunlin, black turnstone, Wilson's snipe, surfbird, sanderling, black oystercatcher, and killdeer.

Distances traveled by shorebirds during migration are generally much greater than those of most other birds. Many Alaskan nesters winter in the southern coastal United States and throughout Central and South America. The Alaska Shorebird Conservation Plan recognizes three sites in Southeast Alaska that serve as resting and feeding areas for large numbers of these long-distant migrants: the Stikine River Delta, Mendenhall Wetlands, and the Yakutat Forelands. The Stikine River Delta supports as many as three million shorebirds during spring migration.

Careful watching of shorebirds in Southeast Alaska can reveal some interesting, bizarre, and sometimes humorous behavior patterns. Perhaps the most obvious and peculiar is the courtship display of the Wilson's snipe. Their loud winnowing or throbbing sound can be heard most often over marshes early in the morning or late into the evening. When approached by humans, some nesting shorebirds behave rather oddly. The distraction displays of the semipalmated plover and killdeer are particularly interesting to watch. In this display

In defense of nests—*Bob Armstrong*

Observing Arctic terns on their nesting grounds can be quite a challenge. Adults not only dive and scream at you; they will, on occasion, strike. Once when I was photographing nesting terns from a blind, as I emerged a tern stabbed me in the forehead with its beak. With blood dripping down my face I hurriedly gathered up my equipment and left. Arctic terns seem to be fairly effective at keeping potential predators away from their nests. However, I have read that if a predator enters the colony during the hours of darkness, the whole colony will abandon the site. Fortunately hours of darkness are few during their nesting season in May and June.

In contrast, Aleutian terns do not defend their nests. Instead their strategy is to periodically relocate their nesting areas. Hence, once predators get used to one area it may be abandoned. In Yakutat I have seen Arctic terns nesting in the vicinity of the Aleutian tern colony. Perhaps the Arctic terns help keep predators away from the Aleutian tern site.

Aleutian tern on nest, Mount St. Elias

the parent bird flutters on the ground as though crippled and utters pitiful cries in hopes of luring you away from its young or nest. If you happen upon a bog in which a pair of greater yellowlegs is nesting, you will be greeted by a shrill, incessant cry, which is repeated over and over until you leave the area. These cries are usually given from the top of a shore pine while the bird clumsily balances itself with feet ill-adapted for gripping tree limbs.

If you approach a small rocky nesting island of the black oystercatcher by boat, you may be greeted by this bizarre

Greater yellowlegs in salt-marsh slough with staghorn sculpin fry.

black shorebird with its long, bright red bill and pink legs and feet. Often it circles around your boat, sometimes quite close, until its curiosity is satisfied.

We always enjoy watching shorebirds feed. The smaller least and western sandpipers dart this way and that, grabbing flies that have been momentarily trapped in the surface tension of the advancing tidewater. Greater yellowlegs prowl our shallow tidal sloughs, grabbing young staghorn sculpins and three-spine sticklebacks that they usually have to manipulate to relax the spines before swallowing. Turnstones turn over small stones and rockweed with their bills, grabbing the creatures living underneath before they can scurry away. Wilson's snipe probe deep into soft mud for worms and other organisms. Sensitive bill tips detect burrowing organisms. Snipe can raise and curve the tip of their upper bill, while still deep in the mud, to seize prey.

Murrelets

Three species of seabirds called murrelets breed in Southeast Alaska. Kittlitz's murrelets and marbled murrelets are closely related; ancient murrelets are more distant kin. Like most seabirds they nest on land but forage at sea on small fishes and planktonic crustaceans. Marbled murrelets range from central California to the Aleutians; Kittlitz's range from northern Southeast to western Alaska; ancient murrelets nest from British Columbia westward across the Aleutian Islands to Siberia.

They differ markedly in nesting habits. Kittlitz's murrelets and marbled murrelets sometimes fly far inland to find suitable nesting sites, but also nest near salt water. Kittlitz's murrelets typically nest on barren scree slopes, in cirques, on nunataks, usually near glaciers, although in the Aleutians they also nest on fairly flat ground. Marbled murrelets nest on moss wads and witches' brooms (formed by dwarf mistletoe parasitic on branches) in large conifers, but also on mossy rock ledges and sometimes in rocky crevices. Use of ground nests increases in northern and western parts of their range.

Ancient murrelets, in contrast, always nest near the shore, which is surely expedient, given that adults do not feed their chicks on the nest. Chicks have to jump out of the nest, and scrabble over the shore to the water; only then will their parents feed them. Ancient murrelet nests are concentrated in colonies, in contrast to the other two species, whose nests are spread out.

All murrelets have many predators. Eagles, peregrine falcons, goshawks,

Watching a marbled murrelet nest—*Bob Armstrong*

On June 30, 2009, two friends discovered a ground nest of a marbled murrelet with egg on Douglas Island near Juneau. In Southeast Alaska, murrelets lay a single egg, either on moss-covered branches of old-growth trees or on the ground. Since very little information was available about ground nests, my friends decided to make periodic observations and invited me along to take photographs. We watched the nest from about eighty feet away and I could take photographs with a small digital camera attached to a spotting scope—a process called digiscoping.

The nest was on a small mossy ledge near the top of a nearly vertical cliff adjacent to a waterfall. Once the chick fledged it had to fly about a mile to salt water and begin feeding on its own, because marbled murrelet parents no longer attend their young once they leave the nest.

The egg hatched about July 27 and after that we visited the area about once a week and I was able to photograph the chick at various stages of development until the brown and black down was lost and the ready-to-fledge nestling had black and white juvenile plumage. The chick left the nest (fledged) on September 1 or 2, a little over a month after hatching.

After fledging we visited the nest site and found it surrounded by a white ring of feces and by an accumulation of shed down feathers. Peering over the edge of the cliff where the nest was located was quite scary. If I were to launch myself from the nest site I would have certainly perished without the help of wings. To survive, the murrelet had to fly the total mile to salt water—or perhaps swim out the stream—because they cannot take off again from flat ground.

We eventually published our observations, with photographs, in the *Journal of Western Birds*. We suggested that the prevalence of coastal, high-gradient streams, cliffs, and rocky outcrops in rugged terrain may offer potential nest sites with good access for takeoff and landing, factors necessary for tending the nest by adults and eventual fledging of the youngster.

Above Murrelet chick, at twenty-three days old, well camouflaged in its ground nest. • *Below* Same chick at thirty-five days, just before fledging, in bolder black-and-white ocean colors.

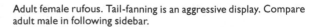

Adult female rufous. Tail-fanning is an aggressive display. Compare adult male in following sidebar.

and sharp-shinned hawks prey on adults. River otters, foxes, glaucous-winged gulls, western gulls, and northern fur seals are additional threats. Ravens take eggs and chicks; at night, owls take ancient murrelet chicks running to the sea. Even Keen's mice eat pipped eggs and little chicks if no parent is present.

Foraging sites of the three species in breeding season tend to differ. Kittlitz's commonly feed in glacial fiords. Marbled murrelets forage in a variety of inshore locations and sometimes even in freshwater lakes. Ancient murrelets typically forage well offshore.

In breeding season Kittlitz's murrelets forage on juvenile capelin and pollock, sand lance, Pacific herring, Pacific sandfish, krill, and other crustaceans. They may eat more crustaceans than marbled murrelets do.

Breeding marbled murrelets forage on sand lance, Pacific herring, capelin, smelt, and seaperch. In winter, they include more krill, shrimp, and even squid. Ancient murrelets eat a variety of small fishes and lots of krill.

Conservation concerns for marbled murrelets include loss of forest habitat in the southern parts of their range; this species is endangered down south. Kittlitz's murrelet is at risk because of its restricted habitat and the effect of climate warming in hastening glacial recession.

Rufous hummingbirds

Rufous hummingbirds begin arriving in Southeast Alaska by early to mid-April. The brightly colored males come first and begin courtship displays as soon as the females arrive. After courtship and mating, the male leaves the nesting and rearing of young to the female. The female aggressively defends the nesting site, attacking with vigor any person, animal, or bird that ventures near.

By late June, most male rufous hummingbirds have left for their wintering grounds. Most females and young depart in mid-July to early August. Leaving Southeast seems to be related more to day length rather than food availability. One day, despite your feeder being full, they will be gone.

The rufous is the only common nesting hummingbird in Alaska. Most hummers we see at feeders in late fall and early winter are another species—Anna's hummingbirds—distinguished from the rufous by the lack of any reddish coloration on back, belly, or tail. Also, the male Anna's is the only hummingbird with rose-red color on its crown. A third species, Costa's hummingbird, has been recorded as an accidental in the fall.

Adult male rufous hummingbirds have a brilliant iridescent orange-red throat called a gorget. The color in this gorget is structural, like that of a rainbow or a blue sky, rather than pigmentary, like that of a red shirt, hence its light-refractive iridescence.

Hummingbirds have the highest metabolic rate of any warm-blooded vertebrate in the world except possibly some species of shrews. Because of this, they must feed or refuel almost continuously to remain alive. However, they cannot eat enough by day to survive the night at their daytime metabolic rate. To survive the cool nights in Southeast Alaska, they become torpid, a state of reduced body temperature and metabolism that uses energy twenty times slower than normal sleep.

Many flowers depend on hummingbirds for pollination. These flowers typically produce little or no scent

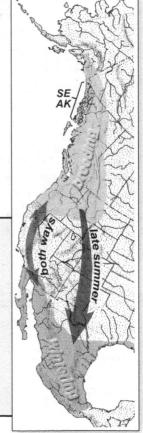

Rufous migration

In early spring rufous hummingbirds leave their wintering grounds in Mexico and head north to nest and raise their young. Traveling up the west coast of North America, some turn inland toward the Rocky Mountains. Others continue north as far north as Prince William Sound.

In mid-July and August, first the males then females and young of the year fly south. Most hummers from southeast Alaska probably follow the Coast Range/Sierra Nevada route. Others travel farther east along the Rockies.

Western columbine (*Aquilegia formosa*).

(which would attract insects), have projecting stamens and pistils that touch the crown or throat of the visiting hummingbird, and lack the landing platforms needed by bees. In addition, they are usually red (a color that bees cannot perceive) and hold large quantities of nectar at the base of a long tube. Flowers thus structured specifically to attract birds as pollinators are termed "ornithophilous."

In Southeast Alaska, only the western columbine and four species of Indian paintbrush have floral characteristics associated with hummingbird pollination. The rufous hummingbird probably invaded Alaska fairly recently, and the spread of most of these hummingbird-adapted flowers has lagged behind that of the birds. The distribution of western columbine in Alaska, however, closely coincides with that of the rufous hummingbird.

Upon arrival in Southeast Alaska, the rufous obtains nectar from flowers adapted for insect pollination, such as blueberries, salmonberries, and rusty menziesia. Only near the end of their nesting season is there a significant bloom of flowers adapted for hummingbird pollination.

To obtain nectar from flowers, the rufous has a long and specially adapted tongue. Split at the end, each half forms a curled trough. Through capillary action, nectar is carried into these troughs, and the bird retracts its tongue to swallow. If you carefully watch a hummer at your feeder, you can see its tongue rapidly darting in and out. In addition to flower nectar, hummingbirds capture and eat tiny insects and spiders, which provide them with a needed source of protein.

The wells in trees that sapsuckers drill (p. 37) appear to be critical early season forage sites for hummers seeking sap and small insects. Rufous hummingbirds may even time their arrival with that of sapsuckers. They're reported to nest near these sap wells and to follow sapsuckers during the day.

Steller's jays

Steller's jays are found in western North America from the Kenai Peninsula in Alaska south through Mexico to Nicaragua. Throughout this range they are typically birds of the mountain and coastal coniferous forests. In Southeast Alaska they're common year-round and, because of their affinity for bird feeders, are well known.

The first European record of the species was an individual shot on Kayak Island, 170 miles miles northwest of Yakutat, by Georg Wilhelm Steller's hunter-assistant. Steller was a German zoologist on Vitus Bering's Arctic expedition in 1741. Both common and scientific names (*Cyanocitta stelleri*) reflect Steller's encounter. The Steller's jay belongs to the family Corvidae, which includes some of the most intelligent birds in the world, intelligence reflected in their social behavior, voice, and food-gathering abilities.

Near nesting sites, jays maintain territories mostly by vocal communication. A simple *too-leer* call tells others to leave the area. Calling saves energy by avoiding physical confrontations.

Beyond the immediate nesting territory, Steller's jays frequently travel about in small groups. Collectively, they mob predators and dominate bird feeders. Each group usually has a pecking order, and a bird's status and dominance can change by mating with a bird of higher status. For instance, the union of a high-ranking female and low-ranking male results in the 'husband' taking on the status of his 'wife.'

Other vocalizations of Steller's jays also indicate their intelligence. For example, they are known for their ability to mimic the voice of other species. The *tee-ar* call is a perfect imitation of the red-tailed hawk. We have noted this call is frequently given by a jay flying to a feeder occupied by other species. As would be expected, the other birds at

Birdbrains—*Richard Carstensen*

Have you ever raised binoculars to study a passing hawk, then sheepishly lowered them, muttering "Oh, it's just a *raven*"? Many perceive ravens and their kin as scroungers or even pests, less worthy of attention than proud raptors or dressy warblers.

It wasn't always this way. Tlingit stories recognize the deep intelligence and ecological importance of ravens and their smaller relatives the crows, magpies, and jays. Northwestern mythology accords Raven a sort of hobo's dignity. He's a creature to be reckoned with. The world is Raven's playroom, and every other creature his toy. Raven's ubiquity is eerie; he uproots mountaineers' snow caches on the ice field, drops from mossy hemlocks onto deer hunters' leavings, surveys for roadkills and Big Macs from power poles, and strides confidently down the sidewalk.

For ravens and crows, curiosity pays. Most birds and mammals mind their own business, with more selective palates and foraging behavior. Ravens, however, use every unsubmerged community in Southeast Alaska. Northwestern crows are beach-oriented, but penetrate into each nearby blowdown and alder tangle and blueberry thicket.

Intertidal ecologists might envy a crow flock's collective knowledge of its territory. A flock may contain about fifty birds, many with over a decade's experience in place, passing on each discovery to precocious offspring. No shell or washed-up fish skeleton escapes their attention. You learn a lot from watching crows. Once, scoping a pair of crows digging in a hummock of foxtail barley, I found them plucking horsefly pupae from their cases. I hadn't realized these flies breed in the intertidal.

Both crows and ravens fly up from rocky beaches to drop mussels, smashing them open, but ravens are most apt to improvise on this theme, observed to yank down pies cooling on second-story windowsills (the ultimate shellfish?). I've even seen them flying with toxic-skinned western toads. Whether they later dropped, peeled and ate them I never determined. Maybe it was just Raven's idea of a good joke on the toad.

Top to bottom: Black-billed magpie; displaying ravens; raven skull.

the feeder quickly disperse. We have also heard them give a close imitation of a bald eagle and a northern goshawk. Once, in a subalpine area, we heard a marmot giving its alarm whistle high up in a tree. Since marmots don't normally climb trees we scanned the tree carefully to document this unusual behavior. Of course, the only live creature we observed was a Steller's jay.

The sex of jays can sometimes be told by their voice. A mechanical-sounding 'rattle' is given by females, whereas only males give a high, muted whistle, usually on one pitch. The most unusual sound they make is their 'whisper song.' This song is surprisingly musical and consists of a medley of whistled and gurgled notes interspersed with snapping or popping sounds run together. The male's whisper song is given in early spring to court the female.

American dippers

The American dipper is a permanent resident of most of Alaska. It is especially common in Southeast, where most streams support one or more pairs. These birds walk, swim, and feed underwater, sing in midwinter, and sometimes build their nests behind waterfalls.

The official common name for this bird comes from the habit of bending its legs so its body moves up and down in a dipping motion. This dipping is most frequent when it is disturbed or closely approached. They rarely dip when feeding or resting. The reason dippers 'dip' is not fully understood. Other names are water ouzel and Anaruk Kiviruk, an Eskimo name that translates as "old woman sunk."

When dippers blink, their eyelids flash white because the lids are covered with tiny white feathers. In search of aquatic insects, fish, and fish eggs, dippers walk underwater against a strong current and swim from one place to another. They walk by grasping stones with their long toes and by keeping their heads down, so the pressure of the running water helps force them against the bed of the stream. Underwater photography has revealed they also use their partially folded wings to propel themselves.

Dippers have several anatomical adaptations that help them underwater. These adaptations include nasal flaps to prevent water from entering the nostrils, a large uropygial preen gland that produces oil for waterproofing their feathers, muscular modifications to aid in the swimming motions of their wings, and probably the ability to see as well underwater as above.

Dippers are well insulated to withstand icy streams and Alaskan winters. Their plumage is unusually dense, and they possess more contour feathers than most other perching birds. Most important, their very heavy coat of down between the feather tracts is similar to that of ducks and other waterfowl. This excellent insulation enables them to maintain a normal body temperature at air temperatures as low as -40°F, with less than a threefold increase in metabolism.

Dippers' circulatory systems are also well adapted to underwater dives. Experiments have shown they can decrease their blood supply to nonvital tissues and organs during diving. Also, they can store more oxygen in their blood than most nondiving birds. This all helps to provide the oxygen needed by the central nervous system and heart while underwater.

The American dipper is highly territorial during their breeding season in spring and summer. Territories may range from a few hundred yards to almost two miles of stream, which they vigorously defend against other dippers. As winter approaches, most birds move downstream and some may even wander between watersheds. During extreme cold, dippers may be forced into the intertidal areas of streams or along saltwater beaches because their normal habitat ices over.

Like other songbirds, the American dipper declares or stakes out its territory by singing. Singing during winter, however, is quite unusual for any songbird in Alaska, and the dipper could be considered almost unique in this respect. Its song, among the most melodious of any songbird's, is difficult to describe but sounds somewhat like a long rendition of some of the best notes of the thrushes and wrens. It is especially delightful to hear during the otherwise almost silent winter. We once timed a dipper's midwinter song that lasted for a full fifteen minutes.

Most of what we know about American dippers in Southeast comes from the dedicated research by Mary Willson and Kathy Hocker. For many years they banded dippers, looked for their nests, sampled their prey, and even analyzed their fecal pellets. Much of this research required miles of bushwhacking along steep-sided mountain streams often crossing the cold, fast moving water. Eventually their results were summarized into a book about the natural history of one of "North America's most charming—and unusual—songbirds."

Watching dippers—*Bob Armstrong*

I really enjoy sitting next to a stream and watching dippers feed. With binoculars and telephoto lenses you can often determine what they are feeding on. Some aquatic insects are fairly large and you can at least identify them to family. Many caddisflies are case builders and the dippers must remove the case before eating the larvae. They usually do this by thrashing the case from side to side or even beating it against rocks. The dippers are very persistent in doing this and the entire event may last several minutes.

When they catch fish they usually bring them to the surface and usually beat them on rocks, wood, or ice to subdue them before swallowing the fish, usually headfirst. This also can last several minutes, which often gives me an opportunity to identify the fish they are eating. So far I have documented, with photographs, pink, chum, sockeye, and coho salmon young, Dolly Varden, threespine stickleback, young sculpins and starry flounders. In other words any young fish in the stream or estuary appears to be fair game.

I once sat on a rock in the middle of a stream and gained the confidence of fledged youngsters and their parents. The youngsters would crawl around over my feet and the adults fed them right in front of me. When the parents weren't around, the youngsters seemed quite capable of feeding on their own. But as soon as an adult came, they would jump up on a rock and beg to be fed.

Dipper nests are balls of moss, commonly on cliff ledges right next to the stream, usually inaccessible to mammalian predators.

Do You Know Where Your Birds Are?

Frequent fliers, part II—*Richard Carstensen*

On its nesting grounds, the northern waterthrush is a common but hard-to-see skulker on brushy margins of streams and ponds. Wintering and migrating water-thrushes are easier to locate. Like other neotropical migrants we Alaskans may think of as 'our' birds, the waterthrush only stays here for the three months needed to nest and fledge a family. The banded bird at top was captured near her nest near the Mendenhall Glacier Visitor Center. The lower bird was foraging with egrets in the mud of a tidal mangrove thicket near Manzanillo, Mexico.

AMPHIBIANS

Six species of amphibian are considered native to Southeast Alaska. Three anurans (the order of frogs and toads) are western toad, wood frog, and Columbia spotted frog.

Three known caudates (the order of newts and salamanders) include rough-skinned newt, long-toed salamander, and northwestern salamander.

In addition to these native species, two frogs from the Pacific Northwest have been introduced: Pacific chorus frog and red-legged frog.

Ranges and habitats

Alaskan climate presents challenges to amphibians. There are four times more species, for example, in Washington State. Southeast Alaskan populations of all species except wood frog are near the northern edges of their geographic ranges. (Extreme freeze-tolerance allows the wood frog to survive north of the arctic circle.) Of the eight species of amphibians documented in Southeast, only western toad and rough-skinned newt are widely distributed throughout the mainland and islands of the Alexander Archipelago. Wood and spotted frog and long-toed salamander are reported chiefly near transboundary river systems such as the Taku and Stikine that connect Southeast Alaska to boreal centers of their distribution.

Above: Just kidding; there's no such thing as a toadstool!

Below: Classification of known Southeast amphibians. Asterisks signify introduced species.

Class Amphibia
Order Anura frogs & toads
  Families:
    Bufonidae true toads
      Anaxyrus boreas boreas western toad
    Ranidae true frogs
      Rana sylvatica wood frog
      Rana luteiventris Columbia spotted frog
      Rana aurora red-legged frog*
    Hylidae tree frogs
      Psuedacris regilla Pacific chorus frog*
Order Caudata newts & salamanders
  Families:
    Ambystomatidae mole salamanders
      Ambystoma gracile
        northwestern salamander
      Ambystoma macrodactylum
        long-toed salamander
    Salamandridae newts
      Taricha granulosa rough-skinned newt

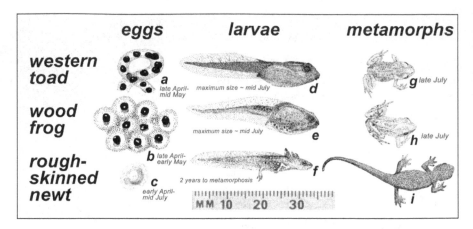

Reproductive stages of Southeast amphibians. Shown to scale; note shrinkage with meta-morphosis. Dates are from Juneau observations: **a)** toad eggs in strings of jelly; **b)** wood frog eggs in softball-sized mass; **c)** newt egg deposited singly—coiled embryo soon to hatch; **d)** toad larva is dark charcoal—dorsal fin starts farther back than on larval frogs; **e)** frog larva more olive brown—dorsal fin attaches well forward of tail; **f)** newt larva has antler-like gills; **g)** toadlet has fat, warty body, and small hind legs; **h)** froglet has smoother skin and legs are more muscular than on toadlets; **i)** unlike anurans, newt metamorphs are proportioned like adults.

That said, amphibians have a way of turning up where we don't expect them. This is due in part to their capture as pets—and subsequent release or escape into new watersheds. Juneau, for example, has four species that aren't supposed to be here. Wood and Columbia spotted frog were likely introduced from Taku River populations. Rough-skinned newts were reportedly trans-planted from a population on nearby Shelter Island. Juneau's Pacific chorus frog probably traveled farther; the nearest native source is in southern British Columbia.

These apparent introductions—intentional or accidental—were illegal. Exotic amphibians have elsewhere displaced native species. Even moving a native amphibian to an adjacent watershed or different pond system can spread disease. Although many of us fondly remember raising tadpoles as children, learning about metamorphosis, even proudly releasing the transformed adults, in today's more dangerous world (risky for the amphibians, that is) possession of amphibians native to our state requires a research or educational permit from the Alaska Department of Fish and Game.

How did toads and newts colonize the islands of our archipelago? Most amphibians are intolerant of salt water. The western toad, in contrast, has been

---

Amphibian pond types

Ponds and lakes used by Southeast amphibians for spawning and larval rearing can be classified according to geomorphic origin. Types include:

Human ponds—Anthropogenic: dredged or backwatered, for gravel extraction or roadside ditching.

Glacial ponds—Kettles and intermorainal swale ponds generally younger than two centuries.

Uplift ponds—On raised former tideland or behind recent storm berms.

Beaver ponds—Created and maintained by beaver. Especially mportant on islands where other pond types are less common.

Fen ponds—In level or gently sloping sedge/herb dominated peatlands.

Bog ponds—In sphagnum-dominated peatlands. In our study we found no amphibians in these acidic, low-nutrient ponds.

Bedrock ponds—Controlled by bedrock. Most larger ponds and lakes.

Riverine ponds—On floodplains of large rivers.

---

seen swimming—albeit sluggishly—in full-strength seawater a mile from shore. But the "wandering pregnant female" hypothesis, invoked to explain some mammalian colonization of islands, doesn't work for toads. Egg-fertilization is external! So not only would a female have to survive the saltwater crossing; once arrived on the island, she'd have to find an equally seaworthy male.

Contemplating the odds against this, one appreciates the extremely high reproductive potential of toads and most other anurans. One western toad jelly-stringer we examined had about 2,500 eggs. Fresh metamorphs are sometimes so abundant we have to step carefully in order not to squash them, bringing to mind one scenario that could launch large numbers of seagoing toads. In warm, desiccating weather, toads reenter freshwater to rehydrate. We see this particularly among quarter-sized yearling toads, which congregate in certain wet meadows on sunny midsummer days. Individuals that make the mistake of bathing in streams with stiff current—as observed in a Glacier Bay toad study in the 1980s—can be swept out into the estuary. During outburst floods, large river systems such as the Taku may periodically flush hundreds of toads and toadlets to sea in this manner.

Because salmon fisheries are economic mainstays in our region, the ecology of streams and rivers has received intensive study. In contrast, there have been almost no studies of small bodies of *still* water, especially the shallow, warm ponds without fish access that appear to offer best breeding habitat for all eight Southeast amphibian species. In 2002, with Juneau ecologist Mary Willson, we embarked upon a two-year survey of amphibians in northern Southeast

Alaska. For this work, we established a pond classification based upon geomorphic origin (sidebar). Our ground-truthing confirmed that even small, thirty-foot-diameter ponds can be accurately mapped and assigned to one of these categories by examination of high-resolution air photos.

Most Southeast amphibians grow up under cover of aquatic plants. During early spring spawning congregations, these plants are only apparent as overwintered stems and runners. By mid-June, however, expanded leaves cast extensive cover over shallow margins of breeding ponds. Emergent, floating-leaved, and submerged plants provide hiding cover for larvae, filter pollutants, oxygenate water, and reduce wave action on margins of larger ponds and lakes. And rooted aquatic plants support a film of epiphytic algae that feed omnivorous tadpoles. In warm, shallow ponds, loose mats of green algae also form at the surface by midsummer, held in place by leaves of vascular aquatics.

Although average temperature hardly varied among ponds we studied, temperature *regime* differed strongly. Most amphibian larvae occupy shallow ponds where temperature amplitude is greatest. Beaver, rich-fen, and uplift ponds provide these conditions. The lower minimum (nighttime) temperatures in such ponds are not a problem. Diurnally feeding amphibians may even seek lower temperatures at night to recover from high daily metabolic demands. On the other hand, the higher (late-afternoon) maximum temperatures in very shallow ponds elevate larval metabolism and enhance algal food production. These warm temperatures also discourage salmonids that prey on amphibian larvae.

Populations of amphibians have declined dramatically around the world in recent decades. Causes include habitat loss, increased UV-B radiation, fungal infection, intensified predation by introduced fish and nonnative frogs, climate change, increased risk of disease, damage to immune systems resulting from pollutants such as pesticides, and combinations of these factors. In the 1990s, concerned about trends in Columbia spotted frog numbers to the south, the US Fish and Wildlife Service conducted surveys of major transboundary rivers throughout Southeast Alaska. Results will provide baseline population estimates to which future surveys may be compared.

In the meantime, however, a possibly more serious decline occurred for which no quantitative data are available. From Skagway to Ketchikan, long-time residents say that western toads, once seen routinely, are now scarce or locally extinct.

Fungal pathogens

Batrachochytrium dendrobatidis (BD) is a chytrid fungus parasitizing vertebrates. Motile zoospores escape from skin of dead animals, swim through water, and penetrate skin of new hosts, causing a fungal skin infection known as chytridiomycosis. BD was discovered in 1998 in Central America and Australia, and has spread to Africa, Europe, North America, and South America. Although BD has a wide temperature range—4–25°C, allowing it to overwinter in hosts—growth halts above 28°C, leading to host recovery in experiments. Linkage to climate change seems possible but is unconfirmed. Some biologists suggest BD only recently evolved, and spread rapidly among the world's amphibians. Species such as bullfrogs withstand higher infection rates, allowing them to serve as vectors. But the appearance of BD in bullfrog-free Southeast Alaska is mysterious.

Since 2005, a growing database of swab samples has been collected from adult and juvenile toads from Prince of Wales Island to Yukon Territory. Toads' ventral pelvic regions—the site of the most intense infection—are swabbed for laboratory analysis. Overall, about a third of the sampled western toads from Southeast and neighboring Canada have tested positive for BD, with the highest infection rate in Yukon populations, and lowest from Admiralty Island. Although isolated populations seem less infected, two of six toads we sampled in the remote Soule River watershed near Hyder tested positive. They were vigorous with no external sign of infection, consistent with findings of other researchers.

Chytrid fungi are abundant parasitic water molds in moist soil throughout Southeast. They normally infect plants, algae, protozoa, and invertebrates. How has this particular chytrid fungus spread to such remote locations? Or *did it* spread? Was the pathogen always widespread and endemic, but only recently grown virulent? Has BD switched hosts, as in the human AIDS epidemic? Is it only virulent in stressed hosts? If so, what is this worldwide stress plaguing a huge variety of host species, in diverse habitats and climates?

Studies elsewhere hint that BD resistance can be developed in previously susceptible populations. Around Juneau, we're hearing reports of greater numbers of metamorphs and yearlings in areas where toads seemed to be in dire straits during our 2002-03 study. Whether that's a real trend, and if it will continue, remains to be seen.

Western toads

Perhaps because true frogs are rare on the archipelago, and many born-and-raised Southeasterners have never encountered them, residents often mistakenly refer to toads as frogs. Unless a frog report comes from a mainland river, or one of the few islands with known frog populations, our first question of observers (phrased politely) is whether they know the difference.

Adult female western toad, almost four inches long. Males are rarely longer than three inches. **Below right**: Tracks in mud, toeing inward.

To anyone who remembers the 'good old days' of toad proliferation—decades prior to about the mid-1980s—the decline of this aggressive colonizer and explosive reproducer is puzzling and sad. Our field notes from the 1980s indicate that on evening walks out the Eagle River trail, north of Juneau, it was common to encounter ten to twenty adult toads. That's more adults than three dedicated toad-hunters managed to find throughout northern Southeast (outside of breeding congregations) during two full seasons of intensive amphibian surveys in 2002 and 2003.

Although the apparent simultaneous decline of toad populations throughout Southeast suggests some global cause such as climate change or disease, it's undeniable that habitat change is also important in some areas. According to a man who spent his boyhood in Mendenhall Valley in the 1950s, the western toad was then "the most abundant noninsect life form." These toads may initially have actually benefited from a construction boom—widespread dredging of gravel ponds and roadside ditches, and deforestation of the lower valley, providing more light and warmth to anthropogenic breeding ponds. Until the 1970s, the valley was largely untransected by the roads or driveways that now make it impossible for a toad to travel fifty yards without risk of being squashed or collected. The western toad is a habitat generalist that responds well to some forms of human disturbance. But at increasing human densities it begins to suffer from barriers to movement in its terrestrial phases.

The pattern of camouflaging bumps is retained throughout a toad's life, as distinctive and persistent as human fingerprints. Our multi-year photo catalog of Juneau-area toads includes about fifty individuals. One male in this collection was a minimum of eight years old when rephotographed in 2009. It's unusual for animals who produce so many eggs and young to also be long-lived. With all the challenges faced by western toads—now including the mysterious chytridiomycosis—those venerable and hopefully fungus-resistant breeders could be key to survival of the species.

In light of declines, all observations of western toads are noteworthy, particularly from areas where distribution is poorly known. Breeding ponds locations are especially important to document. Encounters can be reported to the Alaska Department of Fish and Game. Although photographs are valuable, it's best not to handle wild amphibians—researchers use latex gloves. Toxins in sunscreen or insect repellent easily pass through amphibian skin, and humans may also serve as unwitting disease vectors.

Spotted and wood frogs

If you happen by a wood frog breeding pond in April, it's hard to miss. Loud, duck-like quacks carry twice as far as the soft chirps of arguing male western toads. But spawning takes only a few days, and at other times of year, wood frogs can be furtive and hard to detect. For frogs, they're quite terrestrial in adulthood, unlike the more pond-oriented Columbia spotted frog.

Wood frogs deposit eggs communally, in barely submerged jelly globs quite different from the linear egg-stringers of toads. In winter, wood frog adults hibernate beneath forest litter and snow in a frozen state with no heartbeat, circulation, breathing, or muscle movement. Upon thawing, heartbeat resumes and frogs reactivate. Wood frogs concentrate glucose antifreeze in and around the cells, confining freezing to areas outside their cells as insects do.

Because access to the transboundary rivers requires a special set of skills and equipment, many Southeast outdoorspeople have never enjoyed the unique transitional habitats of the Taku or Stikine River bottoms. Only those priviledged to explore these vast, swampy watersheds (or a few islands off the Stikine) are familiar with the plop of alarmed Columbia spotted frogs launching into side-sloughs and beaver marshes.

An adult wood frog is only about two inches long—half the size of an adult spotted frog, around four inches. It's also distinguished from spotteds by a dark mask from snout to shoulder.

Tadpoles of these frogs are bigger than those of western toads, and already demonstrate the greater wariness that will characterize them as adults. As you approach their pond margin, loose clusters of larvae dash for the bottom cover, quite unlike the seemingly oblivious 'toadpoles.'

Rough-skinned newts

Rough-skinned newts—our second most widely distributed amphibians—are named for their pebbly backs. Unlike frogs and toads, they lay their eggs singly, attached inconspicuously to submerged plants. Larvae may require two or more years to complete metamorphosis, and sexual maturity may take four to five years. Some adults remain in ponds year-round, but we've found them under logs and rocks up to one hundred yards from known breeding ponds.

Many rough-skinned newt populations possess a potent neurotoxin that easily kills most animals including humans. Research in the Lower 48 indicated this toxicity varies inversely with exposure to garter snakes, important predators on newts. Surprisingly, rough-skinned newts we sent to these scientists from a Juneau population—supposedly introduced from nearby Kichxaak', *wing island* (Shelter Island), far north of garter-snake range—turned out to be highly toxic!

How did newts colonize Southeast Alaska after the great ice age? Like western toads, rough-skinned newts are somewhat tolerant of salt water. They forage in the intertidal and survive brief immersion. As for transboundary rivers—clearly our portals for several frogs and salamanders—there's only one newt record on the lower Stikine, and none so far for Canadian headwaters. But in 2009 we found newts near Hyder, suggesting potential source populations in the boreal interior.

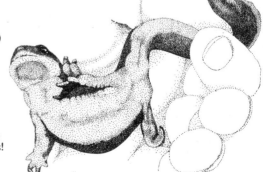

Male rough-skinned newt (*Taricha granulosa*) has an elongated vent compared to females. Cryptically colored above, *Taricha* is bright orange below. As with monarch butterflies, this is an "eat-me-at-your-peril" notice to would-be predators. So far, Alaskan newts have tested negative for chytrid infection; in fact, the danger is to those who contact *them*. Never lick your fingers or rub your eyes while handling newts!

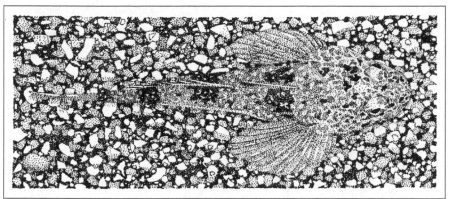

Staghorn sculpin juvenile, camouflaged against the bottom of a salt-marsh slough.

FISH

Southeast Alaska has thousands of freshwater lakes, ponds, rivers, and streams. About 15,500 miles of shoreline break up the marine waters into a myriad of fiords, channels, lagoons, bays, and open ocean. Together, our fresh and salt waters support millions of fish. A total of 521 fish species are known to occur in all of Alaska. Of these, 309 or 59 percent are in the waters of Southeast.

In contrast to other states and countries, fish in most of Southeast Alaska still live in a relatively pristine and pollution-free environment. Our rivers are mostly free of dams and discharges by large industries so detrimental to fish elsewhere. Our towns and cities are small and usually not located along major fish-producing rivers. Yet, wherever people concentrate, damage to fish habitat occurs. Channelized streams and altered wetlands are commonplace in and near all towns and cities. Clear-cut logging to stream banks without provision of protective buffer strips has damaged fish habitat throughout the region, and extensive damage to fish habitat in Washington and British Columbia has reduced the numbers of salmon migrating to and through Southeast waters. For instance, multiple dams on the Columbia River decimated chinook salmon populations that once fed in the inside and offshore waters of Southeast Alaska.

Most of our fish are native. Only two exotic (nonnative) freshwater species (Arctic grayling and brook char) and one marine species (American shad) have been introduced. Both freshwater species were introduced into a variety of waters but appear to have established a foothold only in lakes barren of other

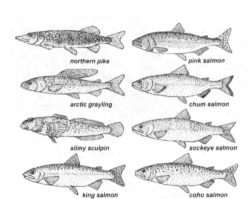

northern pike

arctic grayling

slimy sculpin

king salmon

pink salmon

chum salmon

sockeye salmon

coho salmon

A sampling of Southeast Alaska's freshwater and anadromous fishes. Grayling are not native to Southeast, but have been introduced to some lakes. Not to scale.

species. American shad were introduced from the Atlantic coast to the Sacramento River in California around 1870. The fish rapidly spread to other rivers as well as at sea, reaching Alaska by 1904. A few Atlantic salmon have been caught by commercial fishermen in Southeast, apparently escaped from fish-farming pens in British Columbia. Although native to Southeast Alaska, rainbow trout have also been successfully stocked in a few barren lakes throughout the region.

Freshwater and anadromous fish—Salmon, trout, char, stickleback, and sculpin complete the list for most of Southeast Alaska's fresh waters. In freshwater systems with sea access, sculpin and stickleback may be the only true year-round residents.

For anadromous salmonids (salmon, trout, and char), whose life cycles occur in both salt and fresh waters, the ocean provides bountiful food necessary for rapid growth. Many spend two or more years feeding at sea (chinook, sockeye, chum, steelhead); others spend between one and two years at sea (pink and coho) or only a few weeks or months (Dolly Varden and cutthroat). In winter, most salmon, except some kings, leave our inside waters for food-rich areas in the Gulf of Alaska. Lakes and streams blocked to migrating fish usually contain resident Dolly Varden and sometimes cutthroat trout. Here their growth is quite slow. Resident fish in streams seldom grow longer than seven inches and in lakes seldom longer than a foot (see exceptions under *Cutthroat trout*, p. 191). Slow growth of fish in freshwater lakes and streams is related to cold waters and nutrient-poor soils of surrounding coniferous forests.

Marine fish—In contrast to our fresh waters, the marine waters of Southeast Alaska, including the eastern Gulf of Alaska, contain hundreds of fish species. The most common are flatfish (flathead sole, southern rock sole, yellowfin sole,

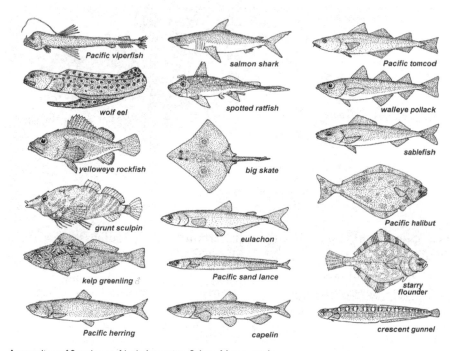

A sampling of Southeast Alaska's marine fishes. Not to scale.

arrowtooth flounder, Pacific halibut), cod (Pacific cod, walleye pollock), rockfish (Pacific ocean perch, rougheye rockfish, yelloweye rockfish, dusky rockfish, silvergray rockfish), sculpins (great sculpin, spinyhead sculpin, buffalo sculpin), skates, sablefish, herring, smelt, salmon, char, Pacific sand lance, and threespine stickleback. Other common marine fish include eelpouts, snailfish, poachers, pricklebacks, gunnels, ronquils, kelp greenlings, wolf-eel, prowfish, and tube-snouts.

Southeast Alaska has about seven of the thirty or so shark species found on the west coast of North America; the salmon shark is probably our most common and most voracious. These fast swimmers grow to a length of about ten feet. In the Gulf of Alaska they eat salmon, often destroying those caught in nets as well as damaging the nets themselves. The legendary white shark occasionally migrates to Southeast, where it has been seen most often off the west coast of Tàan, *sea lion* (Prince of Wales Island) and, during strong El Niño events, off Yaakwdáat, *canoe rebounded*, (Yakutat Bay). The relatively small (two to four

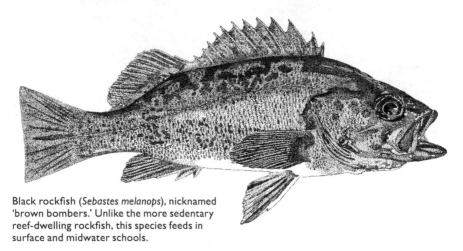

Black rockfish (*Sebastes melanops*), nicknamed 'brown bombers.' Unlike the more sedentary reef-dwelling rockfish, this species feeds in surface and midwater schools.

feet) spiny dogfish can be common in certain areas of Southeast. Fishermen should be cautious with these fish, as they have mildly toxic fin spines and can also inflict severe bites.

At least seven species of skate occur in Southeast. These flattened fish have enlarged pectoral fins that act like wings, which propel them as if they were slowly flying through the water. They are bottom dwellers and take in water for respiration through openings called spiracles, located on their topsides, rather than through their mouths, like most other fish. The Aleutian and Alaska skates are common in the Gulf of Alaska off Southeast. Most skates attain two to four feet in length, but one species, the big skate, may reach up to eight feet. On occasion beachcombers in Southeast find the empty egg cases of big skates and long-nose skates. These cases are quite distinctive and look like rectangular pouches about four to eight inches long with a 'horn' at each corner. The eggs incubate in their cases for a long time, averaging about nine months for the big skate.

Another common, unusual-looking marine fish is the curious and oddly named spotted ratfish. It has a large rabbit-like head, huge green eyes, forward-facing chisel-like teeth, and a body that tapers back to a remarkably long, rat-like tail, which accounts for its common name. Ratfish behavior is as weird as their looks. During elaborate courtship maneuvers, the males undergo striking changes in color. Later, females may take up to thirty hours to extrude their egg cases, which then hang from their bodies in a long filament for another four to six days.

Southeast marine waters abound with huge schools of small, slim, silvery fish, often seen breaking the water's surface when pursued by predators. Many

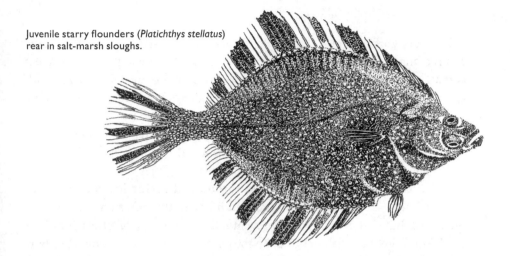

Juvenile starry flounders (*Platichthys stellatus*) rear in salt-marsh sloughs.

people use the misnomer needlefish, a family of fish occurring farther south. The species most often seen here are Pacific sand lance, Pacific herring, eulachon, and capelin. Collectively, these fish form the most important component of the diet of most mature salmon, trout, and char while they are at sea. Many other creatures, such as humpback whales and marbled murrelets, also rely on these fish as a food source. Pacific herring support a multimillion-dollar commercial fishery. They are used for bait and cut into fillets for human consumption. Herring eggs (roe) are considered a delicacy in Japan, where they command a high price.

In the depths of our marine waters live some very bizarre-looking fish. In general, these deep-sea fishes have light organs called photophores, and some have large mouths with numerous long, fang-like teeth. The purpose of their photophores is not well known, but they may be used for recognition, especially at night or in the dark depths of the sea. They may also serve to illuminate their surroundings or attract food. The small Pacific viperfish (to ten inches) has huge fangs protruding from its mouth. One of the largest deep-sea fish in our region is the long and slender longnose lancetfish, which may reach almost seven feet in length. It has a large, sail-like dorsal fin, long daggerlike teeth in the roof of its mouth, and is hermaphroditic (bisexual). The North Pacific daggertooth, northern pearleye, northern lampfish, and barreleye are other bizarre fish that only researchers, using mid- to deepwater trawls, are apt to see alive. Most of the rest of us can only marvel at them preserved for study in museum jars.

Four members of the cod family—Pacific cod, Pacific tomcod, walleye pollock, and saffron cod—occur in Southeast Alaska marine waters. The Pacific cod is of major commercial importance along the North Pacific coast, where it is marketed for the fresh and frozen market and made into fish sticks. With global cod declines, walleye pollock has been increasingly targeted by domestic and foreign fisheries, especially for popular imitation crab (surimi). These fisheries impact many Alaskan marine mammals and seabirds. A cod look-alike is the commercially important sablefish, or black cod—so fatty it tastes like butter—caught in trawls, in traps, and on longlines.

Flatfish, including flounders, sole, turbot, and Pacific halibut, are abundant in Southeast waters. Flatfish start out life with their eyes on either side of their head, but as they grow, one eye eventually migrates to the other side of the head. This allows the fish to lie flat on the ocean bottom, some completely buried and hidden, with just their eyes exposed. Many regard the Pacific halibut as our finest fish for eating. Heavily sought by commercial and sport fishermen, halibut are among our larger species of fish. Females often exceed one hundred pounds (one five-hundred-pound halibut was caught near Petersburg).

We have around thirty species of rockfish in our marine waters. Known for their tasty flesh, rockfish are bass-like in appearance, with somewhat compressed bodies and large mouths. Most adults range from one to two feet in length. One, the rougheye rockfish, may grow to three feet and live up to 205 years. Rockfish are among the longest-lived and latest-maturing of all fish (sidebar: *Harvesting longevity*, p. 211). Most Southeast species have a maximum age of over sixty. As their name implies, many live in reefs and rocky areas. Some species are attracted to old shipwrecks, where they live their entire lives.

A search of our rocky intertidal waters usually reveals pricklebacks and gunnels. There are numerous species of these eel-like fishes, often erroneously called blennies, which do not occur in our region. Small sculpins are often seen darting this way and that in shallow tide pools.

We may never see many of the numerous other groups of marine fish occurring in our waters. We know little about many of their life histories; new species are no doubt out there waiting to be discovered.

Dolly Varden char

Dolly char live in some of the most beautiful waters in the world. Imagine a long, winding fiord bordered by snowcapped mountains, cliffs with waterfalls

Bounties on Dolly Varden—*Bob Armstrong*

A bounty program destroyed over six million Alaskan Dolly Varden between 1921 and 1940. Dolly Varden were then thought to be a serious predator on salmon young and eggs. Bounties ranged from 2½ to 5 cents per Dolly Varden tail.

In 1939, almost twenty years after the bounty program was instigated, biologists were called in to investigate its effectiveness. They found that the bounty program was one of the greatest boondoggles in the history of Alaskan fisheries. They discovered that many, and in some instances the majority, of tails turned in for bounty were from rainbow trout and salmon, the very species they were attempting to save. For instance, in the US Bureau of Fisheries office in Yakutat, of 20,000 tails examined by biologists, 3,760 were from rainbows, 14,200 from coho salmon, but only 2,040 from Dolly Varden.

Since the early 1940s, numerous studies have been done to determine whether or not Dolly Varden were a serious predator on salmon young and eggs. These studies showed that they were not eating salmon fry in numbers sufficient to harm salmon populations. In fact, most of the predator control program was based on the feeding habits of another species, the Arctic char.

The studies also indicated that Dolly Varden may actually benefit salmon. For example, Dolly Varden eats drifting salmon eggs dug up by the nest-building activities of salmon. These eggs, if not eaten, eventually die and develop fungus, which may infect and kill the healthy live eggs and yolk-sac fry in the gravel. Another possible benefit is that while in lakes, Dolly Varden feed heavily on, and may help control, freshwater snails that are an intermediate host of a parasite

Dolly Varden male with kype, a hooked lower jaw. In salmon, hook is on upper jaw.

infecting the eyes of coho and sockeye salmon young, eventually causing blindness. Even competition for space between Dolly Varden and more serious salmon young predators, such as cutthroat trout, may reduce overall predation of salmon young by all species of fish.

cascading to the salt water's edge, a river teeming with Pacific salmon that snakes its way up the valley through ancient forests of Sitka spruce and western hemlock—this is a typical home of the Dolly Varden char in Southeast Alaska.

Walking up one of these streams, you begin to see the almost motionless, well-camouflaged schools of adult Dolly Varden. Occasionally an individual fish darts out of the school to grab something. Each pool of significant size seems to have a school of about fifty to one hundred char. Most seem to be waiting patiently for something to happen. Some wait for spawning to begin from

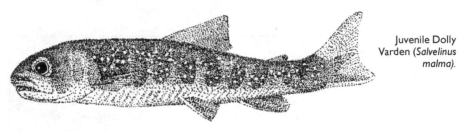

Juvenile Dolly Varden (*Salvelinus malma*).

one to three months after they entered the stream. Others, for no apparent reason, leave the stream for the ocean, and then enter another stream a few miles down the coast. In the riffles between the pools, each pair of spawning salmon seems to have a small number of Dolly Varden in close attendance. These char wait for the numerous salmon eggs that are knocked out of the gravel during the salmon's nest-building activities. They gorge themselves on these nutritious eggs until they are quite rotund.

In the streams' side channels, undercut bank areas, quiet shallow-water areas, and side tributaries, you see many small Dolly Varden ranging from one to five inches in length. They are the progeny of Dolly Varden that have previously spawned in the stream. Most occupy territories, vigorously defending them from other Dolly Varden and young coho salmon.

Continuing to walk along the stream, you begin to realize that Dolly Varden occupy almost all available habitats, in such a great variety of sizes, and exhibiting so many different types of behavior, that you suspect great complexities must exist in their life cycles.

One of these complexities is migration. Each fall in Southeast Alaska, thousands of Dolly Varden migrate from the sea into lakes, where they spend the winter. Most have never been in lakes before, and come from the numerous small- to medium-sized streams that intersect our shorelines. This run of Dolly Varden into lakes also includes fish that originated in a particular lake system, fish that completed spawning in other streams along the coast, and immature fish on their second or third annual trip from the sea.

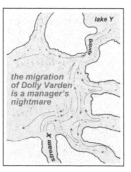

the migration of Dolly Varden is a manager's nightmare

In spring, all Dolly Varden leave their overwintering lakes and migrate to sea. The mature fish then continue directly to the mouth of the stream in which they hatched, and enter it to spawn. The immatures, which usually number in the thousands from each lake, move apparently at random between lakes and streams, and between streams, making the fish appear more abundant than they really are and creating a manager's nightmare.

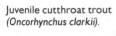
Juvenile cutthroat trout
(*Oncorhynchus clarkii*).

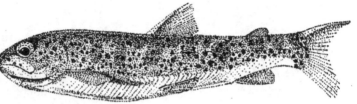

Most streams in Southeast Alaska serve as both spawning grounds for adults and early rearing habitat for their young. Although some large rivers such as the Taku, Stikine, and Chilkat are used by Dolly Varden in winter, they usually do not overwinter in streams.

Dolly Varden can benefit greatly by overwintering in lakes. Because of ice cover there are few, if any, predators. Fresh water may be several degrees cooler than the sea in winter, so fish need fewer calories and less food. And they may live longer because they do not need to burn energy to avoid predators, search for food, or swim to maintain themselves in currents as they do in streams or in the ocean.

It is uncertain whether Dolly Varden can overwinter at sea. Bob Armstrong's tagging showed that most, perhaps all, winter only in fresh water. Attempts in Norway to rear Arctic char (a close relative) year-round in salt water failed; all the fish died. Perhaps Dolly Varden cannot tolerate seawater for extended periods.

Cutthroat trout

Throughout their range, cutthroat trout, like the canary in the mine, are sensitive indicators of environmental change. Once native cutthroat trout abounded throughout the west, but now, except for places like Yellowstone Lake and River in Yellowstone National Park, many populations have vanished. Widespread introductions of exotic (nonnative) races of rainbow trout and brook char and a host of other human changes to the environment caused their demise.

Southeast Alaska is fortunate to have many streams, rivers, and lakes with good cutthroat habitat. In addition, the Alaska Department of Fish and Game prohibits introduction of nonnative fish species, so many genetically pure populations of cutthroat are found here. They may be sea-run (anadromous), spend their entire life in a lake-stream system, or reside only in streams.

Sea-run cutthroat are usually associated with lakes and a few of the larger, slow-moving rivers. Most of these anadromous populations are found south of

Frederick Sound. Each year the fish go to sea in May and June and return to fresh water in September and October. In Southeast Alaska, approximately 2,500 freshwater systems contain sea-run salmon, trout, or char, but fewer than one hundred watersheds contain significant numbers of sea-run cutthroat trout. A good run of sea-run cutthroat may be about 3,000 fish, and of these, only about three- to four hundred may be maturing females that will spawn the following spring. In addition, the fish are relatively slow growing, taking about five to six years to reach a length of ten to twelve inches. These factors make our sea-run cutthroat trout very sensitive to overharvest.

Sea-run cutthroat may also depend on different watersheds for spawning, feeding, and overwintering. For example, cutthroat tagged at Petersburg Creek were recaptured by sport anglers in a total of fourteen streams in the Petersburg area. These streams varied in distance from Petersburg Creek from one-half mile to forty-four miles. This could mean that cutthroat also behave somewhat like Dolly Varden in that spawning fish return home to specific tributaries, while nonmaturing fish do not always go back to a home stream on a feeding run or when seeking overwintering habitat.

Resident cutthroat trout are found in most landlocked lakes at lower elevations in Southeast. In a few of these systems you may find large, trophy-sized cutthroat trout of three to eight pounds. In contrast, most sea-run cutthroat seldom exceed one to two pounds. Some lake-resident cutthroat grow large because they prey heavily on small kokanee (landlocked sockeye salmon), and they are longer-lived than sea-run individuals. Lake residents may live up to nineteen years, whereas few sea-run individuals live beyond eight years. Other resident cutthroat have evolved ways to live their entire lives in streams so small you can easily step over them. Since these fish reach a length of only a few inches, they are ignored by most anglers.

Coho salmon

In Southeast, most adult coho salmon leave the sea and begin entering their spawning streams and rivers between July and November. The young hatch from their eggs in early spring and remain protected in the gravel of streambeds, nourished by absorbing the material in their yolk sacs. Most emerge from the gravel during May and June.

The freshwater life of these young coho may last only a few days or weeks,

***Winter survival tactics**—Bob Armstrong*

In Southeast, fish are not subject to the extensive freezing of more northern Alaskan waters. Nevertheless, significant migrations and behavior changes prepare them for winter. For instance, most salmon, except some kings, leave our inside waters for more food-rich areas in the Gulf of Alaska. Dolly Varden and cutthroat trout migrate from the sea into lakes and deeper portions of large rivers. Young salmon, trout, and char in streams make significant moves before winter to avoid areas that freeze. Pacific sand lances bury themselves in sand during the winter period of low food supplies.

At Hood Bay Creek on Admiralty Island, I observed large schools of young Dolly Varden and coho salmon moving upstream in the fall. My subsequent studies showed that these fish were seeking headwater spring areas. During extreme cold, these springs were the only significant ice-free areas in the stream. At Lake Eva on Baranof Island, about 100,000 Dolly Varden and 2,000 cutthroat trout entered the lake before winter during our study of these fish. In Southeast lakes the water temperature may be only slightly above freezing in winter; hence the fishes' metabolic rate and resulting food requirements are less than if they remained in the warmer salt water. In lakes there are no currents to swim against, and they are usually covered with ice, so no predators can get to the fish. One fall, I helped mark all the Dolly Varden entering Lake Eva. The following spring we counted 94 percent of these marked fish leaving the lake, an amazing overwinter survival.

or may last from one to five years. During this time, the young coho can be found in almost all bodies of water accessible to them. They may live in streams, glacial rivers, beaver ponds, lakes, side sloughs, and even intertidal portions of some streams.

Those living in streams usually set up territories, chasing and nipping at other fish in order to defend the most favorable feeding areas. Since most of their food comes from insects drifting in the currents, certain areas of a stream are more productive than others. In contrast, coho living in still waters such as ponds, lakes, and sloughs may not defend territories. In these situations, the food may appear from almost any direction, so territorial behavior would be of little advantage.

Juvenile coho
salmon
*(Oncorhynchus
kisutch).*

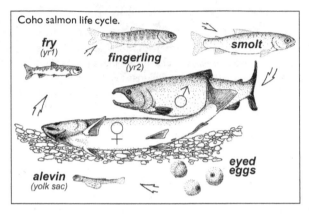

Coho salmon life cycle.
fry (yr1)
fingerling (yr2)
smolt
eyed eggs
alevin (yolk sac)

Streams have a certain carrying capacity (total number of fish the stream will support) for coho young. When this limit is reached, thousands of excess coho young may migrate to sea within days or weeks after emerging from the gravel. These very young fish eventually perish at sea because they have not developed the physiological and behavioral processes that would allow them to grow and develop normally in the ocean. These processes require one to four years in fresh water, at which time the coho successfully migrate to sea as smolts.

Some fisheries biologists believe that these excess coho young are driven to sea by individuals that have already established territories. In Alaska, competition for territories may be high because a large proportion of a population of young coho remains in fresh water for at least two years before going to sea. In other Pacific Coast states and British Columbia, most coho young go to sea as year-old smolts, reducing competition for territories among those remaining in the streams.

Research at the Auke Bay Biological Laboratory in Juneau has revealed that many coho young move into the intertidal portions of streams where territorial fish like older coho and Dolly Varden young do not live. In summer these areas are generally warmer, with more small crustaceans (isopods and amphipods) than stream reaches above tidal influence. Coho young grow faster in these warmer, food-rich areas, and then move upstream in the fall when water temperatures drop.

Most research into the early life history of coho salmon points to one common denominator, the overall importance of small streams and tributaries to maintenance of populations. One study showed that during periods of flooding, coho young moved into side tributaries to escape tremendous velocities of water in the river main stem. Another study revealed that coho young moved into spring-fed tributaries and portions of streams with upwelling ground-

Pink and chum—the Southeast entrée

Pinks are by far the most abundant of our five salmon species. Easily captured in spawning riffles, they're the main course of bears building fat stores for hibernation. Coastal bear numbers are up to eighty times denser than interior populations lacking salmon. Pinks are important to eagles because they're small enough to be carried to the nest when eaglets are largest and hungriest. Dead and dying pinks later feed fledgling eagles inept at obtaining live fish. A host of other fish feed on pink fry: coho smolts, Dolly Varden, cutthroat trout, and at least three species of sculpin.

In terms of pure tonnage, chum salmon are second only to pinks. Run timing can be as important as biomass. In the Chilkat River, upwellings of warm water keep portions of the channel ice-free into November, when spawning chums feed up to 3,500 bald eagles. That late chum run enhances eagle reproductive success over a wide geographic area. Large-bodied chums have more fat than pinks and are favored by bears. Chum salmon fry in fresh water feed young salmon, trout, char, sculpins, mergansers, and kingfishers.

water for the winter. Since spring-fed areas are warmer in winter, coho could avoid severe icing elsewhere in the watershed. In a study of the Juneau streams, biologists found that some of the smallest streams contained unusually high numbers of young coho.

Protection of these small streams is difficult, and development has harmed coho habitat. Channelization of intertidal portions of streams for flood control and to protect neighborhoods or airports renders these areas much less productive as coho habitat. Urban development often eliminates streamside vegetation and canopy of smaller streams.

Removal of coniferous trees along streams by logging and other activities can be detrimental to young coho in ways that are not obvious. For example, trees that fall into streams provide excellent cover, creating pools and velocity shelters for young coho in streams that otherwise plunge rapidly from mountains to sea. When trees are removed from stream banks, the natural cycle of decay and replacement of an important form of coho salmon habitat is lost.

Stream sections with deep pools, beaver ponds, logjams, and undercut banks with tree roots and debris lose fewer fish during freshets and maintain higher numbers of coho in winter than sections without these habitat characteristics. In winter, the coho young generally avoid riffles, glides, and pools without cover.

The importance of coho salmon to humans is evident in the commercial and sport fisheries of Southeast. In some years coho bring in more money than any other commercial salmon fishery in Southeast and sport fishers usually harvest more coho than any other species of salmon.

Coho salmon typically spawn later than other species of salmon. Most populations enter fresh water in September and October, and most spawning takes place in late October and November. Thus, these late-running stocks are available to feed other animals after fish from earlier stocks have disappeared. In addition, coho carcasses may become frozen as streams ice over, so they are often available to hungry birds and mammals during midwinter thaws and even into spring. Due to the abundance and distribution of their young in streams and adjacent ponds they also provide food for many other creatures such as mink, otters, dippers, kingfishers, and mergansers.

Threespine sticklebacks

Threespine sticklebacks are widely distributed in Southeast Alaska and are particularly abundant in lakes, ponds, slow-moving streams, and estuaries containing emergent vegetation. Two forms of threespine stickleback occur in Southeast—a marine form and a freshwater one.

The marine form lives in the sea for most of its life, migrating into fresh water or estuaries in spring to breed. In early autumn the offspring and adults leave streams and estuaries and move out into salt water. Some remain near shore through the winter, and others move out to open sea for considerable distances. Large numbers of three-spine sticklebacks, for example, have been taken at the water surface up to 496 miles from shore in the Gulf of Alaska. The marine form is best distinguished by numerous (twenty-two to thirty-seven) bony plates along its sides and by its bright silver color.

The freshwater form remains in streams, lakes, and ponds throughout its life. This form is best distinguished by only a few (zero to nine) bony plates on its sides and an olive color mottled with indistinct bars. Marine and freshwater forms spawn at one to two years of age, and probably die after breeding. Maximum life span is about four years.

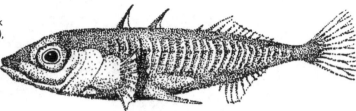

Threespine stickleback
(*Gasterosteus aculeatus*),
marine form.

The males of both forms become brilliantly colored at breeding time, making them one of the most attractive of the small fishes residing in our waters. Colors include a blue or green eye, bright red or orange underparts, a red lining to the mouth, and translucent silver scales on the back.

With a small hand seine we've captured hundreds of these fish in only a few minutes. Other fish and birds take advantage of the stickleback's amazing abundance and availability. They're an important food of cutthroat trout and Dolly Varden char. Terns, kingfishers, yellowlegs, mergansers, herons, and otters feed heavily on them.

Nest-building male sticklebacks

A male stickleback builds a nest by sucking up sand or mud and depositing it away from the construction site. In the resulting depression, he glues together pieces of vegetation with mucus secreted by his kidneys, until a dome-shaped structure is formed. He then wiggles into the structure to form a tunnel. He defends the nest by attacking any other colored male that swims near.

When a female whose belly bulges conspicuously with eggs approaches, the male courts her with a zigzag swimming motion while retreating toward the nest. He repeats these movements until the female follows him to the nest, where he points out the entrance with his snout. If the female likes the nest, she will wiggle into the tunnel and eventually deposit between fifty and one hundred eggs. At once, the male enters the nest and sheds sperm over them. He may repeat this courtship with several females until the nest becomes stuffed with eggs.

The male cares for the fertilized eggs and the young. At frequent intervals he fans the nest with his large pectoral fins, creating a flow of water that improves the supply of oxygen to eggs. The eggs hatch in about two weeks, and as young begin emerging from the nest, the male darts about catching them in his mouth and spitting them back into the nest. About ten days after hatching, the young begin to disperse, and the male no longer attempts to retrieve them.

Stickleback just hatched.

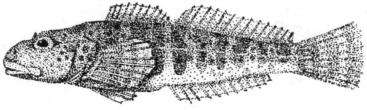

Coastrange sculpin
(*Cottus aleuticus*).

Sculpins

Sculpins are bottom-dwelling fish that scoot about the rocks and sit propped on large pectoral fins. Marine species live in tide pools or in shallow or deep marine waters. Freshwater species live in lakes, rivers, and streams. Most species range in length from two to ten inches, but a few, such as the great sculpin, may reach a length of two and a half feet. They have various names but are most often called sculpins, Irish lords, and bullheads. There are more species of sculpins in Southeast than of any other kind of fish—fifty-six species in four families.

Sculpins are among the most abundant fishes in Alaska. In a study of coastrange sculpin, estimates reached 10,000 per half mile in one Southeast stream. Although sculpins can be hard to detect visually, seining small streams—especially at night—sometimes captures them in unexpected numbers. Along the Beaufort Sea coast in northern Alaska, more than 69 percent of all fish were estimated to be fourhorn sculpins. Pacific staghorn sculpins seem to be everywhere in Southeast marine and tidal waters. At least fishermen seem to catch them more frequently than any other species of fish, especially if their bait nears the bottom.

Sculpins have some of the most unusual habits of any Alaskan fish. For instance, the Pacific staghorn sculpin hums when under stress. Attempt to take one from your hook and you may feel the vibration from its humming. In territorial defense, the male fourhorn sculpin also produces a low-pitched humming sound with a frequency of about 125 cycles per second. One species, the tiny grunt sculpin, obtains its name from the half-grunting, half-hissing sound it makes when removed from the water. The female grunt sculpin chases a male until she traps him in a rock crevice, then keeps him there until she lays her eggs.

Male sculpins may carry territoriality and defense of nesting sites to an extreme. The slimy sculpin 'barks' at an opponent by quickly opening and closing its large mouth. Barking is usually followed by a quick dart at the opponent and by fighting. In contrast to most fishes, in which territorial behavior is

Pacific sand lance *(Ammodytes hexapterus).*

mostly ritual, the loser of a fight between two male slimy sculpins may be killed.

Female sculpins usually lay their adhesive eggs in clumps attached to the surface or underside of rocks. Males of many sculpin species guard the eggs, sometimes keeping them clean by fanning them with alternate movements of their large pectoral fins, and by removing debris and dead eggs with their mouths. Males may be so attentive to their duties that they do not feed until the eggs have hatched.

Sculpins feed many other fish and birds. In Southeast Alaska, the abundance of young Pacific staghorn sculpins in shallow intertidal areas makes them easy prey for yellowlegs, kingfishers, herons, terns, dippers, and mergansers. Most of the prey that we observe river otters capturing and eating is staghorn sculpins. Sculpins are also a potentially good source of food for humans. The staghorn sculpins' abundance, ease of capture in shallow waters, relatively large size (up to eighteen inches), and edibility make them potential survival food for someone stranded along Southeast Alaska's coastal waters. Foragers should be aware, however, that the eggs of this fish are poisonous.

Pacific sand lance

Pacific sand lance are small (six to eight inches), thin, silver-sided fish. They have a long pointed snout, projecting lower jaw, and no paired ventral fins. They are present in a variety of habitats, including offshore waters, tidal channels, and along sandy beaches, where they typically form dense schools and burrow in sand and fine gravel.

This little fish is among the most important in our marine waters, since most fish-eating birds, mammals, and other fish feed on them. When food habits of fish and seabirds are studied, sand lance usually shows up as the major food item. At times sand lance make up more than 50 percent of the diet of Arctic tern, horned and tufted puffin, common murre, pigeon guillemot, king and coho salmon, Pacific halibut, Dolly Varden, and several species of rockfish in Southeast. They appear to be the primary food of marbled murrelet. Studies

Eagles, crows, and sand lance—*Bob Armstrong*

In 1987 the late Pete Isleib of Juneau and I found a sand lance burrowing area on the Mendenhall Wetlands near the Juneau airport.

We were walking on the wetlands near Mendenhall River when we saw some eighty-five bald eagles feeding on something in a sandy area not far from the mouth of the river. Through a spotting scope we were able to see that the eagles were walking around and rapidly moving their feet up and down, almost as if they were dancing.

Hundreds of sand lance, apparently panicked by the activity, were popping up out of the sand and lying on the surface exhausted. The eagles were having a feast.

Several years later my friend Mary Willson and I went out and saw northwestern crows digging sand lance in the same area. They generally captured sand lance in eight digs or less, much to the amazement of nearby gulls which could not find them.

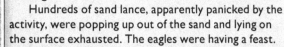

Above: *Crows digging sandlance.*   •   **Below**: *Half-buried in sand.*

also indicate that sand lance may be important food for harbor seal, humpback whale, and even herring, which feed on their larvae.

Sand lance do not have a swim bladder, and they sink to the bottom unless they make continuous undulating movements. To conserve energy and escape from most predators, sand lance bury themselves completely in the sand at night, and are reported to spend most of the winter months resting in the substrate. This behavior enables the fish to efficiently use fat reserves acquired the previous summer to maintain metabolism and to allow gonads to mature. Remaining buried and inactive in a relatively predator-free environment while food supplies such as zooplankton are much reduced is a highly successful survival adaptation.

When Pacific sand lance bury themselves in shallow, intertidal areas, they can be exposed to air at extreme low tides. But the little fish seem to have physiological mechanisms to deal with that, since they can survive for at least five hours in damp exposed sand. Exactly how they do this is not known. Perhaps they can somehow use oxygen from the air.

Look for sand lance along sandy beaches and sandy intertidal sloughs at or near low tide. Often their presence is revealed by the feeding frenzies of gulls, terns, and bald eagles. The larger gulls usually alight on the water, then jab for the sand lances, while the Arctic terns and smaller Bonaparte's gulls hover and then plunge after their prey. Eagles may swoop and take them from the water in their talons or stand alongside a water-filled pocket in the sand, waiting patiently for a sand lance to emerge.

Watching sand lance is fun. When startled, they may dive headfirst into the sand. Then, apparently by wiggling upward in an arc, they may poke their heads out of the sand to look around. If you move suddenly, they wiggle backward into the sand until completely covered. Sometimes as you walk about in the shallows, they panic and squirt out of the sand, madly rush about, then dive back in. If you grab one, hang on—upon escaping, they instantly disappear into the sand.

Bob was involved in compiling a review of the biology, predator relations, and annotated bibliography on sand lance. This entire publication can be accessed for free at: *alaska.usgs.gov/science/biology/seabirds_foragefish/products/publications/sandbib1.pdf*.

From this review we learned that the fish may choose only very select areas for burrowing. Since they spend such long periods within the sand, it is essential that the substrate be well supplied with oxygen. We have found concentrations of sand lance buried where the substrate almost seemed to be in suspension. Identification and protection of burrowing areas may be essential for future maintenance of these important little fish.

Forage fish—*Bob Armstrong*
In Southeast we are blessed with large numbers of small, schooling fishes that are typically called forage fishes, because so many other creatures feed on them. Two of our most important ones are Pacific herring and eulachon.

Humpback whales feed on herring all year long in our waters. Steller sea lions feed on herring in winter and spring.

Herring eggs on rockweed (Fucus).

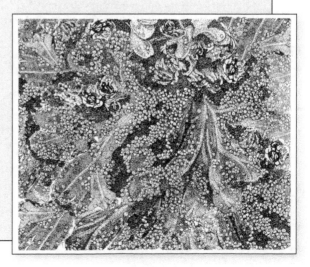

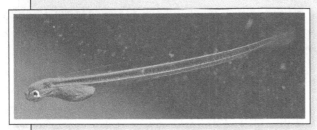

Left: *Recently hatched herring.*

Below: *Eulachon swarming in Alsek River. So fat-rich they can be ignited after drying, candlefish break the winter fast for predators and scavengers of land and sea.*

Sometimes sea lions swim next to foraging humpback whales, collecting herring that escape from the whales' jaws. In Lynn Canal, just off the Juneau road system, huge numbers of herring spend the winter in sort of a dormant state at the bottom of a deep trench. A couple of whales can dive deep enough to feed on them. This causes the herring to swim upward where the sea lions can prey on them. This is a good example of humpback whales benefiting sea lions. This whole interaction can be observed in winter from the Shrine of Saint Therese.

Not too far away, in Berners Bay, large numbers of eulachon gather in preparation for spring spawning in nearby rivers. Here sea lions herd eulachon such that whales can take advantage of the concentrations.

When herring spawn, large numbers of bald eagles gather, swooping down on the distracted fish. Surf scoters and white-winged scoters dive for submerged herring eggs, sometimes gathering in huge flocks as they migrate northward to their nesting grounds. Other marine predators of herring are seals, porpoises, orcas, ducks, loons, and horned grebes. Gulls gobble the eggs at low tide.

Eulachon runs attract thousands of predators, so these feebly swimming fish run a high-risk gauntlet. Hundreds of bald eagles and tens of thousands of gulls forage for days on the bounty of fish. Many Thayer's gulls fuel part of their long northward migration by feeding on eulachon. Sea lions may use the rich food source to lay on fat for the breeding season, when they fast for long periods.

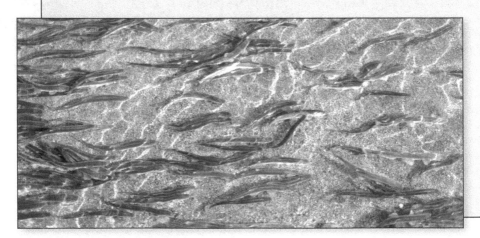

Weathervane scallop
(Patinopecten caurinus).

INVERTEBRATES

Although the invertebrate fauna of Southeast Alaska is abundant and diverse, research has addressed only a few commercially important species. The vast majority of our invertebrates are poorly known scientifically. The abundance of Alaska's biting insects is legendary, of course, and a full account of these alone would fill several volumes.

Some Southeast invertebrates are highly edible. Commercial and sport fisheries target a variety of marine invertebrates. Commercial fisheries take tanner crab, golden king crab, spot and pink shrimp, pinto abalone, Pacific geoducks, sea cucumbers, and sea urchins. The last two groups find an eager market in Japan.

Sport fishers set pots for red king crab, Dungeness crab, and shrimp, while divers take pinto abalone, scallops, and some sea cucumbers. Some steamer and butter clams are harvested despite the ever-present danger of paralytic

Top to bottom (not to scale): Spot and pink shrimp (*Pandalus platyceros* and *borealis*) support pot and trawl fisheries, respectively. • Quarter-sized adult shore crabs (*Hemigrapsus spp.*) are rare in glacier-influenced waters of the northern Tongass. But on the central and southern islands, dozens may hide under each large beach rock, prey for bear, mink, and otter. • Dungeness crab (*Cancer magister*) males reach legal size of six and a half inches at four to five years of age.

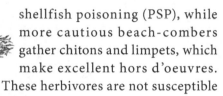

shellfish poisoning (PSP), while more cautious beach-combers gather chitons and limpets, which make excellent hors d'oeuvres. These herbivores are not susceptible to PSP.

Most of our invertebrates are less tasty. One of our most impressive is the Pacific banana slug, an enormous terrestrial mollusk, yellow or olive with blackish blotches. This herbivore is often seen grazing on mushrooms and sometimes on devil's club leaves, if a nearby lady fern frond offers access. Creamy white banana slugs are common on the southern and central Tongass. They eat salmonberries and can disperse viable seeds.

One of the most common beetles in the forest is the half-inch-long net-winged beetle, a scavenger on decaying vegetation. Its all-red, matte-finish color contrasts strikingly with the dark green foliage it frequents. We also have many large purplish-black ground beetles of the carnivorous family Carabidae. Southeast's butterfly list is short compared to those of drier bioregions; with large, delicate wings these insects are challenged by our heavy summer rainfall.

Other insects form tiny galls on blueberry stems, and midges (tiny flies) make roselike deformities on Barclay willows. Many of our most notorious insects also belong to the order Diptera, whose members have but a single pair of wings. In addition to black-and-yellow-banded hover flies, who hang like miniature helicopters over flowers, and fragile craneflies with almost impossibly long legs, we have many species of mosquitoes, black flies, 'no-see-ums,' deer flies, and horse flies, invertebrates who eat *us*.

Culiseta alaskaensis is a large, slow-

Above: Boat-backed ground beetle (*Scaphinotus*)—a carabid predator of slugs and snails—on lanky moss (*Rhytidiadelphus loreus*). • **Left**: Green sea urchin *(Strongylocentrotus droebachiensis)*. Spines shed from shell.

Right: Rose-like galls created by midges on buds of willow (*Salix barclayi*.) • **Below**: Larvae and pupae of black flies (family Simuliidae) attach to rocks in fast-moving streams.

flying mosquito with spotted wings. After spending the winter in a protected spot such as a crack in the bark of a tree, the female emerges in early spring and seeks a blood meal as a prerequisite to development of her eggs, laid on the surface of small ponds with emergent vegetation. Somewhat later in spring, smaller, fast-flying mosquitoes of the genus *Aedes* appear. They overwintered as eggs laid the previous fall and spent the early part of spring going through larval and pupal stages in fresh water.

Among other cues, such as odor and carbon dioxide emission, mosquitoes find their warm-blooded prey by sensing the heat given off by their victim's body, and we have found that there's nothing like a strenuous hike in the mountains to attract mosquitoes.

Black flies are small humpbacked flies with very short antennae. Females are biters, slicing small chunks of skin from the victim and then lapping up blood that trickles from the wound. Their larval stages are aquatic. 'No-see-ums' (but 'bite-um-like-hell') are tiny biting midges, easily identified by their minute size; often they're seen only when a glint of light betrays their tiny wings. Their bites are annoying but usually lead only to small reddish inflammations on the skin. Again, the larvae are aquatic, restricted to running waters.

Deer flies and horse flies are in the same family (Tabanidae). Once again the females are bloodsucking (males feed on flowers). Deer flies are smaller, brownish, and have dark spots on their wings, while horse flies are enormous blackish flies that usually have clear wings. At least one species has bright green eyes. The only kind thing we can say about deer and horse flies is that after landing on their victim, they take so long to bite that we have ample time for a well-aimed swat.

Because many of these blood-feeding insects have aquatic larvae, they

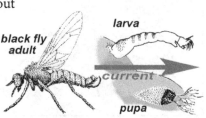

larva

black fly adult

current

pupa

> **Yes, ice worms really exist**
> Naturalists first noted ice worms in 1887 on Muir Glacier in Glacier Bay. They are segmented worms—the annelida, including earthworms—and range from half- to over one inch long. Most live within irregularities caused by melting along ice crystal margins. At dusk they move to the surface of the glacier, to feed on ever-present algae that wash into drainage furrows.

are important in freshwater food chains and help support fish populations and, in turn, fish-eating birds and mammals.

Many Alaskan terrestrial insects have ingenious adaptations enabling them to survive cold winters and thrive despite the shortened growing season. They bask in the early morning sunshine until their bodies warm up, or loiter in bowl-shaped blossoms, which shelter them from cold winds. They may over-winter as eggs, larvae, pupae, or adults, often having glycerol-like antifreeze compounds in their tissues to prevent freezing. Finally, in many species, individuals may survive for more than a year, rather than racing through the entire life cycle in a single season.

In contrast to terrestrial insects, which tend to shut down during winter, a majority of aquatic insects are active, growing, and abundant all winter. They

> **Invasive slugs**
> Until recently, invasive slug species have been of interest primarily as pests in Southeast gardens. But they may ultimately have broader implications. • **Above**: *Deroceras*. Variously called marsh, field, or milk slugs. Gray with clear slime and breathing hole (pneumostome) in rear of mantle. This genus has occupied human-disturbed habits throughout Southeast for many decades. • **Below**: The more recently arrived orange-banded arion (*Arion fasciatus*) has forward-positioned pneumostome and prominent "skirt." Bright orange goo rubs off the mantle. This aggressive slug arrived in Gustavus around 1998, and in Juneau several years later. Unlike *Deroceras*, it was not content with garden produce, but spread to wild habitats such as uplift meadow, even consuming wild iris (*Iris setosa*), toxic to most herbivores.
>
>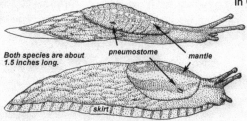
>
> *Both species are about 1.5 inches long.*   pneumostome   mantle
>
> skirt

Bugs on the snow—*Bob Armstrong*

Some aquatic insects emerge from our streams as adults in midwinter and crawl about on the snow. Their purpose is mating. I usually take photographs of them and with the help of John Hudson (an entomologist) we can at least identify them to family. The larger ones have been caddisflies and stoneflies and the smaller ones have been dance flies and midges.

These events seem to occur after a couple days of above-freezing temperatures, especially if the sun is shining. By emerging in midwinter, it may be easier to find a mate with lower numbers of species flying about, and there are fewer predators such as insect-eating birds and dragonflies. I do, however, find wolf spiders crawling on the snow at the same time, no doubt looking for a midwinter feast.

Very tiny creatures called springtails can also be seen on the snow in midwinter. Springtails are insect-like invertebrates, but despite the fact that they have six legs, they are not considered insects, belonging instead to a group called Hexapods.

1) caddisfly 2) stonefly 3) dance fly 4) springtail 5) wolf spider.

thrive because water shields them from cold air temperatures. Below 40°F, some species slow down or stop growing, but remain active. Others, however, with specialized biochemistry and enzymes, continue growing even at 32°F.

Mussels

The Pacific blue mussel forms extensive beds in the upper mid intertidal zone in Southeast Alaska. They grow to three inches long and have relatively thin, smooth shells. In most individuals the shell is blue-black, for maximum absorption of heat from the sun, but some are chestnut brown.

Adult and larval cranefly (family Tipulidae).

The Pacific blue mussel attaches to rocks and other hard objects by a cluster of exceptionally strong strands called byssal (rhymes with whistle) threads. To form these golden threads, the mussel attaches its foot—a narrow orange structure—to a rock, to the shell of another mussel, or to a piling. Then, using a special gland, it secretes a solution of structural proteins and enzymes through a groove along the lower edge of its foot. When the foot finally pulls away from the attachment point, the byssal thread is left. Dozens anchor the mussel. In quiet muddy bays, beds may be formed by mussels attaching mostly to each other. These beds form shelters for innumerable tiny marine creatures living between the mussels and among the byssal threads.

The Pacific blue mussel spawns in spring. Eggs and sperm are shed into the sea, where fertilization and early development take place. Soon a tiny creature called a veliger larva is formed. On its head end are cilia, minute whiplike structures for propulsion. Cilia also stream water toward the mouth, collecting tiny unicellular algae called phytoplankton. The veliger floats in a dilute soup of phytoplankton that blooms in response to increasing daylight hours.

Eventually the veliger settles out of the plankton and selects a piece of real estate where it will become an adult mussel. By this time, it has secreted a minute, glassy double shell and crawls over the rocks. At this stage, called a plantigrade, the mussel secretes threads, but for some time can break them and move around, to avoid being smothered by accumulating sediments. This mobility is probably one reason for the blue mussel's successful colonization of quiet, muddy substrates. Settlement is highly variable from year to year.

After settlement, young mussels feed in a manner quite different from that of the planktonic stages. Shells open slightly to draw water through delicate gills. Phytoplankton and detritus from decomposing kelp sticks to mucus coating the gills. Cilia guide trapped food toward the mouth, a process called filter feeding. Particles as fine as 0.00002 inch in diameter are removed. Among the many kinds of phytoplankton collected are those causing paralytic shellfish poisoning. So mussels should not be eaten here.

Northwestern crows pick up mussels, fly into the air, and drop them onto rocks below to break them open. Scoters swallow mussels whole and crush them in their gizzards. River and sea otters eat them, and even black bears forage in the intertidal for mussels. All of these predators are susceptible to paralytic shellfish poisoning.

Crabs also eat mussels, chipping away the shells with heavy pincers. Many species of sea star eat mussels by pulling shells apart. Mussels torn off rocks by wave action also may be caught by tentacles of large anemones lurking in deeper waters.

The mussel's revenge—Several species of marine snails eat mussels by first boring a hole in their shells. Locally, the frilled and file dogwinkles remove

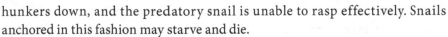

Pacific blue mussels (*Mytilus trossulus*) seal shut when exposed to air, but open to filter-feed when the tide comes back in.

numerous mussels from the population every year. But unlike other fixed marine invertebrates, such as oysters, the beleaguered mussel can to some extent defend itself. It can attach new byssal threads to the shell of the rasping predator and then anchor the snail either to the rock or to the shells of other mussels. The attacked mussel then hunkers down, and the predatory snail is unable to rasp effectively. Snails anchored in this fashion may starve and die.

Pacific blue mussels that successfully avoid all these predators may live for only about three years, but in nature entire beds of mussels are often obliterated by storms, only to be replaced by recruitment of young another season.

Clams

Pacific littleneck and butter clams are among the most abundant shellfish on protected Southeast beaches of mud, sand, and gravel. The littleneck clam or 'steamer' has short siphons ('little necks') and therefore lives only one to three inches beneath the surface. Butter clams with longer siphons can burrow as deep as fourteen inches. Littlenecks tend to live higher on the beach—up into the lower mid intertidal zone just below beds of mussels and brown rockweed—while butters extend from the lower intertidal to almost one-hundred-foot depths.

Littlenecks and butters are easily distinguished by their shells. The shell of a littleneck is up to two inches long, often with brown tepee-like markings in juveniles. Shells are marked with fine, concentric growth lines intersecting delicate radial lines. The dark elastic hinge is hidden between the shells.

In contrast, butter clams are up to five inches long. Butter clams have only fine, concentric growth lines, and radial lines are lacking. The hinge ligament of butter clams is conspicuous.

In Alaska, littleneck clams need at least eight years to reach harvestable size. By comparison, steamers in southern British Columbia require only three years. The difference in growth rates probably results from the colder temperatures of Alaskan waters. Comparable information on butter clams is not available, but we know they can live twenty years or more in Alaskan waters, and it is probable that they, too, have a slow growth rate. These slower growth rates are of economic importance because often such animals produce fewer offspring and are more susceptible to local extermination.

Predators of clams include various species of sea stars. The common mottled sea star finds steamers easy prey, while the many-armed sunflower star targets larger butter clams. Sea stars dig the clam from its burrow, fasten dozens of tiny suction cups (tube feet) to shells, and exert enormous force to pull them apart. Even if shells gape only a fraction of an inch, a sea star can evert its stomach through its mouth, sliding the delicate stomach tissues through this narrow slit to digest the clam's muscles until shells can no longer be held closed.

Lewis' moon snails and arctic natica snails prey on clams by drilling a hole through the shell and stick their feeding organs through it to rasp at the soft tissues within. Moon snails also may surround clams with their huge 'foot' until the shell relaxes enough to open.

Of course, humans eat clams too. Steamers and butter clams are prized edibles. But periodic blooms of toxic phytoplankton (sidebar, *PSP*), make eating untested clams like playing Russian roulette, Southeast Alaskan style. While it's true that spring and summer are most dangerous, even winter clamming is risky because toxins can remain in clam tissues up to two years after original contamination. Removing siphons may help, but there can still be fatal

continued after sidebars

Above: Lyre whelk (*Neptunea lyrata*), a large subtidal predator on mollusks.

Left: Little-neck clam or steamer (*Leucoma staminea*) is distinguished from other local molluscs by fine radial lines running perpendicular to concentric annuli. Largest littlenecks are generally not the oldest. Outermost rings may be too tight to count. This two-inch clam could be much older than the eighteen years suggested by annual rings!

Harvesting longevity—Richard Carstensen

Whether studying clams, fish, deer or trees, northern researchers and naturalists frequently learn that life-span data from southern climes are inapplicable here. Underestimating longevity has serious consequences, especially for wild flora and fauna treated as commercial, sport, or subsistence species.

Mollusks Until recently, most clams have not been recognized as particularly long-lived species; concentric rings formed on the valves were simply counted out to the edge of the shell. However, it's now known that annuli become more tightly spaced at the edge of the shell on older animals, rendering accurate counts from external indicators impossible. Today it's common to section part of the hinge and examine the annual growth lines microscopically. Using these internal growth lines, a 103-year chronology has been developed for long-lived geoducks.

Kristen Munk, a biologist and growth-pattern specialist, applied these techniques to clams from beaches around Juneau. Results were sobering. Hinge-section ages for butter clam greatly exceeded the externally evident shell ages, with specimens over seventy years old reported. Harvested littleneck clams often exceed ten years and sometimes twenty years old; the oldest littlenecks are often small and round, earning them the name 'walnuts.' Imagine, then how many centuries of growth are represented by a bucket of littlenecks; one well-fed deer produces more venison in a single year! Clam diggers have extinguished edible mollusks from favorite beaches, and recolonization potential remains unknown.

Groundfish While salmon are famous for rapid growth and early mortality, most Pacific groundfish—bottom-oriented marine species—generally demonstrate the opposite reproductive strategy. As on land, many of our high-latitude sea creatures grow more slowly and live longer than their counterparts from lower latitudes.

Most fish are aged by examining their sagittal otoliths, a pair of small bones in the inner ear. Charred in flame, or rendered translucent with clearing solution, annuli are counted, as with trees or sectioned animal teeth. Also as in trees, slower growth in later life creates tighter, less-distinct rings. Otolith age-reading is an art as much as a science.

Published studies indicate that Pacific groundfish species of deep, cold water tend to live longer than shallow warm-water species. Quillback rockfish are an

Right: *The maximum recorded ages of groundfishes in the eastern North Pacific and Bering Sea. Our state's oldest and second-oldest documented fish—a 205-year rougheye and a 157-year shortraker rockfish—both came from Southeast Alaska. Data from Munk (2001).*

groundfish species	age
sablefish	94
Pacific cod	25
walleye pollock	28
lingcod	33
Pacific halibut	55
yellowfin sole	34
rougheye rockfish	205
shortraker rockfish	157
quillback rockfish	90
black rockfish	55
China rockfish	78
yelloweye rockfish	121

Recording ten-foot diameter Sitka spruce on Tàan, sea lion (Prince of Wales Island). We expect giants to be old, but what other ancient organisms are we overlooking and endangering?

important commercial species, sold at fish markets. With a reported longevity of ninety years, quillback can be older than the people eating them! Unfortunately, fish market workers can rarely identify the rockfish species at their counters for the conscientious consumer.

Trees As with clams, the largest tree in a given acre is rarely the oldest. In 2005, while assessing sustainability of Tongass timber practices in the Ground-truthing Project, my loyalties began to shift from great size to great age. Unfortunately, it's generally not possible to determine the age of a tree based upon diameter and height. Sections of its growth rings are required. Also, most hemlocks and cedars more than a few centuries old have heart rot. (Sidebar; *Twenty years of learning*, p. 50.)

In their book *The Olympic Rain Forest*, Ruth Kirk and Jerry Franklin describe conifers that reach maximum size for their species on Washington's fertile coast:

> "Despite huge size . . . Olympic Peninsula lowland trees are not particularly long-lived. Instead, they follow a live-fast, die-young pace. . . Ages here typically range up to about 400 years for Sitka spruce and western hemlock . . . Spruce almost twice this age flourish in southeast Alaska, where soils are less optimum . . . Alaskan spruce . . . grow relatively slowly, which seems to foster longevity."

Even red alders, considered 'weedy,' short-lived trees in the lower 48—rotten and leaning at eighty years—can live (like spruces) twice that long in Southeast Alaska. The phrase "old-growth alder" would be an oxymoron in Oregon, but I've seen many individuals and even a few stands

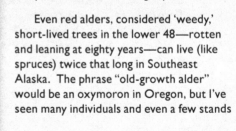

Coring a twenty-three-inch-diameter red alder on Chichagof Island. A pencil-thick sample is removed and annual rings counted. This still-vigorous tree was at least 150 years old.

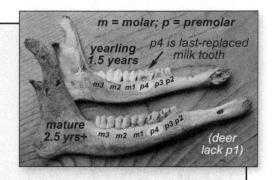

m = molar; p = premolar

yearling
1.5 years

p4 is last-replaced
milk tooth

m3 m2 m1 p4 p3 p2

mature
2.5 yrs+   m3 m2 m1 p4 p3 p2

(deer
lack p1)

Mandibles from Sitka black-tailed deer.
Young animals have high, sharp cheek teeth.
After four years, age estimation from tooth-
wear becomes less precise.

deserving of that distinction on the Tongass.

Although red alders in Alaska grow more slowly than those in Oregon, they reach commercial size about ten times faster than do Alaskan yellow-cedar, as well as providing better fish and wildlife habitat throughout successional development. Alders are therefore better suited than red- or yellow-cedars to sustainable forestry. So far, however, few mill owners are interested in easily regenerated species. Disincentives include low board-foot value for alder, contrasting with very high prices and raw-log export loopholes for cedar; these are termed "perverse subsidies" by the Resilience Alliance (*www.resalliance.org/index.php/resilience*).

Deer Black-tailed (and white-tailed) deer are considered to be fast-growing, rapid-turnover game species—the "alders" of North American wildlife. Where heavily hunted, five years is exceptionally old. Age estimates from molar wear and configuration are reliable for young animals, but speculative in older deer. For better accuracy an incisor is sectioned and stained for counting of annual growth rings. In one study of 113 female Colorado mule deer, the 4 oldest (3.5 percent of sample) ranged from ten to thirteen years. How does that compare with Alaskan blacktails?

In 1985, 54 Sitka black-tailed does were collected on Chichagof Island for assessment of reproductive potential. Tooth-sections revealed that 4 (7.5 percent of sample) were at least fifteen years old. Although this study has not been replicated, it hints that Sitka blacktail maximum age could be much greater than commonly assumed for North American deer.

"Harvest"—a term borrowed from agriculture—is of dubious merit when applied to seas or forests where cycles of birth-to-death are less visible, less understood, and less amenable to control. The consequence of overharvest is quickly obvious to a farmer, who sinks or swims financially on personally owned land. But when "harvesting" wild "resources" from public lands and waters, it's harder to assign blame, or to instill restraint. For some managers and harvesters, exhaustion of one species is simply a cue to move on to another one, perhaps equally ill-suited to commercial or even casual extraction. This frontier mentality is a bull in the china shop of long-lived species.

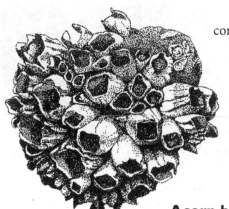

concentrations in contaminated digestive glands.

To be safe, your best bet is to get your clams at the grocery store. Commercial canners test harvested clams regularly to detect dangerous levels of toxins, but such complex laboratory testing procedures are expensive and not available to the general public.

Acorn barnacles

Acorn barnacles are small, whitish volcano-shaped creatures permanently attached to hard surfaces such as rocks and boat hulls. When exposed by the receding tide, they close their plates and wait. When the tide returns, two pairs of tiny plates open at the top of the 'volcano.' Six pairs of feathery appendages called cirri comb their dinner from the water, extracting tiny drifting animals (zooplankton), microscopic algae (phytoplankton), or edible organic particles. This food is then removed from the cirri and transferred to the mouth.

In Southeast Alaska we have five species of acorn barnacle. Highest on the shore is a tiny species with brownish plates, the little brown barnacle. This species is more resistant to exposure than the others and can live where the sea covers it less frequently. Adult little brown barnacles rarely exceed a quarter of an inch in diameter.

A little lower on the shore live two species rather similar in appearance; both have smooth white plates and reach about half an inch in diameter. One of these, the common acorn barnacle, leaves a white scar on the rock when the individual is broken off. The other species, northern rock barnacle, leaves no scar. Both may be abundant

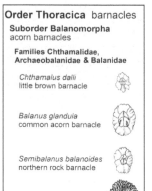

Order Thoracica barnacles
Suborder Balanomorpha
acorn barnacles

**Families Chthamalidae,
Archaeobalanidae & Balanidae**

Chthamalus dalli
little brown barnacle

Balanus glandula
common acorn barnacle

Semibalanus balanoides
northern rock barnacle

Semibalanus cariosus
thatched barnacle

Balanus crenatus
crenate barnacle

Above: Common acorn barnacle leaves a white scar on the rock when it breaks off. • **Left**: Our acorn barnacles, listed in order of their zonation, from high to low intertidal.

Paralytic shellfish poisoning (PSP)

PSP is caused by toxins that accumulate in digestive glands and siphons of clams and mussels straining microscopic plants from seawater. Toxins are produced by a microscopic alga called a dinoflagellate. Resting stages (cysts) of dinoflagellates occur in marine mud. At some unknown environmental cue they hatch, and the swimming stage may multiply at staggering rates to produce a bloom.

Consumed PSP toxins are harmless to clams and mussels, but can be passed on to animals that prey on them. Invertebrate predators such as moon snails are likewise unharmed and can carry even higher concentrations of PSP than the clams they eat. Cooking and freezing do not lower toxin levels. Invertebrates such as limpets and chitons that graze algae never carry PSP.

In humans, symptoms of PSP include a tingling around the mouth and lips, which may lead to general paralysis, respiratory failure, and death. There is no antidote for PSP, but patients may be given oxygen until paralysis wears off.

Some species of dinoflagellate contain a red pigment. Blooming produces the red tide that strikes various parts of our coast each year. From 39,000 feet in a commercial jetliner, we've seen tongues of red tide sweeping along the coast and penetrating into inlets and bays. Red tides don't always indicate contaminated shellfish, since some species of dinoflagellates don't form the toxins associated with PSP. On the other hand, some species (such as *Alexandrium catenella* on our coast) are so toxic they can make shellfish poisonous even when populations are too low to cause a noticeable red tide. Clams from Kulisawu X'áat', *slender island* (Porpoise Island, near Glacier Bay) were toxic every time tested. The poison (called saxitoxin) from these clams was used by the US military in World War II.

Alexandrium catenella, *a toxic dinoflagellate in plankton.*

down into the middle intertidal, often home to extensive mussel beds.

Somewhat below common acorn and northern rock barnacles, one may find the much larger thatched barnacle, up to two inches across the base. Its outer plates are decorated with distinctive downward-pointing spines.

Common acorn barnacle (*Balanus glandula*) feeding. Fine bristles on cirri (feeding appendages) strain plankton and detritus.

In lowest intertidal and subtidal grows the crenate barnacle, *Balanus cre-natus*. Like the common acorn barnacle, it has a smooth white shell and leaves a scar when broken off the rock, but grows much larger and has a relatively small opening to its 'volcano.'

Barnacles were originally thought to be mollusks related to clams and snails, but life history study revealed they are crustaceans, related to crabs and lobsters. They brood fertilized eggs until a nauplius develops, shaped like a rutabaga with horns and three pairs of locomotory appendages.

Nauplii are usually released during a plankton bloom, ensuring food availability. They drift, feed, and molt in the plankton until a new stage, the cypris, forms a clam-like shell with six pairs of swimming legs. The cypris, which does not feed, may be eaten by juvenile salmon.

The cypris eventually settles onto a rock, attaching with one antennule and 'tasting' the rock with the other. If the spot is satisfactory, the cypris glues itself down permanently, within a few hours changing into a translucent, milli-meter-long adult.

Acorn barnacles feed sea stars, drilling snails such as dogwinkles (*Nucella spp.*) and are the sole food of green ribbon worms and rough-mantled sea slugs. These predators either drill holes in the shells of the barnacle or pull the plates apart to expose the soft and nutritious tissues within. Barnacles may also be eaten by larval flies in the family Dryomyzidae.

Most other directly attached marine invertebrates release eggs and sperm into the water, where fertilization occurs. Barnacles, faced with the same prob-lem of being literally glued to the spot, have solved the problem of how to court fair lady by evolving what must be proportionally the longest sex organs of any animals. They are also hermaphroditic. This means that any individual barna-cle can mate with any neighbor, since they are all both male and female at the same time.

Competition and survival—Although it seems odd that fixed-in-place organ-isms might possess survival and combative behavior, in fact the acorn barnacle has such skills. As it feeds and grows, if it encounters many others of its own species, each individual tends to grow taller and narrower. If the growing bar-nacle encounters individuals of another species, however, then a competition for space ensues, with one species characteristically bulldozing, growing over, or crushing other species off the rock. In this manner, the common acorn bar-nacle routinely removes smaller little brown barnacles from the rock.

Female and male bluets (*Enallagma*), common damselflies, often remain attached long after mating.

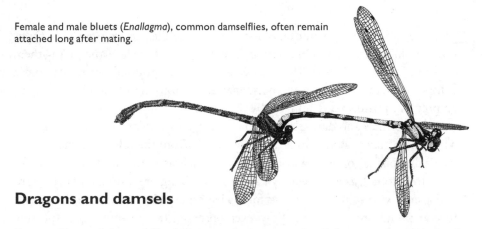

Dragons and damsels

Dragonflies and damselflies belong to the insect order Odonata, a word derived from two Greek words meaning "toothed jaws." Although they do not sting or bite humans, they are real dragons to other insects. The true dragonflies, suborder Anisoptera, hold their wings spread horizontally when at rest and their eyes are connected across the top of the head. Damselflies, suborder Zygoptera, have widely spaced eyes, and hold their wings together above the body, or partly open as in the spreadwing damselflies, when at rest. Sixteen species of dragonflies and three species of damselflies are known to occur in Southeast Alaska.

Larval stages of dragonflies and damselflies abound in our lakes, ponds, and marshes with aquatic vegetation providing dissolved oxygen, shelter, and food for insects and fish on which they feed. These larvae possess a hinged lower lip called a labium that folds under the head. When prey is within striking distance, the larva extends its labium at lightning speed, grasping the target with hooks or teeth.

Adult dragonflies and damselflies are well equipped for predation. Among insects they are masters of flight. Most insects raise and lower their wings by muscles attached inside the body. Contraction of these muscles changes the shape of the body, causing wings to lever up and down simultaneously. In dragonflies and damselflies, however, special groups of muscles are attached directly to the wings. This enables the insect to move each of its four wings independently, resulting in great agility. In pursuit of prey they can fly backward, or suddenly stop and turn while in rapid forward flight. Some species fly at thirty-five miles per hour. Furthermore, they can silently sneak up on prey; wings beating slowly don't hum. Only when zooming through dense vegetation do they alert us by rattling of wings against the leaves.

The iridescent eyes of dragonflies and damselflies are composed of thousands of small facets covering almost the entire side of the face and giving them an enormous visual field. Their heads are also exceptionally movable, and a complex system of joints in the neck enables them to maintain a precise focus on prey, even while being buffeted by the wind.

Dragonflies and damselflies feed on a variety of other insects. The smaller damselflies may snatch aphids and mosquitoes from the foliage as they flit by. Large dragonflies often chase larger insects such as moths and other dragonflies. Their long legs are specially adapted for seizing prey, situated far forward and armed with spines. These legs form a basket used by the dragonflies to capture and hold prey in flight. We've even observed them capturing and eating yellow jackets.

Dragonflies and damselflies mate in flight. The male curls the tip of his abdomen forward and deposits a sperm packet in a chamber below his second abdominal segment. While still in flight he clasps the female by the neck with special claspers located at the tip of his abdomen. The female picks up the sperm packet with the tip of her abdomen. Later she deposits fertilized eggs in or close to water. Many damselflies remain joined even after they have mated, and you can often see them flying about in pairs with the male in the lead.

Watching our dragons and damsels can be fun and educational. Their large size and habit of concentrating along shores of ponds, lakes, and marshes make them easy to observe. Armed with a pair of close-focusing binoculars, a little patience, and a dry place to sit, you can see many fascinating aspects of their behavior. Watch their incredible flight patterns and how easily they outmaneuver and capture other insects. Think about their ability to capture around three hundred insects, including mosquitoes, every day.

Caddisflies

Larval caddisflies are best known for constructing elaborate cases, using materials ranging from twigs to sand grains to carefully cut pieces of leaves and even fairly large pebbles. But some caddisfly families in Southeast don't build cases at all. Common net-spinners spin intricate, rectangular mesh nets that strain food such as algae, fine organic particles, and small aquatic insects from the current. Green rock worm caddisfly larvae are free-living and crawl among rocks in search of other insects to prey upon. Tube-making caddisflies live in fixed retreats made of silk for filtering zooplankton and insects from slow currents, especially at lake outlets.

Abundant in our lakes, ponds, and streams, caddisfly larvae are important food for fish. American dippers and some sandpipers also seem to specialize in caddisflies and can often be seen thrashing them about to get rid of the case.

Our largest caddisfly larvae are called giant case makers. They typically construct large cylindrical cases from pieces of leaves and bark, cut to size and sewn together. These are very active and when a couple are put in an aquarium or pan they often race about entering and leaving each other's case. Also when a larva is removed from its case it will quickly set to work constructing a new case with any suitable material available.

Adult caddisflies have a fluttering, moth-like flight; in fact, some types are easily mistaken for moths because they tend to fly at night. But unlike moths, which have feather-like branched antennae, caddisflies have filament-like, unbranched antennae. They have four somewhat transparent wings, which they fold tent-like above their body when resting.

The mouth structure of adult caddisflies is best suited for lapping, so they cannot bite you. In fact, many adults don't feed at all; their only activity is mating. Their mating flights or nuptial dances are enchanting to watch. Often they circle with whirring wings just slightly above the water surface, paddling vigorously with middle legs, female in front and male in hot pursuit. Other species may dance vertically in the air with long antennae diverging.

The easiest caddisflies to find and observe are the case-builders. If you look carefully along the shallow margins of a stream, you may see these tiny houses and the protruding, caterpillar-like forepart and six tiny legs of the little inhabitant, as it pulls its house along. Whitish caddisfly larvae hide their soft bodies inside these houses for

spruce needle case
free-living larva
bark case
caddisfly adult

Caddisfly larva on granite pebble, in case of sand grains. A mason could be proud of a chimney this well crafted.

Anywhere there is water—*Bob Armstrong*

Aquatic insects are apt to show up anywhere there is fresh water. In 2002 a new species of Apataniid case-maker caddisfly was discovered at Nugget Falls near Mendenhall Glacier in Juneau. Despite searches in similar habitats all over Juneau, that species, *Manophylax alascensis*, has been found only at this single location.

These grazers of microscopic algae live in a rather unique habitat—a thin film of flowing water on vertical bedrock faces along the margins of this powerful waterfall. During rainy periods, some larvae venture outside the areas kept wet by the falling water and spray. When the sun returns, the water dries out from under them forcing the larvae to make a slow and steady retreat back to moist habitat.

I have visited this site several times to watch the tiny larvae climb the rock faces as they feed. With a thin film of rapidly flowing water over them they inch their way around in short jerks while still managing to hang on to the smooth vertical rock. Their cases are beautifully crafted of tiny small rock fragments and decorated with a little moss or algae.

camouflage and protection from predators. Cases also provide ballast and streamlining, preventing larvae from washing away in swift current. Case design aids oxygen extraction as larvae undulate within, pulling steady currents of fresh water across filamentous gills on abdominal segments.

When full-grown, a caddisfly larva makes a cocoon for its resting stage, or pupa. When wings are fully developed, the pupa cuts its way out of the cocoon and swims to the water surface, crawling out on a rock or stick. The adult eventually bursts open the pupal skin and flies away. Mating flights begin and the cycle is repeated.

Butterflies

Despite the seemingly hostile Alaskan climate, eighty-five species of butterflies have been found throughout the state. According to Dr. Kenelm Philip of the University of Alaska in Fairbanks, our butterflies survive the winter cold by two strategies. Some use the insulating qualities of snow to protect them from extreme temperatures. Others living in areas with little snow contain natural antifreeze chemicals in their bodies. Because interior Alaska gets more summer sun than Southeast, it has far more butterfly species, in spite of its more severe winters.

Mourning cloak
butterfly (*Nymphalis
antiopa*) and caterpillar.

Butterflies go through four stages of life: egg, larva, pupa, and adult. Their eggs, which are about the size of a pinhead, are deposited by the female, usually on the underside of a leaf. Each female butterfly may lay up to five hundred eggs during her rather brief adult life.

The eggs eventually hatch into larvae—the familiar caterpillars—who feed almost constantly on leaves of whatever plant is their specialized food. Usually this is a flowering plant or tree, which they recognize by its aromatic oils. Butterfly larvae appear never to eat ferns or mosses. Caterpillars are extraordinarily specific in feeding habits, and each species will usually feed only on a small number of closely related plant species. If a suitable food plant is not available, the caterpillar will starve to death rather than eat something else.

The caterpillar grows rapidly and molts several times until it finally produces a pupa or chrysalis. The pupa is immobile and neither eats nor drinks; its mouth and anus are both sealed over. While in the pupal stage, the butterfly reorganizes itself into a winged adult. When this process is complete, the chrysalis splits open and a fully formed adult butterfly emerges.

Southeast tough on butterflies—Adult butterflies need warmth and sunshine. Our cool and cloudy summers don't support a large or diverse butterfly fauna. However, thirty-three different species have been identified from Southeast.

Order Lepidoptera

Families:

Hesperiidae
Carterocephalus palaemon arctic skipper

Papilionidae
Papilio machaon old world swallowtail
Papilio zelicaon anise swallowtail* (stray, 1 specimen)
Pterourus canadensis Canadian tiger swallowtail

Pieridae
Pieris marginalis margined white
Pieris angelika arctic white*
Pieris oleracea mustard white*
Anthocharis sara sara orangetip
Colias philodice clouded sulphur
Colias palaeno palaeno sulfur

Lycaenidae
Lycaena dorcas dorcas copper*
Lycaena mariposa mariposa copper
Lycaeides idas northern blue
Everes amyntula western tailed-blue
Plebejus saepiolus greenish blue
Agriades glandon arctic blue
Glaucopsyche lygdamus silvery blue
Celastrina ladon spring azure
Plebejus optilete cranberry blue

Nymphalidae
Danaus plexippus monarch*
  (stray, 1 specimen)
Boloria chariclea arctic
  fritillary*
B. epithore Pacific fritillary*
Speyeria mormonia mormon
  fritillary
Speyeria zerene zerene
  fritillary
Vanessa cardui painted lady*
Vanessa atalanta red admiral
Aglais milberti Milbert's
  tortoiseshell
Polygonia faunus green
  comma
Polygonia satyrus satyr
  anglewing
Nymphalis antiopa mourning cloak
Nymphalis vaualbum Compton tortoiseshell
Oeneis chryxus chryxus arctic*
Coenonympha kodiak Kodiak ringlet

* Species recorded outside the Haines/Skagway area.

Butterflies of Southeast Alaska This list, compiled by Dr. Kenelm Philip, totals thirty-three species in five families. Two species in the genus *Vanessa* occasionally migrate to Southeast. Only nine of these species were found outside the Haines/Skagway area.

Inset: red admiral chrysalis.

Most of these records come from the Haines/Skagway area, sunnier and drier than the rest of Southeast. We have only seen nine species of butterflies outside of the Haines/Skagway area (and heard reports of two more from Prince of Wales Island). Two species—red admiral and painted lady—are occasional migrants to our region. Sometimes the Milbert's tortoiseshell seems to be every-where. Another, the mourning cloak, appears during rare periods of extended sunny weather.

Our most common and obvious species is the margined white. Wings are mostly white on top and cream-colored to yellowish underneath. Wing veins may have light to heavy gray-olive or brown scaling, earning the alternative common name "veined white."

Although adults seem to feed on a wide variety of flowers, margined whites lay eggs only on plants of the mustard family. They may have two broods per year, with adults emerging in May to early June and again in August. Eggs are laid singly, usually on undersides of leaves. Caterpillars are forest green with darker or yellowish back and side stripes. They are solitary and well camou-flaged on the green leaf.

Margined white butterflies are not considered pests of the garden. In fact, their caterpillars feed on plants considered weeds by most gardeners. They are beneficial as pollinators of flowers and as a thing of beauty to watch in our otherwise butterfly-poor environment. They're passed over by insect-eating birds, as both pigments and body fluids are toxic.

Pseudoscorpions

Beachcombing between tidelines is popular among Southeast residents, who take advantage of the extreme low tides of spring to treat lingering cabin fever. One fascinating animal, the pseudoscorpion, can be found by diligent searching beneath rocks in the upper intertidal barnacle zone near freshwater streams.

"Pseudoscorpion" means "false scorpion." These animals resemble miniature scorpions, without the long tail and terminal sting. Like scorpions, spiders, and mites, pseudoscorpions are arachnids, or arthropods with four pairs of walking legs. Intertidal arachnids are extremely rare, making our local pseudoscorpion almost unique.

What tiny creatures! Most species of pseudoscorpion are less than a third of an inch long. Our intertidal species *Halobisium occidentale* is one of the largest.

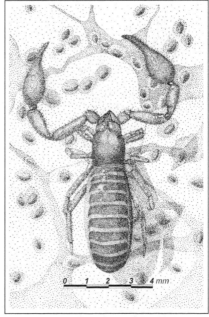

Pseudoscorpion pincers are used to capture and manipulate prey, build nests, hold a mate, and fight. When a pseudoscorpion walks forward slowly, it holds these pincers out in front, suggesting a flamenco dancer with castanets. Tiny bristles on the pincers detect vibrations of moving prey. In feeding on prey such as small insects or mites, pseudoscorpions inject digestive juices, wait for the juices to decompose flesh, and then suck out the body contents. When finished, only the indigestible hard

Glossy chestnut brown *Halobisium occidentale*, on intertidal rock with freshly colonized baby barnacles. Large white patches are scars where common acorn barnacles have peeled off.

0   1   2   3   4 *mm*

outer cuticle remains. Pseudoscorpions feed infrequently and can withstand several weeks or months of starvation. They're eaten in turn by centipedes, spiders, beetles, and birds.

Crab spiders

Our local crab spider is also called the goldenrod or flower spider because of its habit of lurking on flowers, waiting for prey. The females, about a third of an inch long, are twice the size of males and either ghostly white or butter yellow, with a broad, brick-red stripe down each side of the abdomen. Individuals can change color slowly, and it is reported that white spiders placed on goldenrod flowers turned yellow in about eleven days. The adaptive value of this color change is that the spiders find camouflage in white flowers early in the season and then transfer to yellow flowers, which may be more abundant later in summer. A crab spider holds its crablike front legs outstretched, waiting for an insect to visit the flower on which it sits. The spider's venom is highly toxic to flies or even bees much larger than itself. Such insects are grabbed, bitten, paralyzed, and eaten with dispatch.

There are many species of crab spiders—family Thomisidae—in North America. Ours is probably the common Pacific Northwest flower crab spider, *Misumena vatia*.

*Crab spider hangs beneath blossom of white bog-orchid (*Platanthera dilatata*).*

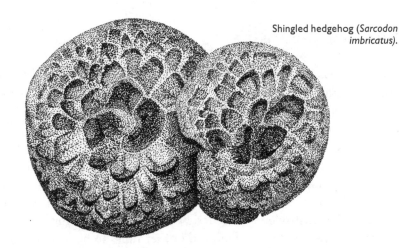

Shingled hedgehog (*Sarcodon imbricatus*).

FUNGI AND LICHENS

Recognizing that fungi are neither plants nor animals, biologists have split them off into their own taxonomic kingdom. Like primitive terrestrial plants such as mosses and ferns, fungi release prodigious numbers of unicellular microscopic spores. Germinating spores produce minute threadlike growths. These 'hyphae' fuse into the fruiting bodies we call bracket fungi, coral fungi, and many more familiar cap-and-stalk mushrooms.

We've identified and photographed some 230 species, classified by their microscopic spore-producing structures. One is a zygomycete related to bread mold. About twenty are ascomycetes (cup fungi, morels, and relatives). Some two hundred are basidiomycetes, including well over one hundred mushrooms with gills under their caps, and about ten are slime molds.

Southeast Alaska has a rich and varied fungal community, thanks to abundant wood and other organic materials and to the wet climate. Our list of 230 is probably just a small fraction of the total fungal species. Growing knowledge of these fungi heightens our pleasure in outdoor activities. When fungus season starts each summer (or spring, for a few species), old friends are greeted with delight.

Many of the ascomycetes can lichenize; that is, fungal species associate with a particular species of terrestrial alga to make what we call a lichen. Lichens grow on rocks, on soil, and on trees and shrubs. Those growing on other plants are called epiphytic and abound in Southeast Alaska's heavy rainfall.

Forest mushrooms

Every year, late in summer and throughout fall, mushrooms burst forth in an overwhelming diversity of shape, texture, color, and odor. Tiers of orange and yellow chicken-of-the-woods mushrooms troop up trunks of dead conifers, while an unusual resinous fragrance cloaks the plush, deep blue-violet caps of violet corts on the ground below. The haunting odor of Amaretto liqueur leads delighted hikers to tawny almond waxy caps nestling in a carpet of moss, beautiful mushrooms with thick, snow-white gills suspended beneath rosy-tan caps.

It is tempting to conclude this rich diversity of mushrooms is designed for our visual and gastronomic pleasure. But scientists unraveling the intricate forest fabric have found mushrooms and other fungi to be links between forest plants and small rodents, such as squirrels and voles.

Forest fungi have three different life styles: saprophytic, parasitic, and symbiotic or mycorrhizal. Saprophytic fungi decompose already dead wood and other organic material. Parasitic fungi attack and injure or kill living organisms. Mycorrhizal fungi establish mutually beneficial relationships with roots of trees, shrubs, and other vascular plants, and sometimes facilitate the parasitism of trees by plants lacking chlorophyll.

Saprophytes—Fungi are essential to decomposition in the forest. The chicken mushroom, for example, grows as a tangled mat of hyphae within the rotting wood of dead trees. The hyphae grow only at their tips, secreting digestive enzymes into wood. The fungi resorb some of the resulting decomposed nutrients, such as simple sugars and amino acids. But eventually most of the nutrients are released, washing into the surrounding soil, vital stimuli for the growth of green plants. Fruiting bodies of chicken-of-the-woods mushrooms blossoming from tree trunks release millions of spores to settle and germinate on other dead trees.

The belted woodconk, (*Fomes pinicola*, or bear bread), forms horizontally oriented conks, parasitic on spruce and hemlock. If the tree falls, new conk growth is reoriented to let the spores fall vertically. Annual growth layers—six on this conk—reveal how long the tree has been down.

Parasites—Parasitic fungi are also composed of hyphae spreading into the wood of trees. But these species attack living and apparently healthy trees, injuring or killing them. Examples include the multilayered red-brown butt rot, which attacks the living roots of Sitka spruce. Another is the honey mushroom, which attacks many kinds of forest trees and is particularly common on alders in our area.

Mycorrhizae—Other species of fungi are incompetent as saprophytes or parasites and instead obtain most of their organic nourishment by infecting the roots of forest plants, a mycorrhizal association. A wide variety of forest trees, shrubs, herbs, and other plants carry mycorrhizae ("fungus-roots") on and within their roots.

Host plants supply the dependent fungus with carbohydrate energy, sugars, amino acids, and vitamins. In return mycorrhizal fungi extend finely divided hyphae through soil to host roots, sharing water, phosphorus, nitrogen, potassium, and calcium. Conifers infected with mycorrhizae are twice as drought-resistant as uninfected trees. Tree seedlings may languish unless infected by mycorrhizae in their first year of growth. Fungal growth is equally dependent on trees.

The interdependence of host plant and mycorrhizal fungus has intrigued and amazed scientists. Mycorrhizal fungi produce hormones that stimulate production of new root tips by the host plant and lengthen the life span of these roots. Mycorrhizae also protect delicate roots from invasion by disease-causing microbes such as water molds, secreting antibiotics into the soil around the roots. Mycorrhizae help aerate soil and increase water retention, both essential for plant health. Fungal growth is attracted to and enhanced by substances released from tips of healthy plant roots.

Mycorrhizal fungi are themselves infected with nitrogen-fixing bacteria. These bacteria absorb organic nutrients from the fungi and in turn fix nitrogen, which stimulates fungal growth and ultimately, growth of the host tree. Water and nutrients pass among trees, their mycorrhizae linked like an interstate highway system. In forests studied elsewhere, young saplings receive nutrients from older, larger trees that serve as hubs in underground mycorrhizal networks.

The interaction of plants, mycorrhizal fungi, bacteria, and forest rodents is complex. For example, some species of mycorrhizal fungus—fly agaric, king

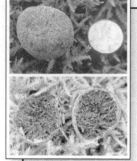

Sectioned truffle (Elaphomyces muricatus) with penny for scale.

Furtive but fragrant

Some ectomycorrhizal fungi are truffles that grow entirely underground. Unlike fungi that fruit above ground and scatter spores on the wind, truffles cannot reproduce unless animals such as squirrels, mice, or voles dig them up and eat them. When a flying squirrel, for example, eats a truffle, the spores mix with yeast and nitrogen-fixing bacteria. This blend ferments and is eventually excreted in squirrel pellets. Truffle spores are thus spread throughout the forest, where they germinate into fungi that help trees thrive.

Truffles work hard to be sure they'll be eaten. When mature they emit strong odors. Smelling like fruit, fish, cheese, or garlic, they lure hungry rodents to dig into the ground after them—savory meals with ulterior motives of their own.

boletus, lackadaisical laccaria, and chanterelle—can associate with a wide variety of plants. Others may be restricted to a single host. *Suillus*, for example, is mycorrhizal, but only grows in association with shore pines. Furthermore, forest trees often require infection by different species of mycorrhizal fungi at different stages in their life cycle, or may be infected by many species simultaneously.

Aboveground and underground fungi—Mycorrhizal fungi can be divided into two kinds, depending on whether their fruiting bodies are produced aboveground (epigeous species) or underground (hypogeous species).

Examples of epigeous mycorrhizal fungi found in Southeast Alaska fill a good-sized field guide. Members of the bolete, waxy cap, gomphidius, russula, chanterelle, and hedgehog families, plus species in the nearly ubiquitous genera *Amanita, Armillaria, Cortinarius, Hebeloma, Inocybe, Laccaria, Ramaria, Rozites, Tricholoma*, and many others are mycorrhizal fungi producing fruiting bodies above ground.

Spores of such species are discharged into the air from gills or fleshy spines, or from tubes. Fruiting bodies of these species take up moisture rapidly after a substantial rainfall and seem to burst through the soil. In Southeast, red-backed voles feed heavily on epigeous mushrooms, and red squirrels often cut off mature mushrooms and carry them up into the trees, where they lodge them in branch crotches. Although fungi have little fat and lag far behind seeds and nuts in caloric value, they're rich sources of B vitamins and contain valuable concentrations of minerals.

Hypogeous fungi, or truffles, resemble small potatoes, with a firm outer layer enclosing masses of spores. In Southeast Alaska, several truffles species of the genus *Rhizopogon* occur with conifers. The "true" and "false" truffles of fungal gourmets are culinary attributes, not ecological distinctions.

Fly agarics

Summer's end is always accompanied by monsoon-like rains throughout Southeast Alaska, and suddenly the forests are decorated with mushrooms of a bewildering variety and number. Many of us delight in cooking with wild mushrooms. But indiscriminate collecting is dangerous because numerous poisonous species also occur in our area. Some are easy to recognize. Most gorgeous and unmistakable is the fly agaric, native throughout cooler regions of the northern hemisphere. One has to wonder if this isn't a kind of warning "don't-eat-me" coloration, as found in toxic monarch butterflies or rough-skinned newts. The fly agaric probably originated in Beringia, where Alaska once connected to Siberia.

Also called the fly amanita, this may be the most depicted mushroom on earth. It has a scarlet cap that may fade to orange and yellow with age. The cap is covered with pale, cottony, pyramidal warts, remnants of the universal veil that enclosed the entire mushroom when younger.

The fly agaric is the toadstool of fairy tales and also the hallucinogenic species figured prominently in the folklore of Asia, Europe, and North America. Native peoples have used the fly agaric for centuries as a ritual hallucinogen, to communicate directly with spirit guides. As early as 2000 BC, the Aryan civilization worshipped the fly agaric as the god Soma. *Amanita muscaria* develops symbiotic mycorrhizal relationships with a variety of northern trees, including pine, spruce, cedar, and birch.

Fly agaric (*Amanita muscaria*).

Life-threatening toxins

Since almost all species of *Amanita* are known or suspected to be poisonous, mushroom eaters should recognize and avoid them. Mushrooms with white, flaky scales on the cap, a cuplike volva at the base, or a well-developed ring on the stem should not be tasted. (Caution: the ring may have dropped to the ground on older specimens.) Young *Amanitas* outwardly resemble edible puffballs; slice all putative puffballs in half vertically; true puffballs are structureless inside, while young *Amanitas* have developing cap, gills, and volva.

Toxins present in the fly agaric are ibotenic acid and muscimol. Symptoms usually appear within an hour of consumption and include excitement, confusion, profuse sweating, severe hallucinations, and delirium lasting four hours or longer, followed by a coma-like sleep and if lucky, recovery within twenty-four hours. But fly agaric can kill. Also, repeated use causes irreversible liver damage. Different geographic races, and perhaps even individual mushrooms, vary in the amount and proportion of toxins. Those who eat this mushroom to alter perception are courting disaster in both the long and short term.

If you suspect that you may have eaten a poisonous mushroom, induce vomiting and call a physician or poison control center immediately.

Short-lived fungus-eater flouts long-term liver damage.

Splash cups

Splash cups are ingenious devices developed by both fungi and plants. They use the kinetic energy of falling raindrops to disperse seeds or spores, or in some cases to assist pollination or fertilization.

Typically, a splash cup is an elastic, thimble-shaped fruiting structure between a quarter of an inch and a half inch across the open top, with sloping inner surfaces. These features enable the cup to extract the maximum amount of kinetic energy from falling raindrops, which scatter its mature seeds or spores. In maturity, splash cups face upward to catch rain.

Bird's nest fungi—Probably the best examples of splash cups are found in a small group of unusual fungi called bird's nest fungi.

Like many other fungi, the major part of the body of a bird's nest fungus is composed of a mass of fine hyphae, the white threads that grow within the fibers of old wood and decompose it. When environmental conditions are right, the fungus may produce the characteristic fruiting structures responsible for its common name. Tiny buttons grow on the surface of the rotting wood, enlarging to about the size and shape of small thimbles. At maturity, a thin membrane over the surface of the thimble ruptures to reveal numerous 'eggs' within the 'nest.' Each of these eggs, or peridioles, contains masses of spores. The peridioles are actually lentil-shaped, but within the thimble, they look like tiny eggs in the nest of some miniature bird.

Common gel bird's nest—In Southeast Alaska we have found two species of bird's nest fungus, the common gel bird's nest and the white-egg bird's nest. In the common gel bird's nest, the peridioles lie free within a gelatinous material in the nest. When a large raindrop or drop of water from the vegetation above the nest hits the opening, the force of the water is redirected upward and outward, causing a peridiole to be splashed as much as several inches away from the parent nest. Biologists think that the peridiole later weathers to release its spores, which can then germinate and grow as hyphae down into the wood, to continue the rotting process. This species is particularly common on old dead canes of salmonberry and thimbleberry and is easily recognized because the gray to tan nest is fuzzy on the outside.

White-egg bird's nest—In the white-egg bird's nest, the nest is a rich brown and has walls with smooth external surfaces. Each peridiole is attached to the wall of the fruiting cup by an elastic anchoring thread fastened to a small knob on its undersurface. This anchoring thread probably aids in ejecting the peridiole, possibly by acting as a

Common gel bird's nest (*Nidula candida*). 'Eggs' or peridioles are ejected by the impact of a raindrop in the cup.

Splash cup mechanics in plants
Good examples of splash cups that disperse seeds are seen in fruiting structures of flowering plants such as swamp gentian and alpine mitrewort, a saxifrage found in  subalpine meadows. At maturity, its fruit is cup-shaped and open at the top, the tiny seeds lying loosely within. The swamp gentian is found in bogs from sea level to subalpine and usually blooms in mid to late summer.

Flowers with small, cup-shaped blossoms, such as buttercups and anemones, can also use the force of raindrops to splash pollen from ripe stamens to receptive female structures, assuring seeds will be produced.

Mosses, too, form splash cups at one stage in their life cycle, but here it is sperm cells that are splashed into receptive female cups where fertilization occurs. Splash cups of mosses are composed of tight circles of special broad, overlapping leaflike structures.

Swamp gentian (Gentiana douglasiana). Some species of liverworts (moss relatives) form splash cups on the upper surface of the flattened plant body, or thallus. For example, lung liverwort (*Marchantia polymorpha*) on trail-sides and other disturbed habitats forms splash cups throughout most of the year. These tiny, bright green cups contain lentil-shaped fragments (gemmae) that bud asexually off the parent body and grow into a new thallus when splashed onto receptive soil.

---

spring to amplify the kinetic force of the raindrop. On launching, the anchoring thread tears off at the base and dangles behind the soaring peridiole. When the thread encounters stems of vegetation, or even hairs on stems or leaves, it clings fast and wraps around them, securing the peridiole. Biologists are not sure what advantage accrues from attachment to living vegetation, but in some species it is known that peridioles eaten accidentally by herbivores can be dispersed to another area and deposited in the natural fertilizer of the animal's dung.

Slime molds

Slime molds are bizarre "creatures" generally regarded as primitive forms of life only tenuously related to other fungi. In fact, slime molds may be related to amoebas, which are single-celled animals. Slime molds may even form a kind of missing link between fungi and primitive animals. Slime molds have remarkable life histories. At one point in its life cycle, each individual slime is

Alien life forms?

The spring of 1973 was particularly rainy in the eastern United States and throughout this area people reported finding weird bloblike creatures apparently growing in their backyards. One terrified woman reported that an original blob seemed to have been obliterated by heavy rains, but when she searched again, she discovered three more had appeared in its place! Some blobs were red and pulsating and were reported to climb telephone poles.

Newspaper journalists speculated the blobs were either mutant microbes taking over the earth or creatures from another planet sent to conquer the human race. This brouhaha was resolved when a prominent mycologist (scientist who studies fungi) identified the blobs as slime molds, which, while usually not well known to laymen, nevertheless have an established track record in the annals of science.

Insect egg-mass slime (Leocarpus fragilis) on electrified cat's-tail moss (Rhytidiadelphus triquetrus).

represented by many thousands of scattered cells that crawl through the forest in amoeboid fashion. Stimulated by some unknown environmental cue (possibly heavy summer rains), some cells secrete a chemical signal that attracts other amoeboid cells.

The attracted cells slowly aggregate and fuse into a large and often colorful slimy mass, giving rise to a blob technically called a plasmodium. The blob often persists for many days and may ooze slowly over the forest floor or climb up onto vegetation.

This slimy mass is the spore-forming stage in the slime mold's life cycle. Microscopic spores are formed by the millions all over the surface of the slime, often causing it to harden and change color. The spores are dispersed on air currents or perhaps by adhering to feet of ground-feeding birds such as thrushes. Under the right environmental conditions, each spore can germinate to release a single amoeboid cell, thus completing the slime mold's life cycle.

As the plasmodium creeps over mosses and vegetation, or within rotting logs, it engulfs and digests bacteria. Many amoebas show the same kind of feeding behavior. Spores landing in water develop into swarm cells, with tiny whiplike appendages for propulsion. Flooding during rainstorms stimulates amoeba-like cells to grow appendages. As puddles dry up, appendages resorb.

Coral slime (*Ceratiomyxa fruticulosa*) is common on rotting wood.

With further drying, slime molds can develop hard coverings and lie dormant for years.

In Southeast Alaska, slime molds are quite common in our forests in midsummer—for example the coral slime and the scrambled-egg slime.

Coral slime—The plasmodium of the coral slime is composed of masses of minute, translucent whitish stalks, each only about a quarter of an inch long. Spores form on outer surfaces of these tiny stalks. A log covered with coral slime looks as if it has a heavy coating of frost, incongruous in the summertime warmth. Coral slime may form small patches a few inches across, or may cover several square feet. This species is very delicate, and we have seen it only on vertical or shaded wood surfaces.

Scrambled-egg slime—The bizarre scrambled-egg slime looks as if someone has dumped the contents of a frying pan unceremoniously onto the ground. The scrambled-egg slime, which forms irregular cushions up to eight inches or so in diameter, has a whitish, somewhat translucent base (the 'egg white'), upon which is heaped a fluffy mound of bright yellow tissue (the 'yolk'): The yellow part is capable of forming spores on its surface, and as it does so it hardens and turns first dirty yellow and then charcoal gray. Slime molds are not known to be edible, and indeed we know of no one, ourselves included, willing to try one.

Lichens

Our coastal rain forests seem almost constantly drenched in fine cold rain or blanketed in winter snow, ideal habitats for a wide variety of lichens. A lichen is an intimate association between two unrelated organisms—a species of fungus and a species of alga. The fungus constitutes the lichen's bulk, forming the house, so to speak. Nestled within the fungal house are clusters of algal cells containing chlorophyll. These make food with assistance from light. The algal contribution, then, is to keep the lichen larder filled.

About forty genera of terrestrial algae are involved in forming lichens, and thousands of species of fungi may lichenize. Within any given species of lichen, however, only one particular species of fungus and one alga are involved. But many lichens also contain a species of blue-green bacterium, making these forms an assemblage of three different species. This raises an interesting point—what is a "species" of lichen, when it actually consists of two or more unrelated organisms?

Lichens are ecologically crucial. Some break down rocks left by retreating glaciers. The fungal parts of these lichens grow directly into the rocks, physically breaking minerals into smaller particles and leading to soil formation. The rocks develop cracks where mineral particles accumulate, which create tiny footholds where mosses and other plants can get established. Lichens also produce chemicals that react with rocks and slowly break them down.

Lichens that contain cyanobacteria are able to absorb, or 'fix,' nitrogen from the air. This nitrogen accumulates in a lichen's body in a form available to plants. Nitrogen is released as rain washes over the lichens, when insects excrete digested bits of lichens, or when lichens die and decompose on the ground. Lichens prepare soil for plants in an otherwise nitrogen-poor environment. This nitrogen fixation is especially important in nutrient cycling within old-growth forests, where alders and other nitrogen sources have long been shaded out.

Arboreal lichens don't parasitize trees, but take advantage of increased light levels above the more darkened forest floor. Some species smother bark lenticels (openings for gas exchange) and can penetrate and damage bark. On the other hand, arboreal lichens may shade older needles of conifers, causing them to drop prematurely. Some think this benefits the tree because old needles shaded by new growth cannot make as much food as the younger needles near the tips of branches.

In Southeast, lichens provide food for mountain goats, Sitka black-tailed deer, northern flying squirrels, red squirrels, mice, and voles. Several bird species use lichens as nesting material or as camouflage on the outside of their nests. Insects seek shelter and lay eggs under lichen lobes, and birds forage for insects among the lichens.

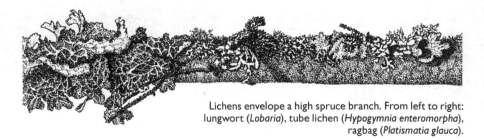

Lichens envelope a high spruce branch. From left to right: lungwort (*Lobaria*), tube lichen (*Hypogymnia enteromorpha*), ragbag (*Platismatia glauca*).

Lichens are sensitive to air quality and indicate air pollution if absent from otherwise appropriate habitats. Trees near pulp mills, for example, are often relatively devoid of lichens. The sulfur dioxide in smoke from such mills oxidizes the chlorophyll in lichen algal cells and kills them. The soil beneath affected trees may not be as rich because of the absence of nitrogen-fixing lichens above.

Lichen forms—Lichens have three growth forms. Crustose lichens adhere tightly to rock or wood and resemble a coat of paint. If you try to pry a crustose lichen from its substrate, it crumbles. One unusual but easily recognized crustose lichen is candy lichen or fairy vomit (*Icmadophila ericitorum*), a blue-green form that grows mostly on well-rotted wood in the forest. Because it usually grows on vertical surfaces, fairy vomit may require well-drained conditions. We have often seen this rapidly growing lichen overgrowing neighboring mosses and leafy liverworts. When reproductively mature, the pastel-green blob is covered with smooth pink bumps, altogether suggesting the forest gnomes may have partied a little too hard.

Foliose lichens are flat and leafy. They adhere much less to the substrate and can either be lifted off with your fingers or pried off with a knife blade. Foliose lichens may grow on rocks, trees, or soil, or among mosses and other plants on the ground. The upper surface of a foliose lichen is usually a markedly different color from its lower surface. In addition, the lower surface may bear rhizines, short rootlike structures serving to anchor the lichen onto its substrate. Pelt lichen—a foliose lichen on the forest floor—bears these rhizines.

Fruticose lichens have erect stems, often elaborately branched. Some arboreal fruticose lichens are hair-like and hang from tree branches. The so-called reindeer moss, a common ground-dwelling fruticose lichen, is not a moss at all. Branched and white, it grows in open areas and is abundant on rubble near

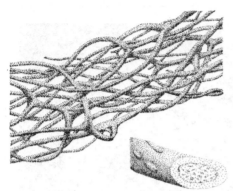 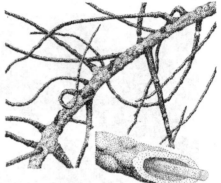

Witch's hair *(Alectoria sarmentosa)* Branches smoother than in *Usnea*, with tiny, elongated bumps. Forks in branches resemble deer antlers. Sectioned branches filled with cottony material.

Beard lichen *(Usnea longissima)* Main branch lumpy or wrinkled, shedding greenish cortex, which remains on side branches. Sectioned branches are hollow with a central cord.

glaciers. This lichen made headlines as a vector for radioactive isotopes. When atmospheric nuclear testing led to the fallout of radioactive elements over the North American and European Arctic, these radioactive atoms were taken up by the reindeer moss and transferred to caribou, which feed on it, and further to Native peoples, who eat caribou. The ability of this lichen to take up radioactive isotopes led to the Nuclear Test Ban Treaty of 1963, something politicians had previously failed to achieve.

Beard- and witch's hair lichens

Coniferous trees, especially those near peatlands, are so heavily decorated with long, draping strands of pale beard and witch's hair lichens that they seem prepared for Christmas year-round. Our beard lichens belong to the genus *Usnea*. They vary from a few inches to several yards in length. Beard lichens can be distinguished from witch's hair lichens by the presence of a central cord that stretches like a thin rubber band. If you pull a strand lengthwise the outer layer will break into segments, revealing this cord, which is most elastic when wet.

Witch's hair lichens belong to the genus *Alectoria*. These lichens are so abundant in our coastal forest that an acre may contain nearly a ton dry weight. These hair-like, pale yellowish-green lichens hang in clumps from trees. Their fine round strands branch several times and clumps of strands are often twisted

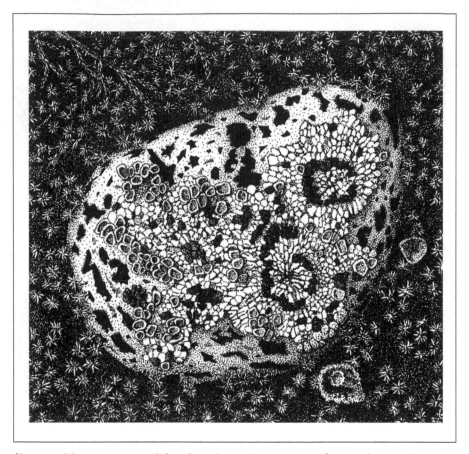

Placopsis gelida, a semi-crustose lichen that colonizes bare rock soon after glacial retreat. Local attempts to develop a size-age relationship (lichenometry) for dating deglaciated surfaces failed because this species has erratic growth patterns. Pixie cup lichens (*Cladonia*) in lower right.

like tangled yarn. A wet strand will stretch when pulled but breaks apart without a central cord.

A local study of a semitame Sitka black-tailed deer revealed that it actively sought both *Usnea* and *Alectoria*, eaten wherever winter storms blew them from the canopy onto shrubs or forest floor. These lichens and others can be especially important to deer in winter when edible plants are scarce or inaccessible.

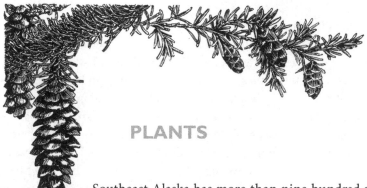

PLANTS

Southeast Alaska has more than nine hundred species of vascular plants (ferns and allies, conifers, and flowering plants). Of these, about fifty species occur primarily in colder boreal regions to the north and east. Among them are the shrubs bearberry, soapberry, and Beauverd spiraea, wild iris, and many arctic flowers. Another sixty or so species occur mostly to the south of our region, barely making it into the state. In this group are Pacific yew, sword-fern, western bracken fern, Pacific silver fir, western redcedar, Douglas spiraea, black twinberry, salal, and many flowering herbs. Some species reach to northernmost Southeast but no farther: red alder, dwarf mistletoe, red huckleberry, Douglas maple, and thimbleberry. The remaining eight hundred or so species occur both north and south of our area.

Few vascular plants are restricted (endemic) to Southeast Alaska, but a handful of species and subspecies are known only from Southeast and the nearby Haida Gwaii Islands. Distinctive endemic flora would not be expected in parts of Southeast glaciated less than 14,000 years ago.

Plants include algae (which most botanists place in a separate kingdom, Protista), liverworts and mosses (bryophytes), ferns and their allies (club-mosses, spike-mosses, horsetails, and quillworts), conifers (the only gymnosperms in our area), and flowering plants (angiosperms).

Douglas spiraea (*Spiraea douglasii*) is common on Prince of Wales Island lakeshores, but absent on the central and northern Tongass. Will it spread northward with warming climate?

Algae—These plants live in marine, freshwater, or terrestrial habitats and can be either microscopic or macroscopic in size. Microscopic species include such unicellular forms as desmids, diatoms, and dinoflagellates. Most of these tiny algae form the phytoplankton (phyto = plant) that 'blooms' in both fresh and marine waters in spring and early summer. Phytoplankton, along with macro algae, contributes to the producer level in aquatic food chains; in marine waters, for example, many species of phytoplankton are grazed by such herbivores as copepods and larvae of many bottom-dwelling (benthic) invertebrates, or are filtered from the water by clams and other animals. Copepods and filter-feeders are then consumed by carnivores such as fish and sea stars. Some microscopic terrestrial algae can enter into special partnerships with certain fungi to form lichens.

Seaweeds—Macroscopic algae include the red, brown, and green seaweeds of our rocky intertidal and shallow subtidal coastlines. These algae are part of the producer level of marine food chains; in addition, dead algal bodies break down to help form detritus that feeds benthic marine invertebrates—mussels, clams, and segmented worms. Some species of macro algae form such luxuriant growths—offshore kelp beds for example—that they attenuate wave action and protect intertidal communities from storm damage. These beds also form structurally diverse habitats important to fish and crustaceans. Some seaweeds are important substrates for herring roe, and most are both nutritious and edible by people and could add significantly to our future diets. Southeast Alaskan gardeners have discovered seaweeds are an excellent organic fertilizer.

Mosses—Mosses and liverworts (bryophytes) are partial to wet climates and flourish in Southeast Alaska. Not only does their reproduction depend on water, but the outer layer of their bodies lacks the protective waxy cuticle that, in vascular plants, helps keep delicate tissues from drying out. Like fungi, they reproduce by wind-dispersed microscopic spores; most species found here are also found throughout the Pacific Northwest. Mosses and liverworts are abundant in all habitats, from just above the high tide

Winged or ribbon kelp (*Alaria marginata*), common at about zero tide level.

Tongass tupelo?!—*Richard Carstensen*

It's hard to imagine Southeast Alaskan vegetation without wet conifer forest and saturated peatland. But this hasn't always been the case. In fact, before successive waves of Pleistocene glaciers gouged our fiordal maze, Southeast wasn't even an archipelago. From late Eocene to early Miocene times (about fifty to twenty million years ago) swampy lowlands near today's Kake and Angoon accumulated fine sediment washed down from surrounding hills. Into those muddy shallows were swept the autumn-shed leaves of a long-vanished forest. Over ensuing epochs, the pond sediment was compacted into mudstone.

Some of this rock can now be broken into flat plates, or even teased apart with the blade of a knife, revealing delicate impressions of deciduous leaf veins. These leaf-prints record a vast Arcto-Tertiary flora that covered all of Alaska, Canada, and Asia when temperate climate extended farther north than today. Tree diversity here was greater than any modern temperate flora.

Paleobotanists wielding rock hammers have studied these deposits and identified beech, elm, maple, basswood, hickory, grapes, figs, walnut, oak, rosewood, sassafras, dawn redwood, and tupelo (today restricted to the southeastern United States).

Eventually, colder, drier climate in the Pliocene drove this rich deciduous flora southward. Only isolated remnants survive in moist uplands such as America's Smoky Mountains and southern China.

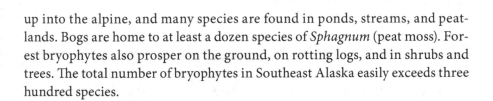

Leaf-vein impressions in mudstone near Angoon.

up into the alpine, and many species are found in ponds, streams, and peatlands. Bogs are home to at least a dozen species of *Sphagnum* (peat moss). Forest bryophytes also prosper on the ground, on rotting logs, and in shrubs and trees. The total number of bryophytes in Southeast Alaska easily exceeds three hundred species.

Ferns—All twenty-seven species of ferns in Southeast Alaska are terrestrial; water ferns and tree ferns do not occur here. The maidenhair fern, lady fern, oak fern, and spiny wood fern are deciduous species, with leaves (fronds) dying off

Fiddlehead, or early sprout stage of lady fern (*Athyrium filix-femina*).

at the end of each growing season. Sword-fern, holly-fern, deer fern, and parsley fern are evergreen. Many species make fiddleheads in the spring, and some are harvested by people.

Some eight species of club-mosses occur in Southeast Alaska; all are slow-growing, evergreen, and terrestrial. Our eight species of horsetail grow in wet meadows, stream margins, ditches and disturbed soils. Quillworts are perennial fern relatives.

Conifers—Only about ten conifers (gymnosperms) occur in Southeast, but several dominate the evergreen forests that define our area. Decomposition of their needles acidifies shallow soil and helps determine what other plants can grow here. Forests also stabilize the water table, preventing excessive runoff and erosion. Both pollen and seeds of conifers are dispersed by wind.

Flowering plants—Hundreds of species of flowering herbs, shrubs, and trees occur in Southeast Alaska. Many depend on wind to carry pollen and seeds, while some are pollinated by birds or insects, and some produce succulent fruits such as berries to entice birds and mammals to disperse their seeds. Flowering-plant families that do particularly well in Southeast Alaska include

Common trees and tall
shrubs of Southeast Alaska.

sedges (Cyperaceae),
grasses (Poaceae), and
heathers (Ericaceae),
the first two probably
because they are wind-
pollinated and the lat-
ter because they thrive
in acidic conditions
found in forest soils
and peatlands.

Mosses

Despite their small
size and often incon-
spicuous growth hab-
its, mosses are impor-
tant members of forest
and peatland commu-
nities in Southeast
Alaska. Hundreds of
different species of

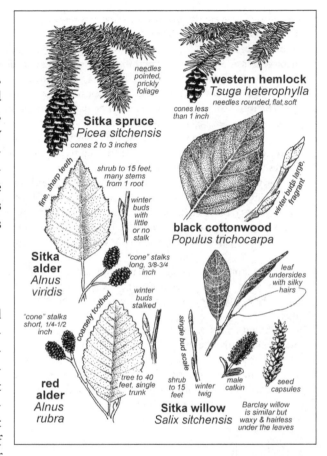

mosses carpet the forest floor, fallen logs, living tree trunks and branches, and
stream banks.

Although the caloric content of moss tissues is nearly as high as that typical of flowering plants, they are relatively indigestible due to their high content
of cellulose and lignin-like compounds abundant in wood. On the other hand,
mosses are rich in polyunsaturated fatty acids, which would be beneficial in the
diets of mammals. Two compounds in mosses—benzyl benzoate and oxalic
acid—are toxic to some insects and mites, so these invertebrates don't eat much
moss. Most birds and mammals are likewise thought not to eat mosses—except
incidentally, while consuming other plants. We've found only one published
record of intentional moss consumption by any of the vertebrates of Southeast

Introduced species—*Richard Carstensen*

Worldwide, the proliferation of nonnative plants and animals is second only to habitat loss as a driver of extinction. In the past few decades, land managers throughout Alaska have recognized the magnitude of exotic plant invasions, and begun to collaborate on surveys, eradication, and public education.

The most comprehensive online information source is the Alaska Exotic Plants Information Clearinghouse (AKEPIC). Querying this database for Southeast Alaska yields 180 introduced species in twenty-four families. Species are ranked from zero to one hundred points, according to potential to spread into wild places, displacing native flora and fauna.

Most threatening on the Southeast list, tied at eight-seven points, are several widely introduced knotweeds in the genus *Fallopia*. Close behind is spotted knapweed (eighty-six points), fortunately much less common. The seed of reed canary grass (eighty-three points) was intentionally included in mixes for roadside stabilization throughout the Tongass, so it's nearly universal on every island with logging roads.

With limited resources, managers have had to prioritize control efforts. When garlic mustard (seventy points) was detected at Juneau, volunteers turned out in large numbers to assist with weed pulls, trying to nip this invasion in the bud.

Habitats most at risk from aggressive nonnative plants are productive, early successional marshes and thickets found along streams and rivers, raised beaches, slide zones, and forest gaps. These habitats are extremely important to songbirds and rearing salmon, to mention just two connections. Preemption of these places by invasive flora—as has already occurred in much of the world—could be devastating to Southeast Alaska.

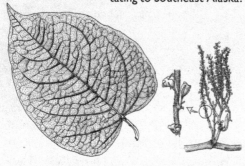

Japanese knotweed (Fallopia japonica) was introduced throughout Southeast as an ornamental but spread along streams and roads. It shades native herbs, clogs waterways, and reduces food for juvenile salmon and streamside insects. Hybrids with F. sachalinensis are common.

Alaska—the bog lemming. And indeed we once examined a dead bog lemming whose mouth was full of well-chewed moss. The most common use of moss by Southeast birds and small mammals is for nest linings.

One invertebrate living almost exclusively on mosses is the microscopic

Sphagnum girgensohnii is the first species of peat moss to appear in forest understories. As noted in *Peatlands* (p. 75) some ecologists consider this species a driver in 'paludification'—the conversion of forest to bog over the course of millennia. This hypothesis is controversial.

water bear, a distant relative of insects. These animals are about a millimeter long, with four pairs of legs armed with sharp claws for clinging tightly to the tiny plants upon which they feed. The water bear uses sharp stylets to pierce moss cells and suck out the contents, leaving behind the indigestible cell walls.

Mosses are not consumed by people but are a possible source of potent therapeutic drugs. One study of mosses and relatives showed that 56 percent of the species tested contained effective antibacterial compounds; one contained chemicals inhibiting growth of fungi.

The value of mosses to a forest community involves more than their worth as food and a potential drug source. Thick beds of moss absorb and retain rainwater together with its cargo of dissolved nutrients (such as phosphorus and nitrates). Without mosses, much of this water would be lost to streams. The moss carpet prevents soil erosion and moistens an underlying network of tree roots that would otherwise dry out during summer warm spells.

Tardigrade, or water bear, a microscopic inhabitant of mosses and lichens.

Buffering of soil acidity is another service of mosses. Nitrogen-fixing bacteria grow best when soil is buffered between certain moderate pH values. These bacteria may be free-living in the soil or associated with the roots of such plants as legumes, alders, and yellow mountain avens.

Alpine adaptations

While enjoying wildflower profusion in lush subalpine meadows and alpine tundra, one can easily observe special adaptations that enable plants to live in these often-harsh habitats.

Lichens are admirably suited to the highest alpine areas because they can live where there is no soil at all, obtaining minerals strictly from rainwater. What soils do exist in the alpine are thin, acidic, and low in nutrients, because water from rainfall and snowmelt leaches out minerals. Plants tolerant of such poor soils, such as lupines and heathers, do well in the alpine. Lupines not only thrive in but enrich poor soils because their root nodules contain nitrogen-fixing bacteria. Excess nitrates seep into soil to increase its fertility and make it more hospitable toward other species.

Heathers—Heathers abound in the alpine, not only because they thrive in acidic soils, but also because they tolerate drought. At first it seems a contradiction to think of any Southeast habitat as dry, but most alpine water is frozen much of the year, unavailable to plants. During summer dry spells, thin alpine soils dry out rapidly.

Southeast's alpine heathers are leathery-leaved and desiccation-resistant.

Alpine azalea (*Loiseleuria procumbens*), arctic willow (*Salix arctica*), and reindeer lichen (*Cladonia*) on a crack in alpine bedrock.

They include white- and Alaskan-moss heathers—both with tiny, white, bell-shaped blossoms—and yellow mountain-heather, with pale yellow lantern-shaped flowers.

Many alpine species are slow-growing but long-lived. During particularly harsh summers they forgo growth, waiting for better conditions. Yellow map lichen, for example, lives for centuries and grows extremely slowly.

On the other hand, where the effective growing season is only two to three months long, fast growth pays for plants that form and disperse seeds before first frost. Perennial plants store nourishment in underground structures, and as soon as snows melt back, sprout and flower rapidly. Cooley buttercup blooms in June at the edge of melting snowbanks. Annual plants do poorly in the alpine because they must start from seed each year, and a single bad year can wipe them out.

While wind-pollinated grasses and sedges do well in the alpine, wind scour forces many plants to grow as low as possible. Cushion growth forms are common. The moss campion, for example, may be a foot in diameter and less than an inch high—so effective at avoiding wind that air temperatures within the cushion can be 40° F higher than air several inches above the plant. The delightful wedge-leaf primrose also huddles close to the ground to avoid wind. The extreme case of ground-hugging among the heather family is alpine azalea, which creeps over rocks on the most exposed and bitter ridgetops.

Many plants that do stick up into the wind protect themselves by wearing fur coats. The woolly hawkweed, a close relative of dandelions, has long hairs on its stems, leaves, and around the bases of its flowers. These hairs insulate against cold and prevent rapid water loss.

***Broad-petaled gentian**—Bob Armstrong*
One of my favorite alpine flowers is the broad-petaled gentian. The large, clustered blooms are a beautiful deep blue or purple color.

They tend to open only on sunny days and bloom into September. Since the flower remains closed during most of our typical cloudy drizzly days, I have wondered what pollinates them. Sometimes I see flower flies on them when they are open. Once I decided to open up a few of the blossoms when they were closed. Much to my surprise they were loaded with tiny insects about 2 mm long. A little research revealed these insects were thrips in the order Thysanoptera. Without magnification they looked like dots moving about and feeding inside the flower. I speculated that an insect that tiny would have no trouble forcing its way past the tightly closed petals. I also wondered how important they are in pollination of these gentians.

Left to right: *Closed on cloudy day. • Open in sun, with flower fly. • Close-up view of thrips.*

The alpine flowering season is shorter than at sea level, and many insects need temperatures above 45°F to fly and pollinate. Plants attract these often-sluggish pollinators with the largest and most colorful flowers possible. Narcissus anemone and mountain marsh-marigold have huge white blossoms with yellow centers that contrast strikingly with their dark green foliage. Arctic cinquefoil and caltha-leafed avens both have large, bright yellow blossoms. Flowers such as Jeffrey shooting-star and arctic sweet coltsfoot may further enhance attractiveness to pollinators by strong perfume.

In adopting dwarfed dimensions for wind protection, alpine plants run into problems. Medium- to large insect pollinators require flowers of adequate size and strength to attract their attention and support their weight. For this reason, many dwarfed alpine plants retain normal-sized flowers, which then look out of scale with the rest of the plant. Good local examples of apparently outsized flowers are mountain harebell—an alpine bluebell—and purple mountain saxifrage.

Excessive sunlight can also be a problem in the alpine, where the air is thinner and less polluted than at sea level. Tender new growth is especially sensitive to ultraviolet rays, and many alpine plants protect rapidly growing parts with anthocyanins, red pigments that screen out the harmful, highest-energy wavelengths of sunlight.

Because seed reproduction is difficult in the short, cool alpine summer, many plants spread vegetatively. Partridgefoot is a member of the rose family that sends out runners like those of strawberry plants. At intervals along these runners, new shoots sprout upward. Alpine bistort, which may also be found at sea level, has tiny bulblets located on its stem immediately below its white flowers. These bulblets can drop off the parent plant, take root, and give rise to completely independent offspring.

Plant dispersal

Unlike most animals, plants stay put where they germinate. This works okay until time for reproduction, when seeds must somehow travel. We compared dispersal strategies of herbaceous and shrubby species in forest versus open beach meadow at Eagle River, northwest of Juneau, categorizing the seventeen most common plants in each habitat according to how they colonize new ground.

Vegetative spread—Many plants partially avoid problems of seed production by extending a network of stems and runners into nearby terrain either above or just below the ground surface. This strategy is more common in forest (86 percent) than in meadow (59 percent). In the more stable forest understory, dim light provides little energy for flowering and fruiting. Plants spreading vegetatively can grow into new areas, reserving relatively expensive seeds for colonizing more remote sites like clear-cuts and new windthrow gaps.

Distribution by wind—The majority of open-meadow plants rely on wind to disperse seed (76 percent of meadow species versus 36 percent of forest species). Very little breeze occurs in the forest understory; there, most airborne seeds and spores are nearly microscopic, easily lifting free to take advantage of the slightest air movement.

Seed head and hooked seed of large-leaf avens (*Geum macrophyllum*). This hitchhiker on fur and pant legs is common along trails and sidewalks.

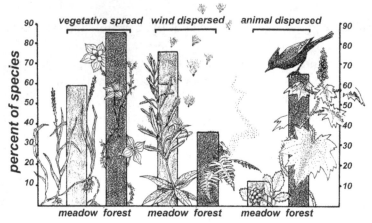

Plant dispersal in meadow versus forest at Eagle River, near Juneau. Because some species have multiple strategies, totals for forest and meadow exceed 100 percent.

Dispersal by animals—While some plants produce seeds with burrs or sticky coverings in order to hitchhike on the coats of mammals and feathers of birds, this strategy is less common in Southeast Alaska than elsewhere. Our most successful animal-dispersed plants produce fleshy fruits such as berries. Berries are offerings to birds and mammals, who repay this gift by eating and distributing seeds. Here we find the most striking differences between the two communities at Eagle River. Only 12 percent of the common meadow species produce berries, but in the forest 65 percent of the common understory plants are berry producers. Why?

The seeds of forest plants are, on average, heavier than those of plants in more open communities. In dark understory, a seed needs more nutrient reserves to sustain the germinating plant until it can begin gathering and producing its own food. But a heavy seed is a burden when it comes to dispersal, so most successful forest understory plants enclose their seeds in edible berries. This allows for heavier, nutrient-rich seeds without sacrificing mobility.

Berries: how to be obvious—A berry 'wants' to be eaten, quite opposite from the needs of nearly all other animals and plants—even the rest of the plant on which the berry grows. While everything else is hiding, running away, trying to taste terrible, or wearing armor or spines, a berry 'tries to be' as delicious and noticeable and available as possible.

A berry faces its own unique set of problems. It's a lavish but immobile expenditure. After fruiting in shady forest, it may take up to five years for a plant to accumulate enough energy to fruit again. So its berry should grow where odds are good it will be found by some creature that spends lots of time in places where that berry would like to have its seeds excreted. And it should avoid being eaten until its seeds are viable; it should stay green and bitter and cathartic until ripe.

It's also a good idea for a ripe berry to be red, a beacon color for birds and primates (including humans) but not visible to insects. In general, flowers love insects (as pollinators), but berries fear them (as seed consumers). This is why so few local wildflowers and so many local berries are red. The obvious exception—blueberry—is also the Southeast Alaskan fruit most visibly infested by insect larvae.

While everything else is competing to survive intact, the berry competes to be eaten. There are many ways to hide, or be speedy, or indigestible, but only a few ways to be obvious. Odor is one, but most birds have a poor sense of smell. Wiggling around is another, but plants aren't very good at that. A berry can only hang out in public places and be colorful. Thus, while there are quite a few specialists at cracking the intricate defenses of the hiders and runners and armor wearers (woodpeckers tweezering larvae from bark, deer digesting twigs), anything can eat a berry, and almost everything does!

In the tropics, different berry-producing species ripen at different times throughout the year, which reduces competition for, yet sustains high populations of generalist berry eaters year-round. In Southeast Alaska, where fruits can ripen mainly between midsummer and late fall, plants have less choice. But there is still clearly a partitioning of ripening seasons, between early fruiters such as salmonberry and late fruiters such as highbush cranberry. And some berries persist in winter, like those of mountain ash, a favorite of grosbeaks, and deerberry, under snowpack with hungry voles. Berries ripening too early or too late face problems. In midsummer most birds are still on breeding territories, too sedentary to be good seed distributors. In addition, most breeding birds forage for insects, as berries aren't often fed to nestlings, who need diets higher in protein. It doesn't pay to ripen so late that only winter resident birds and denned bears remain. The ripening of many temperate-zone berries is timed to late-summer and fall migration, when southbound birds are plundering the forest in search of quick energy.

Berries and tree-fall gaps—Everyone who gathers berries knows more fruit is produced on forest fringes and under well-lit windthrow gaps than beneath

Seeds in bear scat—*Richard Carstensen*

In October 1984, I noticed and flagged a fresh bear scat composed mostly of blueberries. Heavy fall rains were dissolving the pulped berries into the moss and litter. By marking the site, I could return at intervals to see what happened there.

By September 1985, the material of the dropping had washed away, but a plate-sized circle of blackened mosses revealed where it had been. As if to remove any doubt, a small fragment of garbage bag remained—the bear had likely been Hefty, a local yearling overly fond of human food. Rimming the circle was a fairy ring of *Cortinarius* mushrooms. But the most exciting discovery was 150 tiny sprouts of blueberry inside the ring! Obviously, they had germinated from the abundant seeds contained in the bear scat.

I revisited the site in October 1987. Nothing showed where the scat had been. Green mosses had moved back into the circle, and the fairy ring was gone. It hadn't been an auspicious site for blueberries, either—thick, interlocking hemlock canopy admitted little light. But five of the original 150 blueberry plants had survived and entered the young seedling stage, still less than an inch tall, with minuscule, toothed, evergreen leaves.

These young leathery-leaved blueberries are tenacious. They may endure for years under poor light conditions, prostrate and inconspicuous, waiting for their luck to change. Maybe a windstorm will someday open a space in the canopy and give the go-ahead to one of Hefty's sprouts. Our forest is a collaboration of animals and fungi and green things, and every square foot has a history as intriguing as the spot I happened to mark.

6 mm

—7 mm —

A forest collaboration: brown bear, varied thrush, and red huckleberry.

Clockwise from top: *mature autumn branch, young creeping evergreen plant, berry chewed by mouse or vole, and second-year sprout.*

dense, interlocking tree canopies. More energy is available to plants in sunny locations. But there may be more to this story. Studies in eastern deciduous forests found greater rates of fruit removal under canopy gaps than under closed canopy forests. Berries are offered where they know they're wanted. And if birds forage selectively in gaps, they distribute seed selectively there as well.

In our forests, red elderberry is a good example of this process. Young plants are more common in gaps on root masses of recently downed trees than under closed canopies. Elderberry is a common food of birds such as varied thrushes, American robins, and Steller's jays, all of whom favor edges of forest openings. Birds and mammals faithful to specific habitat types help, by seed dispersal, to maintain the distinctiveness of those habitats.

Ferns

Ferns display remarkable anatomical diversity, from tiny floating aquatic forms a fraction of an inch in diameter to tree ferns dozens of feet tall. Of the 12,000 or so contemporary species of ferns worldwide (many more are known only as fossils), about two-thirds are restricted to the tropics. The success of ferns in both tropical and temperate rain forests is due to sustained year-round moisture.

Woodland ferns display a continuum of growth forms ranging from broadly scattered fronds as in oak ferns, through more closely grouped fronds as in parsley fern or licorice fern, to fronds tightly clustered into a circle or rosette, as in sword-fern or hollyfern. Regardless of frond arrangement, every species of forest fern has a

Beech fern (*Phegopteris connectilis*), an example of the scattered-frond growth form.

perennial underground stem, or rhizome, interconnecting the fronds. The difference between a scattered growth form and a rosette is simply the relative length of the rhizome. This means that when you see numerous fern fronds of a single species scattered over a large area, you're probably not looking at many separate plants, but rather at a single plant (or a few plants) of impressive dimensions. Even in Southeast Alaska, ferns may rival small trees in size.

Yellow skunk cabbage

In late February or early March, before the winter snows have completely melted, the first leaf of yellow skunk cabbage pokes up through mucky soil in the forest. A member of the arum family (Araceae), it's a distant cousin of lilies, sedges, and grasses.

This first bright butter-yellow leaf is called a spathe. It forms an erect sheathing enclosure for the thick, fleshy floral spike, or spadix, within. The generic name, *Lysichitum*, meaning "loose tunic," may refer to these yellow spathes. First harbingers of spring, they almost seem to be candles lighting the forest in preparation for the pageant that follows.

Toward the end of March, hundreds of tiny flowers on the spadix begin to bloom, anthers splitting longitudinally to release clouds of pale yellow pollen. At this time, dozens of tiny beetles cover the spadix, apparently eating the pollen and possibly aiding in pollination. This is when the plant releases the odor responsible for its common name, although many find the odor neither skunk-like nor objectionable.

While flowering, the plant's first green leaves also rise above the mud, at first inrolled, forming thick spears, which push up and finally unfold into huge elliptical fans perhaps four or even five feet long. The long delay after appearance of spathe and spadix suggests they are produced entirely from compounds manufactured the previous season and stored underground in the thick roots. Green leaf production continues throughout summer, until as many as thirty huge leaves are present in an immense cluster. They are now making materials for next year's reproductive parts to be stored in the thickening underground parts over winter.

By late summer, the ripened spadix droops to the ground and seeds begin to separate and fall onto the mud. Although seeds may germinate to give rise to new skunk cabbage plants, probably most of them are consumed by such opportunists as Steller's jays.

A matter of taste

Despite the cabbage-like texture of skunk cabbage leaves, they are inedible to humans because their tissues contain long sharp crystals of calcium oxalate. Even a nibble embeds these crystals in the tongue and gums and causes extreme irritation. But bears, geese, and deer seem oblivious to them. Bears dig up the thick underground parts, and mature plants are staple food for nesting Vancouver Canada geese. Skunk cabbage is one of the highest-quality plants available to Sitka black-tailed deer, eaten in early

spring when other forage is in low supply and when deer are in the weakest condition of the year. In April we've seen places where nearly every spathe was clipped off at ground level. This doesn't seem to hurt the plant unless the spadix too is taken (drawing, below right). A month later the only evidence of grazing will be a slight wrinkling of the giant leaf tip. Skunk cabbages may live for seventy years, ten times longer than the deer who prune them each spring. As other young and tender plants become available, skunk cabbages are ignored for a time, but between mid July and October, the mature leaves are again eaten by deer.

Native peoples used the leaves to wrap salmon before baking and to line steaming pits.

Above: *Mating rove beetles (Pelecomalis testaceum) on skunk cabbage spadix in spring.*

Left: *Mature leaves of skunk cabbage are eaten by deer and Canada geese. In this case, high elevation (about 2,000 feet above sea level) suggested deer.*

Right: *Spring spathe, nipped by deer at ground level when young, still shows evidence of grazing. Like a grass, skunk cabbage grows from the base, not the leaf tip— an adaptation to recover from grazing and perhaps from frost kill.*

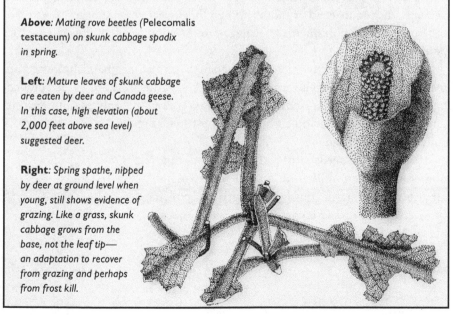

Orchid strategies

Orchids are among the most beautiful of flowers. Most of the 17,000 or so species in the orchid family are found in tropical rain forests, where they are typically epiphytic—growing on trees in a nonparasitic manner for access to increased light above the forest floor. North America has only about 140 orchids, and most are terrestrial rather than epiphytic. About sixteen species are found in Southeast Alaska, mostly huddling inconspicuously in wet meadows and peatlands. The fairy slipper or calypso orchid is a spectacular exception with large pink and purple blossoms. It's found in needle litter beneath spruce and redcedar trees, especially on small islands. Many have been picked, so it's now rare around towns.

Orchid flowers are typically complex in structure and often flamboyant in color. Many are exquisitely perfumed as well. Sepals are often highly colored and petal-like in appearance. The lowermost petal, the lip, is usually broadly expanded and especially colorful; it functions as a landing platform for an insect pollinator.

Many orchids are specifically shaped, colored, and scented to attract a single species of insect. When the insect lands and attempts to feed, pollinia become stuck to its head or thorax. When this insect visits another blossom of the same species, pollinia are transferred to the stigma of that flower, effecting pollination.

In North America, orchids having small whitish or greenish flowers are usually pollinated by male mosquitoes, which visit the blossoms to feed on nectar. These orchids either lack detectable fragrance or emit only a faint perfume. Orchids that are white and emit a heavy perfume are typically moth-pollinated.

In orchids, seeds are extremely small and numerous—over 3 million in a single ovary. After all the machinations involved in getting pollen transferred, the orchid is content to let seeds be dispersed by the vagaries of wind. Orchid seeds are so tiny that there is no room for any of the stored food

Fairy slipper, or calypso orchid
(*Calypso bulbosa*).

reserves present in most other kinds of seeds. For this reason, germinating orchid seeds must immediately set up an intimate relationship with a particular species of fungus in order to survive.

This orchid-fungus relationship is said to be mycorrhizal. The delicate strands of fungal tissue (hyphae) penetrate into the growing orchid and soon pump in water and nutrients from the surrounding soil. Without this fungal pump the orchid could not survive. Orchids transplanted from the wild will languish in your garden, unless you also transfer fungus-laced soil with them. In some species it appears the orchid seed refuses even to germinate unless penetrated and chemically coaxed by fungal hyphae.

Local orchids—Comparing three terrestrial local orchids, we can speculate about their mycorrhizal relationships. Menzies' rattlesnake-plantain (not a plantain at all but an orchid) bears a basal rosette of lustrous evergreen leaves. Although the plant is probably associated with a fungus, apparently it achieves a good measure of independence and can at least make its own food via photosynthesis.

The calypso or fairy slipper orchid has but a single small basal leaf per plant and is probably more nutritionally dependent on its root fungi than is rattlesnake-plantain. As the fungus digests dead organic matter in the soil, some of the resulting nutrients may be passed along to the orchid as a bonus.

Of all the local orchids, coralroots are most heavily dependent on their mycorrhizae. Coralroots are named for underground parts resembling knobby pieces of branched coral. In

Menzies' rattlesnake "plantain" is actually an orchid (*Goodyera oblongifolia*).

Only when walking home with this plant, collected for drawing, did we notice the male *Aedes* mosquito buried to his shoulders in the faintly fragrant lowermost blossom.

fact, these are not roots at all but underground stems, or rhizomes. Coralroots have actually lost all vestige of roots and are utterly dependent on mycorrhizae plugged into the rhizomes. Western coralroot has lost all its chlorophyll and cannot photosynthesize. The erstwhile green leaves have been reduced to purplish scales. Lacking green leaves, individual stems of coralroots can readily live in shady places and can grow in dense clumps rather than spaced well apart to obtain sufficient light.

Comparing these three species of orchids, we may see a progression from partial to complete dependence on mycorrhizae. It appears some orchids are 'burning their bridges' by becoming utterly dependent on certain fungi, unable to survive on their own. This may explain why so many species of orchids are so rare, and possibly why orchids produce so many millions of minute seeds to be scattered at the mercy of the wind. If enough seeds are sent forth, maybe at least one will find some hyphae of the right kind of fungus.

Dwarf mistletoe

Dwarf mistletoes are fascinating flowering plants that parasitize trees in the pine family, including pines, Douglas-fir, true firs, spruces, hemlocks, and larches. In western North America, dwarf mistletoes are serious forest pests that slow tree growth and predispose hosts to attack by insects and fungi, leading to increased mortality. Heavily infected trees may have their cone crop reduced by 75 percent or more.

Dwarf mistletoes probably originated in Northeast Asia and spread to North America across the Bering land bridge during the last great ice age. Once in North America, dwarf mistletoes found a wide variety of host species and so evolved into many different species. Today there are about forty species of dwarf mistletoe worldwide, three-quarters of which occur in western North America.

In Southeast Alaska we have only one. It occurs primarily on western hemlock from Haines southward, most abundantly at lower elevations. Dwarf mistletoe is a long-lived parasite. It requires at least five years from time of infection to produce a new generation of leafless but reproductively mature aerial shoots outside the host tissues. These shoots are about one to four inches high.

In dwarf mistletoes, male and female plants are separate. Small berrylike fruits, each containing a single seed, ripen slowly on female plants. In our local dwarf mistletoe, fruit ripening usually concludes in September to October. At that time, sudden cold weather can trigger an explosive release of the seed. Hydraulic pressure builds up beneath the seeds, and they are shot away at speeds up to sixty miles an hour. Often they travel forty feet or more from the parent tree. Each seed is covered with a sticky coating enabling it to adhere to almost anything it strikes. Many seeds are trapped by overlying host branches, intensifying the infestation of that host. The majority fall to the ground and perish, but some land on nearby trees and spread the disease. Dwarf mistletoe can spread in this manner through a forest at the snail's pace of 1 to 2 feet per year.

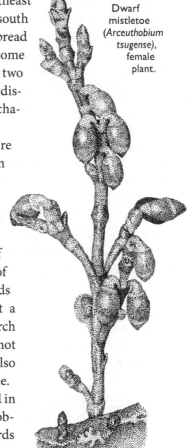

Dwarf mistletoe (*Arceuthobium tsugense*), female plant.

Although dwarf mistletoes first entered our continent near today's Bering Sea, our local species apparently colonized Southeast Alaska from a source about 1,000 miles to the south during the last 10,000 or 12,000 years. This spread into Southeast is equivalent to an annual rate of some 500 or more feet, greatly exceeding the one to two feet per year estimated from the method of seed dispersal described above, and hints that other mechanisms may be involved.

Seeds mature in fall when most birds are migrating south, which wouldn't seem to explain mistletoe's northward movement. But several birds, among them the Steller's jay, overwinter in Southeast Alaska, and random movements of these birds could assist the gradual northward spread of dwarf mistletoe. In fact, seeds of dwarf mistletoes have been found on the feathers of Steller's jays. The jay may preen these sticky seeds out with its bill and then wipe them against a branch, where they can germinate. Jays often perch in tree crowns, and parasites established there not only are best situated for further dispersal, but also damage the most actively growing part of the tree.

Dwarf mistletoe seeds have also been found in feathers of warblers, juncos, red crossbills, and robins and in the fur of red and flying squirrels. Birds and squirrels often build their nests in branches misshapen by dwarf mistletoe infestation, where they may frequently encounter seeds. One study showed seeds stuck to fur or feathers of up to 20 percent of the mammals and birds examined. Radio-tracked birds moved repeatedly between infected and healthy trees.

Seeds stuck to hemlock needles loosen in the rain and either wash to the ground and die, or slide to the base of the needle, where they contact exceptionally thin bark and germinate. Seeds and seedlings of dwarf mistletoes apparently contain enough food reserves to survive the few months that pass before they can penetrate this thin bark and begin to parasitize their new host.

Within the bark of the host branch, roots of dwarf mistletoe spread through those tissues (phloem) that conduct foods manufactured by the host tree, pirating and absorbing them. The parasite also sends sinker roots deeper into the branch to penetrate other specialized tissues (xylem) conducting water and minerals upward into the tree, robbing the host of even its raw materials. Because dwarf mistletoe plants do not manufacture much of their own food, they lack their own phloem tissues.

As the parasite grows, the host branch swells, and additional nutrients are brought to the site, which further favors the growth of the dwarf mistletoe. Its growth also interferes with the normal activity of the host hormones, which may radically alter the regular pattern of branching within the infected region, creating large, bizarrely branched structures known as witches' brooms.

Witches' brooms continue to enlarge in size and may survive more than seventy years. The age of brooms can be determined by cutting the infected branch through the center and counting the distorted rings of wood laid down since the infection began. Brooms that eventually become shaded by continued upward growth of the host may die and be removed by natural self-pruning. Rodents such as porcupines and squirrels also are somehow attracted to the swollen branches of these brooms; they chew on them and can girdle and kill them.

Our dwarf mistletoe occurs as far south as central California, where its preferred host is mountain hemlock rather than western hemlock. This switch in preference with latitude is only one of the many mysteries surrounding the biology of this intriguing plant. It is also unknown why levels of infestation are lower in Southeast than farther south, and why dwarf mistletoe does not accompany hemlock throughout its range almost to Kodiak Island.

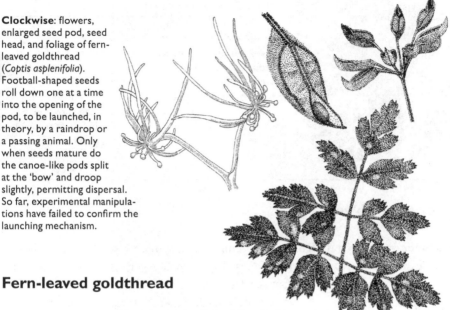

Clockwise: flowers, enlarged seed pod, seed head, and foliage of fern-leaved goldthread (*Coptis asplenifolia*). Football-shaped seeds roll down one at a time into the opening of the pod, to be launched, in theory, by a raindrop or a passing animal. Only when seeds mature do the canoe-like pods split at the 'bow' and droop slightly, permitting dispersal. So far, experimental manipulations have failed to confirm the launching mechanism.

Fern-leaved goldthread

Fern-leaved goldthread is another harbinger of spring in Southeast Alaska; it seems the plant can hardly wait for snow to melt before the stems begin to push up from soft mossy beds in the forest or at the edges of bogs. Early April in Ketchikan or mid-April in Juneau is not too early to begin searching at sea level for blooms of this diminutive member of the buttercup family. At higher elevations fern-leaved goldthread may bloom several weeks later.

Every stem supports two or three exquisite blossoms, each on its own side-branch, or pedicel. These blossoms look decidedly 'unbuttercuppy.' The five to eight white sepals are about half an inch long and almost thread-like. They are strongly reflexed, or arched backward away from the center of the blossom, and somewhat resemble comet tails.

Digging in the soil beneath the stem will reveal the thin, bright yellow roots responsible for half of goldthread's common name. The leaves, attached at the base of the flower stalk, explain the first half of the common name and the specific name *asplenifolia*, which means "having leaves like those of *Asplenium*"— a genus of fern with highly subdivided leaves.

Fern-leaved goldthread stays green all winter, providing important forage for Sitka black-tailed deer. Lacking animal seed distribution, it takes longer than bunchberry or five-leaved bramble to colonize forests after glacial retreat.

Poisonous plants

Baneberry—This tall, handsome member of the often-toxic buttercup family grows in meadows and forest edges. In August, ripening ovaries swell into glossy scarlet berries, each slightly less than half an inch in diameter. Rarely, plants bearing pure white berries are found in our region. Consumption of these enticing fruits can result in severe gastrointestinal sickness and even respiratory paralysis, hence the common name. The poison, protoanemonin, is related chemically to other toxins found in the buttercup family. Children should know and avoid baneberry.

Baneberry (*Actaea rubra*). Early sprout and flower buds on left. Fruits and mature leaves on right. Inside the ripened berries is an unappetizing white pulp.

Water hemlock—This common local member of the parsley family may rank as the most virulently poisonous plant in all of North America. Water hemlock prefers wet places and is common in many freshwater marshes, along edges of slow-moving streams and roadside ditches, and more rarely along the shoreward edges of marine wetlands.

A rather slender plant, it can reach a height of five or six feet. Water hemlock

Leaf venation distinguishes bent-leaved angelica (*Angelica genu-flexa*) from the deadly water hemlock (*Cicuta douglasii*).

leaves are divided into many leaflets having rather sharply toothed margins. A distinctive feature of this species is its veining. Many of the leaf veins run out to the notches between teeth rather than to their tips, as in other parsley-family species. The bases of the leaf stems do not carry large sheaths, as do cow parsnip and bent-leaved angelica.

In midsummer each water hemlock plant carries a large umbrella of tiny white flowers. The umbrella, which may be supported by as many as 3 dozen spokes, is not as flat-topped as that of cow parsnip; the individual sections of the flowering head of the water hemlock are well rounded. These flowers may emit a somewhat musty fragrance.

Water hemlock is supported by a large underground taproot, where the poison, cicutoxin, is concentrated. This part of the plant is most frequently responsible for human poisonings; a single mouthful may be fatal. Early leaves and stems growing from the taproot also contain highly concentrated poison. Although toxins are somewhat diluted with further growth, the entire plant should be considered dangerous.

Internally, the root of water hemlock is divided into a series of chambers separated by complete partitions. These apparently serve as flotation chambers. After bank-collapsing storm flows on small wetland creeks, we've observed clusters of hemlock roots washed up on the levees downstream. Other local members of the parsley family have similar hollow structures to their taproots, but the spaces are not as regular or numerous as those of water hemlock. Even the roots of edible plants in this family are scarcely gourmet eating and should be left to bears, who better appreciate their taste.

Carnivorous plants

The comedy *Little Shop of Horrors* stars Audrey II, a sort of bloodsucking cabbage (Audrey I is the play's human heroine). While bloodsucking plants exist

Common butterwort (*Pinguicula vulgaris*), with flies stuck to the leaves.

only in the imaginations of playwrights, carnivorous plants that eat entire animals are common. Carnivorous Southeast plants include butterworts (Lentibulariaceae family, closely related to Indian paintbrushes) and sundews (Droseraceae family, with no really close kin).

Butterworts—Bog violets, or butterworts, grow in the drier parts of peatlands, alpine slopes, and wet meadows. They also frequent damp pond margins in deglaciated valleys. The species most encountered in Southeast Alaska is the common butterwort. We also have the hairy butterwort, so tiny (only 1 to 1.5 inches high) that it's often overlooked.

Each butterwort has a rosette of thick yellowish green leaves lying rather flat against the surface of the ground. These leaves secrete a greasy or sticky material over their upper surfaces, and any insects landing or crawling on them become stuck fast. Digestive enzymes are secreted, and the prey is consumed. If you examine the upper surfaces of the butterwort leaves, you will see numerous tiny corpses in various stages of digestion.

Butterworts flower in summer, when a single deep-blue blossom with backward-directed spur and a thatch of thick white hairs in its throat is produced on a stem rising perhaps six inches above the dangerous leaf rosette. The blossom is held high above the leaves; it would be disadvantageous for the plant to trap and eat its own pollinators.

Sundews—These *Drosera* species (Greek for "dewy") are also found in muskegs and wet meadows. There are two species in Southeast Alaska, the round-leaf and long-leaf sundews. Both have a cluster of long-stemmed leaves but are distinguished by rounded versus elongated leaf shapes. Both species of sundew bloom in early summer. Dainty white blossoms develop at the top of leafless stems, and the flowers open only during bright sunshine.

In both species, the sundew leaves are covered with a liberal supply of

Flies captured by long-leaf sundew (*Drosera anglica*).

stalked red glands. These glands secrete glistening droplets of thick glue. Any tiny animal that contacts these glands is held fast. The stalked glands bend inward with their captive toward the center of the leaf, where digestive enzymes are released.

Our 2 species of sundew seem to have different 'fishing' strategies. The round-leaf sundew is found in drier parts of bogs and holds its leaves rather flat against the ground. This growth habit likely helps it catch tiny spiders and crawling insects. The long-leaf sundew, on the other hand, lives around the edges of small pools in the bog and holds its leaves more vertically, probably to capture the mosquitoes and gnats that hover about the water.

One interesting question about carnivorous plants is whether they really depend on chance encounters. It's been suggested they secrete sugars or other substances to attract potential prey, but this idea has not been supported by any field experiments or observations.

But why go to all this trouble in the first place? After all, sundews and butterworts are all green plants with a good supply of chlorophyll, and all are capable of making their own food with the help of sunlight. It turns out that most carnivorous plants live in highly acidic conditions, where nutrients such as nitrogen and phosphorus are in limited supply. Animals provide these nutrients, so by eating them, carnivorous plants are able to compete successfully in what might otherwise be marginal habitat.

Devil's club

The ginseng family is a small group of about 70 genera containing 700 species of primarily tropical woody shrubs and vines. Devil's club is the only member of this family in Southeast Alaska. Among Tlingit herbalists, sáxt' is the most widely used medicinal plant.

Devil's club grows in rich tangles, gracing the moist but well-drained, nutritious soil of stream and river banks and steep talus slopes. The roots of devil's club seem to require good lateral movement of soil water, rather than the standing water and acidic muck tolerated by species such as yellow skunk cabbage.

Left: Devil's club in fruit, clustered for easier consumption by bears. • Below: Overwintering stem of devil's club (*Oplopanax horridus*) with next year's bud at top. Leaf scars at nodes on base and midstem show two years' growth.

The generic name of devil's club is partly derived from *hoplon*, a Greek word meaning "weapon." Stems, leaf stalks, and even undersides of the leaf veins are armed with brittle, yellowish-brown spines up to half an inch long. When you brush against this plant carelessly, these spines break off and penetrate your skin. If spines are not extracted, they fester for days. People allergic to substances on these spines have especially inflamed reactions. Off-trail travel on the Tongass entails learning how to weave unpricked between stems and leaves of this magnificent plant. An entire generation of *Discovery Southeast* students on field trips near Juneau elementary schools has learned the slogan—"Save your face; keep your space!"—a reminder to stay well behind the bushwhacker in front of you.

Why is it so heavily armed? Leaves of devil's club are particularly rich in protein, and if they weren't so well protected, they might be the preferred food of many forest herbivores. Even with its spiny protection, we find August leaves browsed to tatters by deer in high subalpine forests.

Each devil's club has several coarse and flexible pithy stems that may rise to more than seven feet or droop to the ground and then turn up at their tips. These prickly stems persist over winter. By mid-May, buds on the tips of these stems swell and open, releasing several large leaves that expand to eighteen inches across. While still young and tender these green shoots can be cooked and eaten as a vegetable; they are also browsed by Pacific banana slugs.

The blade of each leaf is shallowly cut into five to nine lobes, each marginally toothed around a single central drip point, which helps the leaf shed rain easily. These long-stemmed leaves spread out in a nonoverlapping array to catch the maximum amount of light filtering down to them in the dense forest. The leaves, light green in summer, briefly turn lemon yellow before being shed in the fall.

The flower cluster of devil's club appears in June. By

Fruiting bunchberry or ground dogwood (*Cornus canadensis*). One drupe has been chewed by a mouse or vole.

late summer the ovaries of these flowers have ripened into glossy scarlet berries. Despite their enticing appearance, these berries consist of little but a thin skin and meager pulp enclosing two huge seeds, considered inedible by humans, but favored by bears, hermit thrushes, and red squirrels.

Bunchberry

Bunchberry is a trailing forest and peatland plant, a miniature member of the mostly shrubby dogwood family. In the forest, bunchberry seeds germinate only in places where light can penetrate. In darker places bunchberry propagates by means of an underground stem, forming large beds of genetically identical shoots. Vegetative, sterile shoots bear four leaves; fertile shoots carry six leaves, flowers and fruit.

The center of the bunchberry 'flower' is actually a cluster of many tiny blossoms. On each of these tiny flowers, one petal out of four bears a long bayonet-like spine on its tip. Before the blossom opens, these spines stick upward, forming a spiny carpet over the surface of the flower buds. When the blossoms finally open, the petals bend strongly backward away from their centers, and the spines rotate downward and are no longer visible—a unique 180° rotation. Perhaps before blossoms open, the plant finds it advantageous to ward off possible pollinators who can only waste their time; later, when pollen and unfertilized seeds are ready, the armature is lowered.

By early August, after the white bracts that surround the flowers have withered and fallen, orange-to-scarlet fruits ripen. Frequently called berries, these are technically drupes, with mealy pulp surrounding a single seed. Rarely eaten by people, they feed birds and forest mammals. In September we've found sooty grouse gizzards packed with bunchberry seeds so hard-coated they may need to be abraded or chemically softened in order to germinate.

By the time fruits have ripened, the four smaller terminal leaves almost catch up in size with the others. Leaves of bunchberry in the forest are evergreen, even beneath a blanket of snow, an important winter food for Sitka black-tailed deer. In open peatlands, leaves often turn red and are shed in fall.

Blueberries

Both the early and Alaska blueberry are abundant throughout Southeast Alaska. The two frequently grow together and are quite similar, but attention to a few key characteristics will usually distinguish them.

Both species grow best in clearings in the forest or around forest edges, where light is more abundant, and they are often found together with rusty menziesia and red huckleberry. All four shrubs are members of the heather family. Both species of blueberry produce erect perennial stems three to five feet in height. Young branchlets have weakly angled sides, conspicuously red or reddish purple in winter. Bark on the branchlets thickens and turns gray by the second or third year.

In both species the thin leaves of mature plants are deciduous. In the Alaska blueberry, branching leaf veins are relatively less prominent below, and a field lens usually reveals a few glandular hairs along the underside of the midvein. In the early blueberry, the branching leaf veins are more prominent and hairless.

Flowers of these two species are quite different in form and in time of first appearance. Flowers of early blueberry develop before leaves begin to expand, in mid- to late April, depending on the length of the preceding winter. This species seems sensitive to a string of several unusually warm days any time after the leaves are shed in the early fall, and it may flower at inappropriate times. We once observed blossoms in mid-October.

Alaska blueberry usually flowers later in May, when the leaves are already expanded to at least half their final size. Early blueberry is easily forced; cuttings brought indoors in winter and placed in water will produce blossoms in a week, but Alaska blueberry resists forcing. The difference in flowering time between these and other heather-family shrubs reduces competition for pollinators, who are also kept happy by a longer pollinating season.

In both species the blossom is urn-shaped. The coppery pink urn of Alaska blueberry is broader than long; the pistil usually protrudes just outside the

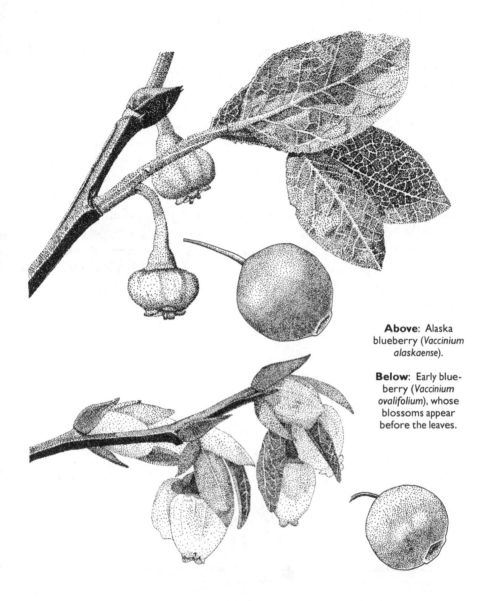

Above: Alaska blueberry (*Vaccinium alaskaense*).

Below: Early blueberry (*Vaccinium ovalifolium*), whose blossoms appear before the leaves.

opening. In early blueberry, the pink-to-white urn is slightly longer than broad; hence the pistil is hidden from view.

Stamens of blueberries are intriguing. Anthers, or pollen sacs, are held upright when pollen is immature, but rotate 180° on ripening. Fine pores appear, dusting out pollen in saltshaker fashion. Such anthers are typical of heathers. Rufous hummingbirds and yellow warblers feed at blossoms of early blueberry, so these birds may be cross-pollinators of this species. Probably more effective is buzz pollination by queen bumblebees, who overwinter and seem to emerge exactly when early blueberry blossoms open.

Fruits of the two blueberry species are also quite distinct. Early blueberry fruits are about half an inch in diameter, bluish black with a whitish coating or 'bloom' of wild yeasts on the surface. They begin to ripen in July. Alaska blueberries are usually glossy bluish-black; they are sometimes called black huckleberries for this reason. They average somewhat larger than those of the early blueberry and are juicier, with a distinctive, almost resinous flavor. Both berries make excellent jams, jellies, and pies, and are often picked and frozen for winter use.

In winter, Sitka black-tailed deer browse the leafless stems of blueberries. Although not as nutritious as evergreen leaves of ground-hugging plants such as bunchberry, the shrubs are easier to find in deep snow, and may take starving deer through the critical period.

Bumblebee *(Bombus mixtus)* on half-dollar-sized flower cluster—one sprig of the musky, plate-sized umbel of cow parsnip *(Heracleum maximum).*

AFTERWORD

When we wrote *The Nature of Southeast Alaska* in 1992, the World Wide Web was one year old, and we hadn't yet heard of it. Our final draft resided on floppy disks; to us, that was cutting-edge technology.

Assembling this third edition, it's natural to look not only backward but forward in time. Twenty years from now—if we're around for a fourth rewrite—will bound books or keyboards even exist? Will great redcedar trees still stand at Su<u>k</u> Dàa, *dry around* (Calder Bay)? What languages will be spoken in the state capitol, and who—or what—will translate them? Will the world celebrate or mourn the Tongass?

Such unanswerable and unsettling questions spring easily to mind as we reflect upon profound changes in technology, politics, and scientific understanding—all transpired since we first committed to paper our dilettante synopsis of this beloved, rain-forest home. For better and worse, the rate of change is accelerating. Climate destabilization outpaces predictions. Smart phones look dumb within two years. On the brighter side, acoustic bat detectors capture range extensions while we sleep. Genetic analysis opens windows into speciation, migration, and endemism that few dreamed of in 1992. Each year, remote sensing technologies such as lidar grow more powerful and affordable, mapping ground contours and canopy structure at unprecedented resolution.

Although we've added more than a hundred new drawings, maps and photos, fifty-two new sidebars, and made sweeping updates and elaborations to chapter narratives—often thanks to technology unknown in 1992—the *Table of Contents* in this third edition looks much the same. Like Tlingit Raven stories, the scaffolding of bedrock-to-bugs natural history has a timeless cadence,

In the late 1800s, Takjik' Àan Kwáan monuments, sternly painted, claimed a small, cleared bluff near the village of Tuxekan, in the Sound renamed in roundabout fashion for a mysteriously vanished ship—the Royal Navy's *Sea Otter*. By the time of this 1994 drawing, a pole-timber stand of laax (redcedar) had enveloped and mercifully hidden the carvings from vandal-plied waterways. In dense shade and toxic bark litter, few plants grew except calypso orchids, sprinkled like cemetery bouquets.

Although the forms of xóots and gooch (*bear, wolf*) have probably since melted into this bluff, they're rising, reinspired, from high school art classes and aromatic woodshops, from the surf of Yaakwdáat, *canoe rebounded* (Yakutat) to the gateway of Kichxáan, *near the eagle's wing* (Ketchikan).

impervious to literary fashion or scientific furtherance. Generations hence, naturalists will still roll silt in their fingers, tracking marine intrusion. They'll still tell harriers from shortears by wing-angle in a glide.

In that light, our book revision is like a potlatch—a ceremony of old forms with new faces. We haul out regalia to show the youngsters. We ask guidance from mentors, living and departed. If honest, we acknowledge our mistakes and uncertainties, modeling curiosity, curbing preconception, celebrating family, and passing out these treasures—our inheritance from land and sea.

The Nature of Southeast Alaska was and remains rather thin in two respects—which bear acknowledgment. First, throughout the book, we've scarcely glanced below the surface of the sea. From a flounder's perspective, that's pretty lopsided. Secondly, to suggest, even unintentionally, that nature is a subject apart from culture, slights those whose tools, food, monuments, clothing, and watercraft grew, surged, and recycled through these verdant, glacier-plowed watersheds. In part, our silence was respectful; some stories are not ours to tell.

But all of us are culture-bearers, with obligations to the past and future. In this third edition, we've tried in a small way to liberate some of the country's more tenured place-names. Translations can be tricky and ambiguous; we hope our errors and misinterpretations are at least benign.

Extremes in recreational transport. As timber declines in importance to the Southeast economy, tourism grows to industrial proportions.

Another invisible frontier, fairly bulging with untold story, involves the hyporheic zone. Pioneers of this adolescent discipline explore the interface of aquifers and streams, where ground- and river waters mingle. If we'd woven breaking news from hyporheic research into our *Streams and rivers* narrative, rewrites would be needed before ink dried on Edition 3. For now, let's only speculate that twenty years out, today's trendy phrase "salmon in the trees" may be remembered as a somewhat over-eager campaign slogan. After all, some of the greatest forests documented by the Landmark Trees Project grow upstream of barrier falls, innocent of rotting salmon for ten millennia. In twenty years, we may better understand the blind denizens and inexorable currents of braiding, underground paleochannels, munching, banking and relocating marine- and alder-spawned nutrients, undergirding productivity of our most generous terrestrial environment—the percolating alluvial bottomland.

In twenty years, if genetic analysis advances at anything like its current pace, anyone—Native or newcomer—curious about his or her maternal (mtDNA) or paternal (Y-chromosome) lineage should be able to backtrack a hundred generations. In concert with archival genealogy, now vastly enhanced by ever-growing online databases, a simple mouth swab will claim for each of us a spreading tree of forbears—some illustrious, some despicable, some anonymous—in statistically predictable proportions. Genealogy can be an antidote to illogical pride—and an impetus for seeking legacies and predecessors that do merit commemoration. When did your people discover this watershed? This continent? Who lived here before them? Does their blood too run in your veins?

When the clamor of advocacy grows shrill and irritating, it helps to go outdoors with children—to reset expectations. For the young, no dogma pulls harder than the first tug on a fishing line, or the thrill of a solved or elusive tracking puzzle. Nourishing that thrill, says Richard Louv (*Last Child in the Woods*, 2005; *The Nature Principle*, 2011), is the fundamental challenge of our age. This is not a good century to be raising the first generation on earth without significant experience in nature.

Digital photography and text-anywhere communication—tools that will someday seem as outmoded as floppy disks—can serve either discovery or narcissism. Young people, especially, are at risk of distraction. Along with bogeymen, lawsuits and lyme disease, says Louv, digital recreation keeps kids indoors. And in adulthood, the higher we climb the digital-workplace ladder, the less we splash up streams, or sit in the mist above deer-cabbage bowls.

Technology's relentless insinuation into research and education has a downside that most recognize but few resist. Device-mastery grows to supercede botany and bushwhacking. During a workshop on "connecting people and place," educators spent as much time exploring tablet apps and virtual interfaces as forests or glaciers. Science, too, demands specialization and instrumentation, each field probing its parochial depths with astounding productivity, but at the expense of interdisciplinary breadth, sometimes training laboratory wizards tone-deaf to the symphony of rocks and berries and butterflies.

Even back in 1992, by insisting on remaining generalists, we felt a bit like throwbacks to an earlier age. In an address to the Fourth Glacier Bay Science Symposium, our friend the Gustavus naturalist Greg Streveler expressed this as rededication to "peripheral vision as an adjunct to [scientific] rigor." Greg cautioned that:

"Many important subjects resist rigorous treatment. We will know a lot about campsite vegetation, but god help wolverines . . ."

A resilient culture has fierce, maternal attachment to watersheds as familiar as forearms, and broad attention to all that sprouts or hatches. It knows the use of every plant, and the pedigree of every bear. It self-replicates through story, fashioning (as the poets remind us) each new axe handle by studying the one in hand. Technology is no enemy of this story. It's the binding of its pages, the shining, stone-whetted blade.

Our story begins in rock, suffers in ice, rejoices in flood. With Xóots (brown bear) we pace raw soil, stalking sea mammals. With Yéil (raven), we soar over alder-healed valleys, watching streams and seas boil silver. With natural history, we animate the past, and brace our companions for the climb ahead.

COMMON AND SCIENTIFIC NAMES

Common and scientific names—We use mostly common names in this book, but often include scientific names in captions. For birds and fish, common names should create few misunderstandings, since the American Ornithologist's Union (AOU) and the American Fisheries Society (AFS) have standardized common names of those species; our common and scientific names follow AOU and AFS conventions (except for capitalization, explained below). Common names for mammals and amphibians—although not standardized—are reasonably consistent throughout North America. For both mammals and amphibians our names generally follow MacDonald & Cook (2007) *Mammals and amphibians of Southeast Alaska.*

Common names for other taxa—invertebrates, fungi, lichens, and vascular plants—can be confusingly inconsistent. For marine invertebrates our common names come from Rita and Chuck O'Clair (1998) *Southeast Alaska's Rocky Shores: Animals.* For mushrooms our names are from David Arora (1986) *Mushrooms demystified.* For lichens, we follow Brodo *et al* (2001) *Lichens of North America.*

The most widely used plant guide applicable to our region is Pojar & MacKinnon (1994) *Plants of the Pacific Northwest.* With a few exceptions, we adhere to common names in that guide for vascular plants and mosses. Scientific names, however, have changed greatly in the past twenty years. For these, we relied mostly upon the E-Flora BC website: *http://www.geog.ubc.ca/biodiversity/eflora/.* In addition to these sources we also recommend Judy Hall (2010) *Native plants of Southeast Alaska*, available in print or on Kindle.

Names for marine algae (seaweeds) are from O'Clair *et al* (1996) *Southeast Alaska's Rocky Shores: Seaweeds.*

Capitalization and abbreviation—The common names of bird species recognized by the American Ornithologist's Union are capitalized. In a general natural history, however, capitalizing one taxa and not others seems biased. For stylistic consistency, in this book we adhere to AOU common names, but do not capitalize them.

In the following lists, where genus name is appended by the abbreviation *spp.* there are multiple species documented or suspected in Southeast Alaska. When we list only genus, the species remains unidentified.

Mammals

arctic fox *(Vulpes lagopus)*
beaver *(Castor canadensis)*
black bear *(Ursus americanus)*
brown bear *(Ursus arctos)*
bushy-tailed wood rat *(Neotoma cinerea)*
California myotis *(Myotis californicus)*
collared pika *(Ochotona collaris)*
Columbian black-tailed deer *(Odocoileus hemionus columbianus)*
Coronation Island vole *(Microtus longicaudus coronarius)*
Dall porpoise *(Phocoenoides dalli)*
Dall sheep *(Ovis dalli)*
dusky shrew *(Sorex monticolus)*
gray whale *(Eschrichtius robustus)*
harbor porpoise *(Phocoena phocoena)*
harbor seal *(Phoca vitulina)*
hoary bat *(Lasiurus cinereus)*
hoary marmot *(Marmota calligata)*
house mouse *(Mus musculus)*
humpback whale *(Megaptera novaeangliae)*
jumping mouse *(Zapus hudsonicus)*
Keen's mouse *(Peromyscus keeni)*
Keen's myotis *(Myotis keenii)*
killer whale *(Orcinus orca)*
least weasel *(Mustela nivalis)*
little brown myotis *(Myotis lucifugus)*
long-legged myotis *(Myotis volans)*
long-tailed vole *(Microtus longicaudus)*
lynx *(Lynx canadensis)*
marten *(Martes americana)*
masked shrew *(Sorex cinereus)*
meadow vole *(Microtus pennsylvanicus)*
mink *(Mustela vison)*
minke whale *(Balaenoptera acutorostrata)*
moose *(Alces alces)*
mountain goat *(Oreamnos americanus)*
mountain lion *(Puma concolor)*
mule deer *(Odocoileus hemionus)*
muskrat *(Ondontra zibethicus)*
northern bog lemming *(Synaptomys borealis)*
northern flying squirrel *(Glaucomys sabrinus)*
northern fur seal *(Callorhinus ursinus)*
northern red-backed vole *(Myodes rutilus)*

Norway rat *(Rattus norvegicus)*
Pacific pilot whale *(Globicephala macrorhynchus)*
porcupine *(Erethizon dorsatum)*
raccoon *(Procyon lotor)*
red fox *(Vulpes vulpes)*
red squirrel *(Tamiasciurus hudsonicus)*
ringed seal *(Pusa hispida)*
river otter *(Lontra canadensus)*
Roosevelt elk *(Cervus elaphus)*
sea otter *(Enhydra lutris)*
short-tailed weasel, ermine *(Mustela erminea)*
silver-haired bat *(Lasionycteris noctivagans)*
Sitka black-tailed deer *(Odocoileus hemionus sitchensis)*
Sitka mouse *(Peromyscus keeni sitkensis)*
snowshoe hare *(Lepus americanus)*
southern red-backed vole *(Myodes gapperi)*
sperm whale *(Physeter catodon)*
Steller's sea cow *(Hydrodamalis gigas)*
Steller's sea lion *(Eumetopias jubata)*
tundra vole *(Microtus oeconomus)*
water shrew *(Sorex palustris)*
wolf *(Canis lupus)*
wolverine *(Gulo gulo)*

Birds

alder flycatcher *(Empidonax alnorum)*
Aleutian tern *(Onychoprion aleuticus)*
American bittern *(Botaurus lentiginosus)*
American dipper *(Cinclus mexicanus)*
American golden-plover *(Pluvialis dominica)*
American kestrel *(Falco sparverius)*
American pipit *(Anthus rubescens)*
American robin *(Turdus migratorius)*
ancient murrelet *(Synthliboramphus antiquus)*
Anna's hummingbird *(Calypte anna)*
Arctic tern *(Sterna paradisaea)*
bald eagle *(Haliaeetus leucocephalus)*
barred owl *(Strix varia)*
Barrow's goldeneye *(Bucephala islandica)*
belted kingfisher *(Megaceryle alcyon)*
black oystercatcher *(Haematopus bachmani)*
black scoter *(Melanitta niger)*
black turnstone *(Arenaria melanocephala)*

black-backed woodpecker *(Picoides arcticus)*
black-legged kittiwake *(Rissa tridactyla)*
black-capped chickadee *(Poecile atricapillus)*
bohemian waxwing *(Bombycilla garrulus)*
Bonaparte's gull *(Larus chroicocephalus)*
brown creeper *(Certhia americana)*
bufflehead *(Bucephala albeola)*
Canada goose *(Branta canadensis)*
Cassin's auklet *(Ptychoramphus aleuticus)*
chestnut-backed chickadee *(Poecile rufescens)*
Clark's nutcracker *(Nucifraga columbiana)*
common goldeneye *(Bucephala clangula)*
common merganser *(Mergus merganser)*
common murre *(Uria aalge)*
common raven *(Corvus corax)*
common redpoll *(Acanthis flammea)*
common yellowthroat *(Geothlypis trichas)*
Costa's hummingbird *(Calypte costae)*
dark-eyed junco *(Junco hyemalis)*
dunlin *(Calidris alpina)*
dusky Canada goose *(Branta Canadensis occidentalis)*
fork-tailed storm-petrel *(Oceanodroma furcata)*
golden-crowned kinglet *(Regulus satrapa)*
golden-crowned sparrow *(Zonotrichia atricapilla)*
gray-crowned rosy-finch *(Leucosticte tephrocotis)*
great blue heron *(Ardea herodias)*
great horned owl *(Bubo virginianus)*
greater white-fronted goose *(Anser albifrons)*
greater yellowlegs *(Tringa melanoleuca)*
green heron *(Butorides virescens)*
green-winged teal *(Anas crecca)*
hairy woodpecker *(Picoides villosus)*
harlequin duck *(Histrionicus histrionicus)*
Harris's sparrow *(Zonotrichia querula)*
hermit thrush *(Catharus guttatus)*
horned grebe *(Podiceps auritus)*
horned lark *(Eremophila alpestris)*
horned puffin *(Fratercula corniculata)*
house sparrow *(Passer domesticus)*
killdeer *(Charadrius vociferus)*

Kittlitz's murrelet *(Brachyramphus brevirostris)*
Lapland longspur *(Calcarius lapponicus)*
Leach's storm-petrel *(Oceanodroma leucorhoa)*
least sandpiper *(Calidris minutilla)*
lesser Canada goose *(Branta canadensis parvipes)*
lesser yellowlegs *(Tringa flavipes)*
Lincoln's sparrow *(Melospiza lincolnii)*
long-billed dowitcher *(Limnodromus scolopaceus)*
long-tailed duck *(Clangula hyemalis)*
mallard *(Anas platyrhynchos)*
marbled murrelet *(Brachyramphus marmoratus)*
merlin *(Falco columbarius)*
mountain chickadee *(Poecile gambeli)*
northern goshawk *(Accipiter gentilis)*
northern harrier *(Circus cyaneus)*
northern pintail *(Anas acuta)*
northern pygmy-owl *(Glaucidium gnoma)*
northern saw-whet owl *(Aegolius acdicus)*
northern shrike *(Lanius excubitor)*
northern waterthrush *(Parkesia noveboracensis)*
northwestern crow *(Corvus caurinus)*
olive-sided flycatcher *(Contopus cooperi)*
orange-crowned warbler *(Oreothlypis celata)*
orchid oriole *(Icterus spurius)*
Pacific wren *(Troglodytes pacificus)*
Pacific-slope flycatcher *(Empidonax difficilis)*
pectoral sandpiper *(Calidris melanotos)*
pied-billed grebe *(Podilymbus podiceps)*
pine siskin *(Spinus pinus)*
purple finch *(Haemorhous purpureus)*
red crossbill *(Loxia curvirostra)*
red-breasted nuthatch *(Sitta canadensis)*
red-breasted sapsucker *(Sphyrapicus ruber)*
red-necked phalarope *(Phalaropus lobatus)*
red-tailed hawk *(Buteo jamaicensis)*
red-winged blackbird *(Agelaius phoeniceus)*
rhinoceros auklet *(Cerorhinca monocerata)*
rock ptarmigan *(Lagopus muta)*
rock sandpiper *(Calidris ptilocnemis)*
rose-breasted grosbeak *(Pheucticus ludovicianus)*

ruby-crowned kinglet *(Regulus calendula)*
ruddy turnstone *(Arenaria interpres)*
ruffed grouse *(Bonasa umbellus)*
rufous hummingbird *(Selaphorus rufus)*
sanderling *(Calidris alba)*
sandhill crane *(Grus canadensis)*
savannah sparrow *(Passerculus sandwichensis)*
semipalmated plover *(Charadrius semipalmatus)*
sharp-shinned hawk *(Accipiter striatus)*
short-billed dowitcher *(Limnodromus griseus)*
short-eared owl *(Asio flammeus)*
snow bunting *(Plectrophenax nivalis)*
song sparrow *(Melospiza melodia)*
sooty grouse *(Dendragapus fuliginosus)*
spotted owl *(Strix occidentalis)*
spotted sandpiper *(Actitis macularius)*
Steller's jay *(Cyanocitta stelleri)*
surf scoter *(Melanitta perspicillata)*
surfbird *(Aphriza virgata)*
Swainson's thrush *(Catharus ustulatus)*
swamp sparrow *(Melospiza georgiana)*
Thayer's gull *(Larus thayeri)*
three-toed woodpecker *(Picoides tridactylus)*
Townsend's warbler *(Setophaga townsendi)*
tree swallow *(Tachycineta bicolor)*
tufted puffin *(Fratercula cirrhata)*
tundra swan *(Cygnus columbianus)*
Vancouver Canada goose *(Branta canadensis fulva)*
varied thrush *(Ixoreus naevius)*
Virginia rail *(Rallus limicola)*
warbling vireo *(Vireo gilvus)*
western grebe *(Aechmophorus occidentalis)*
western sandpiper *(Calidris mauri)*
western screech-owl *(Megascops kennicottii)*
western tanager *(Piranga ludoviciana)*
white-crowned sparrow *(Zonotrichia leucophrys)*
white-tailed ptarmigan *(Lagopus leucura)*
white-throated sparrow *(Zonotrichia albicollis)*
white-winged scoter *(Melanitta fusca)*
willow ptarmigan *(Lagopus lagopus)*
Wilson's snipe *(Gallinago delicata)*
Wilson's warbler *(Cardellina pusilla)*

yellow-rumped warbler *(Setophaga coronata)*
yellow warbler *(Setophaga petechia)*

Reptiles
garter snake *(Thamnophis sirtalis)*

Amphibians
long-toed salamander *(Ambystoma macrodactylum)*
northwestern salamander *(Ambystoma gracile)*
Pacific chorus frog *(Pseudacris regilla)*
red-legged frog *(Rana aurora)*
rough-skinned newt *(Taricha granulosa)*
spotted frog *(Rana pretiosa)*
western toad *(Anaxyrus boreas boreas)*
wood frog *(Rana sylvatica)*

Fish
Alaska skate *(Bathyraja parmifera)*
Aleutian skate *(Bathyraja aleutica)*
American shad *(Alosa sapidissima)*
Arctic char *(Salvelinus alpinus)*
Arctic grayling *(Thymallus arcticus)*
arrowtooth flounder *(Atheresthes stomias)*
Atlantic salmon *(Salmo salar)*
barreleye *(Macropinna microstoma)*
big skate *(Raja binoculata)*
black rockfish *(Sebastes melanops)*
brook char *(Salvelinus fontinalis)*
buffalo sculpin *(Enophrys bison)*
burbot *(Lota lota)*
capelin *(Mallotus villosus)*
China rockfish *(Sebastes nebulosus)*
chinook salmon, king salmon *(Oncorhynchus tshawytscha)*
chum salmon *(Oncorhynchus keta)*
coastrange sculpin *(Cottus aleuticus)*
coho salmon *(Oncorhynchus kisutch)*
crescent gunnel *(Pholis laeta)*
cutthroat trout *(Oncorhynchus clarkii)*
Dolly Varden char *(Salvelinus malma)*
dusky rockfish *(Sebastes ciliatus)*
eulachon *(Thaleichthys pacificus)*
flathead sole *(Hippoglossoides elassodon)*
fourhorn sculpin *(Myoxocephalus quadricornis)*

great sculpin (Myoxocephalus polyacanthocephalus)

grunt sculpin (Rhamphocottus richardsonii)

kelp greenling (Hexagrammos decagrammus)

kokanee (Oncorhynchus nerka)

lingcod (Ophiodon elongatus)

longnose lancerfish (Alepisaurus ferox)

longnose sucker (Catostomus catostomus)

North Pacific daggertooth (Anotopterus nikparini)

northern lampfish (Stenobrachius leucopsarus)

northern pearleye (Benthalbella dentata)

Pacific cod (Gadus macrocephalus)

Pacific hake (Merluccius productus)

Pacific halibut (Hippoglossus stenolepis)

Pacific herring (Clupea pallasii)

Pacific ocean perch (Sebastes alutus)

Pacific sandfish (Trichodon trichodon)

Pacific sand lance (Ammodytes hexapterus)

Pacific staghorn sculpin (Leptocottus armatus)

Pacific tomcod (Microgadus proximus)

Pacific viperfish (Chauliodus macouni)

pink salmon (Oncorhynchus gorbuscha)

prowfish (Zaprora silenus)

pygmy whitefish (Prosopium coulterii)

quillback rockfish (Sebastes maliger)

rainbow trout (Oncorhynchus mykiss)

rougheye rockfish (Sebastes aleutianus)

round whitefish (Prosopium cylindraceum)

sablefish (Anoplopoma fimbria)

saffron cod (Eleginus gracilis)

salmon shark (Lamna ditropis)

shortraker rockfish (Sebastes borealis)

silvergray rockfish (Sebastes brevispinis)

slimy sculpin (Cottus cognatus)

sockeye salmon (Oncorhynchus nerka)

southern rock sole (Lepidopsetta bilineata)

spiny dogfish (Squalus acanthias)

spinyhead sculpin (Dasycottus setiger)

spotted ratfish (Hydrolagus colliei)

starry flounder (Platichthys stellatus)

steelhead (Oncorhynchus mykiss)

threespine stickleback (Gasterosteus aculeatus)

tubesnout (Aulorhynchus flavidus)

walleye pollock (Theragra chalcogramma)

white shark (Carcharodon carcharias)

wolf-eel (Anarrhichthys ocellatus)

yelloweye rockfish (Sebastes ruberrimus)

yellowfin sole (Limanda aspera)

yellowtail rockfish (Sebastes flavidus)

Invertebrates

Alaska falsejingle (Pododesmus macroschisma)

Alaska spoon worm (Echiurus echiurus alaskanus)

Alaskan pink shrimp (Pandalus borealis)

Arctic moonsnail (Cryptonatica affinis)

Arctic natica (Natica clausa)

Baltic macoma (Macoma petalum)

barnacle-eating Onchidoris (Onchidoris bilamellata)

black fly (family Simuliidae)

bluets (Enallagma spp.)

boat-backed ground beetle (Scaphinotus spp.)

bumblebee (Bombus)

burrowing green anemone (Anthopleura artemisia)

butter clam (Saxidomus gigantea)

Canadian tiger swallowtail (Pterourus canadensis)

common acorn barnacle (Balanus glandula)

common net-spinner caddisflies (family Hydropsychidae)

Dungeness crab (Cancer magister)

file dogwinkle (Nucella lima)

frilled dogwinkle (Nucella lamellosa)

giant case maker caddisflies (family Phryganeidae)

giant octopus (Octopus dofleini)

green rock worm caddisflies (family Rhyacophilidae)

golden king crab (Lithodes aequispinus)

goldenrod spider (Misumena vatia)

green ribbon worm (Emplectonema gracile)

green sea urchin (Strongylocentrotus droebachiensis)

hoverflies (family Syrphidae)

ice worm (Mesenchytraeus spp.)

intertidal pseudoscorpion (Halobisium occidentale)
leaf beetle (family Chrysomelidae)
Lewis'moonsnail (Euspira lewisii)
little brown barnacle (Chthamalus dalli)
Lyre whelk (Neptunea lyrata)
Milbert's tortoiseshell (Aglais milberti)
mottled sea star (Evasterias troschelii)
mourning cloak (Nymphalis antiopa)
mustard white (Pieris oleracea)
net-winged beetle (Eros)
northern rock barnacle (Semibalanus balanoides)
Nuttall cockle (Clinocardium nuttallii)
Pacific banana slug (Ariolimax columbianus)
Pacific blue mussel (Mytilus trossulus)
Pacific geoduck (Panopea abrupta)
Pacific littleneck (Leucoma staminea)
painted lady (Vanessa cardui)
pinto abalone (Haliotis kamtschatkana)
purple sea urchin (Strongylocentrotus purpuratus)
purple star (Pisaster ochraceus)
red admiral (Vanessa atalanta)
red king crab (Paralithodes camtschaticus)
red sea urchin (Strongylocentrotus franciscanus)
shore crabs (Hemigrapsus spp.)
shorebugs (family Saldidae)
spot shrimp (Pandalus platyceros)
sunflower star (Pycnopodia helianthoides)
tanner crab (Chionoecetes bairdi)
thatched barnacle (Semibalanus cariosus)
tube-making caddisflies (Polycentropodidae)
weathervane scallop (Patinopecten caurinus)
zigzag darner (Aeshna sitchensis)

Fungi and lichens

beard lichens (Usnea)
belted woodconk (Fomes pinicola)
black seaside lichen (Verrucaria maura)
candy lichen (Icmadophila ericetorum)
chanterelle (Cantharellus cibarius)
chicken of the woods (Laetiporus sulfureus)
common gel bird's nest (Nidula candida)
coral slime (Ceratiomyxa fruticulosa)

false truffle (Rhizopogon)
fly agaric (Amanita muscaria)
foam lichens (Stereocaulon)
honey mushroom (Galerina autumnalis)
king boletus (Boletus edulis)
laccaria (Laccaria laccata)
lungwort lichens (Lobaria)
pelt lichens (Peltigera)
pixie cup lichens (Cladonia)
red-brown butt rot (Phaeolus schweinitzii)
reindeer "moss" (Cladonia sub-genus Cladina)
rock tripe lichens (Umbilicaria)
scrambled-egg slime (Fuligo septica)
suillus (Suillus tomentosus)
tawny almond waxy cap (Hygrophorus bakerensis)
tube lichens (Hypogymnia)
violet cort (Cortinarius violaceus)
western gall rust (Endocronartium harknessii)
white-egg bird's nest (Crucibulum levis)
whiteworm lichens (Thamnolia)
witch's hair lichens (Alectoria)
yellow map lichen (Rhizocarpon geographicum)

Algae

bull kelp (Nereocystis luetkeana)
PSP dinoflagellate (Alexandrium catenella)
ribbon kelp (Alaria marginata)
rockweed (Fucus distichus)
sugar kelp (Laminaria saccharina)
stonewort (Chara)

Plants

Alaska blueberry (Vaccinium alaskaense)
Alaskan moss heather (Harrimanella stelleriana)
Alaska saxifrage (Saxifraga ferruginea)
alpine azalea (Loiseleuria procumbens)
alpine bistort (Bistorta viviparum)
alpine mitrewort (Mitella pentandra)
alpine sweetvetch (Hedysarum alpinum)
Arctic cinquefoil (Potentilla nana)
Arctic sweet coltsfoot (Petasites frigidus)
Arctic willow (Salix arctica)
baneberry (Actaea rubra)

Barclay willow (Salix barclayi)
beach rye (Leymus mollis)
beach strawberry (Fragaria chiloensis)
bearberry (Arctostaphylos uva-ursi)
Beauverd spiraea (Spiraea stevenii)
bent-leaved angelica (Angelica genuflexa)
black cottonwood (Populus balsamifera ssp.
    trichocarpa)
black twinberry (Lonicera involucrata)
bog blueberry (Vaccinium uliginosum)
bog cranberry (Vaccinium oxycoccos)
bog rosemary (Andromeda polifolia)
broad-petalled gentian (Gentiana platypetala)
buckbean (Menyanthes trifoliata)
bunchberry (Cornus canadensis)
caltha-leafed avens (Geum calthifolium)
chocolate lily (Fritillaria camschatcensis)
cloudberry (Rubus chamaemorus)
common butterwort (Pinguicula vulgaris)
common water moss (Fontinalis antipyretica)
lung liverwort (Marchantia polymorpha)
common mare's-tail (Hippuris vulgaris)
common plantain (Plantago major)
Cooley's buttercup (Kumlienia cooleyae)
copperbush (Elliottia pyrolaeflora)
cow parsnip (Heracleum maximum)
creeping spike-rush (Eleocharis palustris)
crowberry (Empetrum nigrum)
deerberry (Maianthemum dilatatum)
deer-cabbage (Fauria crista-galli)
deer fern (Blechnum spicant)
devil's club (Oplopanax horridum)
ditchgrass (Ruppia maritima)
Douglas fir (Pseudotsuga menziesii)
Douglas maple (Acer glabrum)
Douglas spiraea (Spiraea douglasii)
dwarf blueberry (Vaccinium caespitosum)
dwarf fireweed (Chamerion latifolium)
dwarf mistletoe (Arceuthobium tsugense)
early blueberry (Vaccinium ovalifolium)
eelgrass (Zostera marina)
electrified cat's-tail moss (Rhytidiadelphus
    triquetrus)
fairy slipper, calypso orchid (Calypso bulbosa)
false hellebore (Veratrum viride)

fern-leaved gold thread (Coptis asplenifolia)
fern moss (Hylocomium splendens)
few-flowered sedge (Carex pauciflora)
fireweed (Chamerion angustifolium)
five-leaved bramble (Rubus pedatus)
foamflower (Tiarella trifoliata)
forget-me-not (Myosotis scorpioides)
foxtail barley (Hordeum jubatum)
frayed-cap moss (Racomitrium spp.)
goat's-beard (Aruncus dioicus)
goose-tongue (Plantago maritima)
groundcone (Boschniakia rossica)
haircap moss (Polytrichum spp.)
hairy butterwort (Pinguicula villosa)
highbush cranberry (Viburnum edule)
holly-fern (Polystichum lonchitis)
Indian paintbrush (Castilleja spp.)
Indian-pipe (Monotropa uniflora)
Jeffrey shooting star (Dodecatheon jeffreyi)
Labrador tea (Rhododendron groenlandicum)
lady fern (Athyrium filix-femina)
lanky moss (Rhytidiadelphus loreus)
large-leaf avens (Geum macrophyllum)
licorice fern (Polypodium glycyrrhiza)
lingonberry (Vaccinium vitis-idaea)
long-leaf sundew (Drosera anglica)
Lyngbye sedge (Carex lyngbyei)
maidenhair fern (Adiantum aleuticum)
many-flowered sedge (Carex pluriflora)
marsh cinquefoil (Comarum palustre)
monkshood (Aconitum delphiniifolium)
moss campion (Silene acaulis)
mountain harebell (Campanula lasiocarpa)
mountain hemlock (Tsuga mertensiana)
mountain marsh-marigold (Caltha leptosepala)
mountain sagewort (Artemisia norvegica)
narcissus anemone (Anemone narcissiflora)
Nootka lupine (Lupinus nootkatensis)
narrow beech fern (Phegopteris connectilis)
northern bur-reed (Sparganium hyperboreum)
northern horsetail (Equisetum variegatum)
oak fern (Gymnocarpium dryopteris)
one-sided wintergreen (Orthilia secunda)
Pacific alkaligrass (Puccinellia nutkaensis)
Pacific silver fir (Abies amabilis)

Pacific yew *(Taxus brevifolia)*
parsley fern *(Cryptogramma sitchensis)*
partridgefoot *(Luetkea pectinata)*
pinesap *(Monotropa hypopithys)*
pondweeds *(Potamogeton spp.)*
purple mountain saxifrage *(Saxifraga oppositifolia)*
quillwort *(Isoetes maritima)*
rattlesnake-plantain *(Goodyera oblongifolia)*
red alder *(Alnus rubra)*
red elderberry *(Sambucus racemosa)*
red huckleberry *(Vaccinium parvifolium)*
reed canary grass *(Phalaris arundinacea)*
rosy twisted stalk *(Streptopus roseus)*
round-leaf sundew *(Drosera rotundifolia)*
rusty menziesia *(Menziesia ferruginea)*
salal *(Gaultheria shallon)*
salmonberry *(Rubus spectabilis)*
sea milkwort *(Glaux maritima)*
seabeach sandwort *(Honkenya peploides)*
sheep sorrel *(Rumex acetosella)*
shore pine *(Pinus contorta)*
sibbaldia *(Sibbaldia procumbens)*
single delight *(Moneses uniflora)*
Sitka alder *(Alnus viridis)*
Sitka spruce *(Picea sitchensis)*
Sitka valerian *(Valeriana sitchensis)*
slender bog-orchid *(Platanthera stricta)*
small-fruit bulrush *(Scirpus microcarpus)*
soapberry *(Shepherdia canadensis)*
speedwell *(Veronica beccabunga)*
spiny wood fern *(Dryopteris expansa)*
spring-beauty *(Claytonia sibirica)*
step moss *(Hylocomium splendens)*
stiff clubmoss *(Lycopodium annotinum)*
stink currant *(Ribes bracteosum)*
swamp gentian *(Gentiana douglasiana)*
swamp horsetail *(Equisetum fluviatile)*
sweet gale *(Myrica gale)*
sword-fern *(Polystichum munitum)*
tall cotton-grass *(Eriophorum angustifolium)*
thimbleberry *(Rubus parviflorus)*
tufted hairgrass *(Deschampsia caespitosum)*
water-milfoil *(Myriophyllum spicatum)*
water crowfoot *(Ranunculus aquatilis)*

water hemlock *(Cicuta douglasii)*
water sedge *(Carex aquatilis)*
wedge-leaf primrose *(Primula cuneifolia)*
western bog-laurel *(Kalmia microphylla)*
western bracken fern *(Pteridium aquilinum)*
western columbine *(Aquilegia formosa)*
western coralroot *(Corallorhiza mertensiana)*
western hemlock *(Tsuga heterophylla)*
western redcedar *(Thuja plicata)*
western thimbleberry *(Rubus parviflorus)*
white bog-orchid *(Platanthera dilatata)*
white moss heather *(Cassiope mertensiana)*
white spruce *(Picea glauca)*
wild iris *(Iris setosa)*
woolly hawkweed *(Hieracium triste)*
yellow-cedar *(Callitropsis nootkatensis)*
yellow marsh-marigold *(Caltha palustris)*
yellow monkey-flower *(Mimulus guttatus)*
yellow mountain avens *(Dryas drummondii)*
yellow mountain-heather *(Phyllodoce glanduliflora)*
yellow pond-lily *(Nuphar luteum)*
yellow skunk cabbage *(Lysichiton americanum)*

BIBLIOGRAPHY

General—Southeast Alaska

Armstrong, R.H. and M. Hermans. 2004. *Southeast Alaska's Natural World.* Nature Alaska Images, Juneau, AK.

Armstrong, R.H. and M. Hermans. 2007. *Life around Mendenhall Glacier.* Nature Alaska Images, Juneau, AK.

Armstrong, R.H., R.L. Carstensen, M.F. Willson, and M.Hermans Osborn. 2009. *The Mendenhall Wetlands: A globally recognized Important Bird Area.* Nature Alaska Images, Juneau, AK.

Armstrong, R.H., and M. F. Willson. 2014. *Natural connections in Alaska.* Nature Alaska Images, Juneau, AK.

Carstensen, R. 1996. "Southeast Alaska." In Kirk. ed. 1996.

Carstensen, R. 1999. "Heart of the forest." In Servid and Snow. eds. 1999.

Carstensen, R. 2010. "Coming home: The land of old trees." In Gulick. 2010.

Carstensen, R., J. Schoen, and D. Albert. 2007. "Biogeographic provinces of Southeastern Alaska." Chapter 4 in Schoen and Dovichin. eds.

Carstensen, R. 2013. *Natural history of Juneau trails: A watershed approach.* Discovery Southeast, Juneau, AK.

Demerjian, B. 2006. *Roll on! Discovering the wild Stikine River.* Stikine River Books, Wrangell, AK.

Demerjian, B. 2007. *Anan: Stream of living water.* Stikine River Books, Wrangell, AK.

Gulick, A. 2010. *Salmon in the trees: Life in Alaska's Tongass rain forest.* The Mountaineers, Seattle, WA.

Kirk, R. ed. 1996. *The Enduring Forests: Northern California, Oregon, Washington, British Columbia and Southeast Alaska.* The Mountaineers, Seattle, AK.

Lentfer, H. 2011. *Faith of cranes: Finding hope and family in Alaska.* The Mountaineers, Seattle, WA.

Littlepage, D. 2006. *Steller's Island: Adventures of a pioneer naturalist in Alaska.* The Mountaineers, Seattle, WA.

Milner, A. and J. Wood. 1988. *Proceedings of the second Glacier Bay science symposium.* US Department of Interior, Alaska Regional Office, Anchorage, AK.

Nelson, R. 1991. *The island within.* Vintage Books, NYC.

Piatt, J. and S. Gende. eds. 2007. *Proceedings of the fourth Glacier Bay science symposium.* US Geological Survey. Alaska Science Center. Scientific Investigations Report. 2007-5047. Juneau, AK. *http://pubs.usgs.gov/sir/2007/5047/*

Rennick et al, eds. 1991. *Admiralty Island, fortress of the bears.* 18(3). Alaska Geographic Society, Anchorage, AK.

Saupe, S., M. Lindeburg, and G. Schoch. 2012. *Coastal impressions: A photographic journey along Alaska's Gulf Coast.* Alaska Shorezone Program, Anchorage, AK.

Schoen, J. and E. Dovichin. eds. 2007. *A conservation assessment and resource synthesis for the coastal forests and mountains ecoregion in southeastern Alaska and the Tongass National Forest.* Audubon Alaska and the Nature Conservancy, Anchorage, AK.

Schooler, L. 2002. *The blue bear: A true story of friendship, tragedy and survival in the Alaskan wilderness.* Harper Collins, NYC.

Schoonmaker, P., B. von Hagen, and E. Wolf. eds. 1997. *The rain forests of home: Profile of a North American bioregion.* Island Press, Washington, DC.

Servid, C. and D. Snow. eds. 1999. *The book of the Tongass.* Milkweed Editions, Minneapolis, MN.

Smith. W., M. Stotts, B. Andres, J. Melton, A. Garibaldi, and K. Boggs. 2001. *Bird, mammal, and vegetation community surveys of Research Natural Areas in the Tongass National Forest.* USDA Forest Service. PNW-RP-535.

Wood, J., M. Gladziszewski, I. Worley, and G. Vequist. eds. 1984. *Proceedings of the first Glacier Bay science symposium.* USDI Science Publications Office, Atlanta, GA.

Geology and glacial history

Baichtal, J. and G. Streveler. 2000. *Sculptures in granite: A guide to the geology and glacial history of Misty Fiords National Monument, Alaska.* USDA Forest Service. R10-RG-119.

Carstensen R. and C. Connor. 2013. *Reading Southeast Alaska's landscape: How bedrock foundations, glaciers, rivers and sea shape the land.* Discovery Southeast, Juneau, AK.

Connor, C. and D. Haire. 1988. *Roadside geology of Alaska.* Mountain Press Publishing, Missoula, MT.

Hansen, B. and D. Engstrom. 1996. Vegetation history of Pleasant Island, southeastern Alaska, since 13,000 yr BP. *Quaternary Research.* 46(0056): 146-175.

Kruckeberg, A. 2002. *Geology and plant life: The effects of landforms and rock types on plants.* University of Washington Press, Seattle, WA.

Larsen, C., R. Motyka, J. Freymueller, K. Echelmeyer, and E. Ivins. 2005. Rapid viscoelastic uplift in Southeast Alaska caused by post-Little Ice Age glacial retreat. *Earth and Planetary Science Letters.* 237: 548–560.

Mann, D. and G. Streveler. 2008. Post-glacial relative sea level, isostasy, and glacial history in Icy Strait, Southeast Alaska, USA. *Quaternary Research.* 69: 201-216.

Miller, L., H. Stowell, and G. Gehrels. 2000. *Progressive deformation associated with mid-Cretaceous to Tertiary contractional tectonism in the Juneau gold belt, Coast Mountains, southeastern Alaska.* In Stowell and McClellan. eds. 2000.

Miller, R. 1972. *Surficial geology of the Juneau urban area and vicinity, Alaska, with emphasis on earthquake and other geologic hazards.* USGS Open-file Report. 72-2550.

Miller, R. 1975a. *Gastineau Channel Formation, a composite glaciomarine deposit near Juneau, Alaska.* Geologic Survey Bulletin. 1394-C.

Miller, R. 1975b. *Surficial geology map of the Juneau urban area and vicinity, Alaska.* Miscellaneous Investigations Series. I-885.

Riehle, J. 1996. *The Mount Edgecumbe volcanic field: A geologic history.* USDA Forest Service Alaska Region. R10-RG-114.

Stowell, H. 2006. *Geology of Southeast Alaska: Rock and ice in motion.* University of Alaska Press, Fairbanks, AK.

Stowell, H. and W. McClellan. eds. 2000. *Tectonics of the Coast Mountains, southeastern Alaska and British Columbia.* Geological Society of America Special Paper 343.

Tockner, K. and J. Stanford. 2002. Riverine flood plains: Present state and future trends. *Environmental Conservation.* 29(3): 308–330.

Habitats

Alaback, P. 1982. Dynamics of understory biomass in Sitka spruce-western hemlock forests of Southeast Alaska. *Ecology* 63(6): 1932-48.

Alaback, P. and G. Juday. 1989. Structure and composition of low elevation old-growth forests in Research Natural Areas of Southeast Alaska. *Natural Areas Journal.* 9(1): 26-39.

Armstrong, R.H. and M. Hermans. 2005. *Along the Mt Roberts Trail, in Juneau Alaska.* Goldbelt, Mount Roberts Tramway, Juneau, AK.

Arno, S. 1984. *Timberline: Mountain and arctic forest frontiers.* The Mountaineers, Seattle, WA.

Bishop, D., R.H. Armstrong, and R. Carstensen. 1987. *Environmental analysis of lower Jordan Creek and nearby wetlands in regard to planned airport taxiway extension.* Environaid, Juneau, AK.

Brooks, R., E. Peterson, and V. Krajina. 1970. *The subalpine mountain hemlock zone.* Ecology of Western North America. 2:2. University of British Columbia, Vancouver, BC.

Caouette, J. and E. DeGaynor. 2005. Predictive mapping for tree sizes and densities in Southeast Alaska. *Landscape and Urban Planning.* 72(1-3): 49-63.

Carstensen, R. 2007a. "Terrestrial ecological systems." Chapter 5, Section 2 in Schoen, J. and E. Dovichin, eds. *A conservation assessment and resource synthesis for the coastal forests and mountains ecoregion in southeastern Alaska and the Tongass National Forest.* Audubon Alaska and the Nature Conservancy, Anchorage, AK.

Carstensen, R. 2007b. "Coastal ecological systems." Chapter 5, Section 3 in: Schoen and Dovichin, eds.

Carstensen, R. 2007c. "Freshwater ecological systems." Chapter 5, Section 4 in: Schoen and Dovichin, eds.

Carstensen, R. and B. Christensen, 2005. *Ground-truthing Project Final Report.* Sitka Conservation Society, Sitka, AK.

Carstensen, R. 2010. "Coming home: The land of old trees." In Gulick, A. 2010. *Salmon in the trees: Life in Alaska's Tongass rain forest.* Braided River, The Mountaineers, Seattle, WA.

Chapin, T., L. Walker, C. Fastie, and L. Sharman, 1994. Mechanisms of primary succession following deglaciation at Glacier Bay, Alaska. *Ecological Monographs.* 64: 149-175.

Deal, R., C. Oliver, and B. Bormann. 1991. Reconstruction of mixed hemlock-spruce stands in coastal Southeast Alaska. *Canadian Journal of Forest Research.* 21: 643-654.

Deal, R. 2007. Management strategies to increase stand structural diversity and enhance biodiversity in coastal rainforests of Alaska. *Biological Conservation.* 137(207): 520-532.

Elias, S. 2013. The problem of conifer species migration lag in the Pacific Northwest region since the last glaciation. *Quaternary Science Reviews.* 77: 55-69.

Engstrom, D., S. Fritz, J. Almendinger, and S. Juggins, 2000. Chemical and biological trends during lake evolution in recently deglaciated terrain. *Nature.* 408: 161-166.

Everest, F. and G. Reeves. 2007. *Riparian and aquatic habitats of the Pacific Northwest and Southeast Alaska: Ecology, management history, and potential management strategies.* USDA Forest Service. General Technical Report. PNW-GTR-692.

Fastie, C. 1995. Causes and ecosystem consequences of multiple pathways of primary succession at Glacier Bay, Alaska. *Ecology* 76(6): 1899-1916.

Franklin, J., K. Cromack, W. Denison, A. McKee, C. Maser, J. Sedell, F. Swanson, and G. Juday. 1981. *Ecological characteristics of old-growth Douglas fir forests.* USDA Forest Service. General Technical Report. PNW-118.

Hanley. T. and J. Barnard. 2005. Red alder, *Alnus rubra,* as a potential mitigating factor for wildlife habitat following clearcut logging in southeastern Alaska. *The Canadian Field-Naturalist.* 112: 647-652.

Hanley, T., M. McClellan, J. Barnard, and M. Friberg. 2013. *Precommercial thinning: Implications of early results from the Tongass-Wide Young Growth Studies experiments for deer habitat in Southeast Alaska.* USDA Forest Service. Research Paper. PNW-RP-593.

Harris, A. 1989. *Wind in the forests of Southeast Alaska and guides for reducing damage.* USDA Forest Service. General Technical Report. PNW-GTR-244.

Hennon, P. and M. McClellan. 2003. Tree mortality and forest structure in the temperate rain forests of Southeast Alaska. *Canadian Journal of Forest Research.* 33: 1621–1634.

Hocker, K. and T. Schwartz. 2003. *The streamwalker's companion: An introduction to the investigation of Southeast Alaskan streams.* Discovery Southeast, Juneau, AK.

Kirk, R. and J. Franklin. 1992. *The Olympic rain forest: An ecological web.* University of Washington Press, Seattle, WA.

Kirk, R. ed. 1996. *The enduring forests: Northern California, Oregon, Washington, British Columbia and Southeast Alaska.* The Mountaineers, Seattle, AK.

Kramer, M., A. Hansen, M. Taper, and E. Kissinger. 2001. Abiotic controls on long-term windthrow disturbance and temperate rainforest dynamics in Southeast Alaska. *Ecology.* 82(10): 2749–2768.

Lawrence, D. B. 1979. "Primary versus secondary succession at Glacier Bay National Monument." In R. Linn. ed. *Proceedings, first conference on scientific research in the National Parks.*

McClellan, M., T. Brock, and J. Baichtal. 2003. *Calcareous fens in Southeast Alaska.* USDA Forest Service. PNW-RN-536.

Nowacki, G. and M. Kramer. 1998. *The effects of wind disturbance on temperate rain forest structure and dynamics of Southeast Alaska.* USDA Forest Service. General Technical Report. PNW-GTR-421.

Nowacki, G., P. Krosse, G. Fischer, D. Brew, T. Brock, M. Shephard, W. Pawuk, J. Baichtal, and E. Kissinger. 2001. *Ecological Subsections of Southeast Alaska and neighboring areas of Canada.* USDA Forest Service. Technical Publication. R10-TP-75.

Paustian, S. ed. 2010. *A channel type user's guide for the Tongass National Forest, Southeast Alaska.* USDA Forest Service. R10 Technical Paper 26.

Piccolo, J. and M. Wipfli. 2002. Does red alder (*Alnus rubra*) in upland riparian forests elevate macroinvertebrate and detritus export from headwater streams to downstream habitats in Southeastern Alaska? *Canadian Journal of Fisheries and Aquatic Sciences.* 59: 503-513.

Reiners, W. A., I. A. Worley, and D. B. Lawrence. 1971. Plant diversity in a chronosequence at Glacier Bay, Alaska. *Ecology.* 52: 55-69.

Ricketts, T., E Dinerstein, D. Olson, C. Loucks *et al.* 1999. *Terrestrial ecoregions of North America: A conservation assessment.* World Wildlife Fund. Island Press, Washington, DC.

Shelford, V. 1963. *The ecology of North America.* University of Illinois Press, Urbana, IL.

Shepard, M. and T. Brock. 2002. *Landtype associations of the Yakutat Foreland, Alaska.* USDA Forest Service. R10-TP-109.

Stephens, F. R., C. R. Gass, and R. F. Billings. 1970. The muskegs of Southeast Alaska and their diminished extent. *Northwest Science.* 44(2): 123-30.

Streveler, G. 1996. *The Natural History of Gustavus.* Self-published, Gustavus, Alaska.

Wipfli, M., J. Hudson, and J. Caouette. 1998. Influence of salmon carcasses on stream productivity: response of biofilm and benthic macroinvertebrates in southeastern Alaska, U.S.A. *Canadian Journal of Fisheries and Aquatic Sciences.* 55: 1501-1511.

Wipfli, M. and J. Musslewhite. 2004. Density of red alder (*Alnus rubra*) in headwaters influences invertebrate and detritus subsidies to downstream fish habitats in Alaska. *Hydrobiologia* 520: 153–163.

Wipfli, M. 2005. Trophic linkages between headwater forests and downstream fish habitats: Implications for forest and fish management. *Landscape and Urban Planning.* 72(1-3): 205-213.

History and culture

Bryson, G. 2009. *DNA tracks descendants of Tlingit Haida and Tsimshian in Southeast Alaska.* News from Indian Country. *http://www.indiancountrynews.com/*

Connor, C., G. Streveler, A. Post, D. Monteith, and W. Howell. (2008). The Neoglacial landscape and human history of Glacier Bay, Glacier Bay National Park and Preserve, Southeast Alaska, USA. In Matthews, J. ed. *The Holocene: An interdisciplinary journal focusing on recent environmental change.* SAGE Publications, UK.

Colt, S., D. Dugan and G. Fay, 2007. *The Regional Economy of Southeast Alaska.* Report to the Alaska Conservation Foundation by the Institute of Social and Economic Research. University of Alaska, Anchorage, AK.

Crowell, A., W. Howell, D. Mann, and G. Streveler. 2013. *The Hoonah Tlingit cultural landscape in Glacier Bay National Park and Preserve: An archaeological and geological study.* National Park Service.

Cruikshank, J. 2005. *Do glaciers listen? Local knowledge, colonial encounters, and social imagination.* University of Washington Press, Seattle, WA.

Dauenhauer, N. and R. Dauenhauer. eds. 1987. *Haa Shuka, our ancestors: Tlingit oral narratives.* University of Washington Press, Seattle, WA.

Dauenhauer, N. and R. Dauenhauer. eds. 1994. *Haa Ḵusteeyí, our culture: Tlingit life stories.* University of Washington Press, Seattle, WA.

Dauenhauer, N., R. Dauenhauer, and L. Black. eds. 2008. *Anóoshi Lingít Aaní Ká: Russians in Tlingit America. The battles of Sitka, 1802 and 1804.* University of Washington Press, Seattle, WA.

DeArmond, R. 1978. *Early visitors to southeastern Alaska: Nine accounts.* Alaska Northwest Books, Portland, OR.

Deur, D. and N. Turner. eds. 2006. *Traditions of plant use and cultivation on the Northwest Coast of North America.* University of Washington Press, Seattle, WA.

Durbin, K. 1999. *Tongass: Pulp politics and the fight for the Alaska rain forest.* Oregon State University Press, Corvallis, OR.

Edwards, K. 2009. *Dictionary of Tlingit.* Sealaska Heritage Foundation, Juneau, AK.

Emmons, G. and F. deLaguna. 1991. *The Tlingit Indians.* University of Washington Press, Seattle, WA.

Goldschmidt, W. and T. Haas. 1998. *Haa Aaní. our land: Tlingit and Haida land rights and use.* University of Washington Press, Seattle, WA.

Hope, A. 2003. *Traditional Tlingit country: Tlingit tribes, clans and clan houses.* Map by Sealaska Heritage Foundation, Juneau, AK.

Howe, J. 1996. *Bear man of Admiralty Island: A biography of Allen E. Hasselborg.* University of Alaska Press, Fairbanks, AK.

Isto, S. 2012. *The fur farms of Alaska: Two centuries of history, and a forgotten stampede.* University of Alaska Press, Fairbanks, AK.

Louv, R. 2005. *Last child in the woods: Saving our children from nature-deficit disorder.* Algonquin Books, Chapel Hill, NC.

Louv, R. 2011. *The Nature Principle: Human restoration and the end of nature-deficit disorder.* Algonquin Books, Chapel Hill, NC.

Mackoviak, J. 2010. *Tongass timber: a history of logging and timber utilization in Southeast Alaska.* Forest History Society, Durham, NC.

Moss, M. and J. Erlandson, 1992. Forts, refuge rocks and defensive sites: The antiquity of warfare along the North Pacific coast of North America. *Arctic Anthropology.* 29(2): 73-90.

Muir, J. 1915. *Travels in Alaska.* Houghton Mifflin, Boston, MA.

Newton, R. and M. Moss. 2009. *Haa Atxaayí Haa Kusteeyíx Sitee: Our food is our Tlingit way of life: Excerpts from oral interviews.* USDA Forest Service. R10-MR-50.

Olson, W. 1993. *The Alaska travel journals of Archibald Menzies, 1793-1794.* University of Alaska Press, Fairbanks, AK.

Olson, W.1994. "A prehistory of Southeast Alaska." In Alaska Geographic Society. eds. *Prehistoric Alaska.* 21(4).

Orth, D. 1967. *Dictionary of Alaska place names.* USGS professional paper 567. US Government Printing Office, Washington, DC.

Rakestraw, L. 2002. *A history of the United States Forest Service in Alaska.* USDA Forest Service. R10-FR-5.

Redman, E. 2011. *The Juneau Gold Belt: A history of the mines and miners.* Green Igloo Press, Cavan, Ireland.

Shoaf, B. 1998. *The taking of the Tongass; Alaska's rainforest.* Running Wolf Press, Ketchikan, AK.

Schurr T., M. Dulik, A. Owings, S. Zhadanof, J. Gaieski, M. Vilar, J. Ramos, M. B. Moss, F. Natkong, and the Genographic Consortium. 2012. Clan, language, and migration history has shaped genetic diversity in Haida and Tlingit populations from Southeast Alaska. *American Journal of Physical Anthropology.* 48(3): 422-435.

Streveler, G. 2007. "Peripheral vision as an adjunct to rigor." 236-237 in Piatt and Gende. eds. *Proceedings of the fourth Glacier Bay science symposium.* US Geological Survey. Scientific Investigations Report. 2007-5047. Juneau, AK.

Thornton, T. 2008. *Being and place among the Tlingit.* University of Washington Press, Seattle, WA.

Thornton, T., ed. 2012. *Haa L'éelk'w Hás Aani Saax'ú. Our grandparents' names on the land.* University of Washington Press, Seattle, WA.

Vancouver, G. 1984. *George Vancouver: A voyage of discovery to the North Pacific Ocean and round the world. 1791-1795.* W. K. Lamb, ed. The Hakluyt Society, London, England.

Mammals

Allen, B. and R. Angliss. 2013. *Alaska marine mammal stock assessments, 2012.* National Oceanic Atmospheric Administration. Technical Memorandum. NMFS-AFSC-245.

Pacific Wildlife Foundation. *Important Cetacean Areas.* http://www.pwlf.org/ica/ica6.html

Anderson, P. 1995. Competition, predation, and the evolution and extinction of Steller's sea cow, *Hydrodamalis gigas. Marine Mammal Science* 11(3): 391–394.

Brown, C. ed. 2004. Elk management report of survey-inventory activities, 2001-2003. Alaska Department of Fish and Game, Division of Wildlife Conservation.

Calambokidis, J. et al. *SPLASH: Structure of Populations, Levels of Abundance and Status of Humpback Whales in the North Pacific.* Final report for US Department of Commerce. Cascadia Research, Olympia, WA.

Carstensen, R. 2013. *Common tracks of Southeast Alaska*. Discovery Southeast, Juneau, Alaska. *http://www.juneaunature.com/publications/books-booklets/*

Conroy, C., J. Demboski, and J. Cook, 1999. Mammalian biogeography of the Alexander Archipelago of Alaska: A north temperate nested fauna. *Journal of Biogeography*. 26: 343–352.

Cook, J., A. Bidlack, C. Conroy, J. Demboski, M. Fleming, A. Runck, K. Stone, and S. MacDonald. 2001. A phylogeographic perspective on endemism in the Alexander Archipelago of southeast Alaska. *Biological Conservation* 97: 215-227.

Cook, J., N. Dawson, and S. MacDonald. 2006. Conservation of highly fragmented systems: The north temperate Alexander Archipelago. *Biological Conservation*. 133: 1-15.

Elbroch, M. 2003. *Mammal tracks and sign: A guide to North American species*. Stackpole Books, Mechanicsburg, PA.

Flynn, R., S. Lewis, L. Beier, and G. Pendleton. 2007. *Brown bear use of riparian and beach zones on northeast Chichagof Island: Implications for streamside management in coastal Alaska*. Alaska Department of Fish and Game. Wildlife Research Final Report. Juneau, AK.

Friends of Admiralty. 2001. *Brown bears of Admiralty Island*. Juneau, AK.

Gende, S. and T. Quinn. 2004. The relative importance of prey density and social dominance in determining energy intake by bears feeding on Pacific salmon. *Canadian Journal of Zoology*. 82: 75-85.

Hanley. T. and J. Barnard. 1999. Spatial variation in population dynamics of Sitka mice in floodplain forests. *Journal of Mammalogy*. 80(3): 866-879.

Herrero, S. 2002. *Bear attacks, their causes and avoidance*. The Lyons Press, Guilford, CT.

Higdon, J., O. Bininda-Emonds, R. Beck, and S. Ferguson. 2007. Phylogeny and divergence of the pinnipeds (Carnivora: Mammalia) assessed using a multigene dataset. Biomed Central. *Evolutionary Biology*. 7: 216.

International Whaling Commission. 2007. *Humpback whale population estimates. http://iwc.int/estimate*.

Jackson, J. 2010. The future of the oceans past. *Philosophical Transactions of the Royal Society, Biological Sciences*. 365(1558): 3765-3778.

Kirchhoff, M. and D. Larsen. 1998. Dietary overlap between native Sitka black-tailed deer and introduced elk in Southeast Alaska. *Journal of Wildlife Management*. 62(1): 236-242.

Kirchhoff, M. and C. Farmer. 2007. Ecological classification of deer habitat in the Tongass National Forest, Alaska. *Northwestern Naturalist*. 88(2): 73-84.

MacDonald, S. and J. Cook. 1996. The land mammal fauna of Southeast Alaska. *Canadian Field Naturalist*. 110(4): 571-598.

MacDonald, S. and J. Cook. 2007. *Mammals and amphibians of Southeast Alaska*. Museum of Southwestern Biology. Special Publication 8.

Mathews, E. and G. Pendleton. 2007. "Declines in a harbor seal population in a marine reserve, Glacier Bay, Alaska, 1992–2002." In Piatt and Gende. eds. *Proceedings of the fourth Glacier Bay Science Symposium*. US Geological Survey. Scientific Investigations Report. 2007-5047. Juneau, AK.

Nagorsen, D. 2002. *An identification manual to the small mammals of British Columbia*. Royal BC Museum, Victoria, BC.

Peacock, E., M. Peacock, and K. Titus. 2007. Black bears in Southeast Alaska: The fate of two ancient lineages in the face of contemporary movement. *Journal of Zoology* 271: 445–454.

Person, D. 2009. *Habitat use and survivorship of Sitka black-tailed deer in Southeast Alaska: A* regional meta-analysis and synthesis. Alaska Department of Fish and Game. Annual research performance report.

Smith. W., M. Stotts, B. Andres, J. Melton, A. Garibaldi, and K. Boggs. 2001. *Bird, mammal, and vegetation community surveys of Research Natural Areas in the Tongass National Forest*. USDA Forest Service. PNW-RP-535.

Steller, G. 1751. *De bestiis marinis, or, the beasts of the sea*. Miller, W. transl. University of Nebraska Libraries. Faculty Publications. Paper 17.

Stewart N. and B. Konar. 2012. Kelp forests versus urchin barrens: Alternate stable states and their effect on sea otter prey quality in the Aleutian Islands. *Journal of Marine Biology*. 2012(92308).

Turvey, S., and C. Risley. 2006. Modelling the extinction of the Steller's sea cow. *Biology Letters*. 2: 94-97.

Wallmo, O. ed. 1981. *Mule and black-tailed Deer of North America*. University of Nebraska Press, Lincoln, NB.

Wilson, D. and S. Ruff. eds. 1999. *The Smithsonian book of North American mammals*. Smithsonian Institution Press, Washington, DC.

Willson, M. and R. Armstrong. 2009. *Beavers by the Mendenhall Glacier in Juneau, Alaska*. Nature Alaska Images, Juneau, AK.

Wynne, K. 1992. *Guide to marine mammals of Alaska*. Alaska Sea Grant Program, University of Alaska, Fairbanks, AK.

Birds

Alaska Department of Fish and Game. ND. *Marbled murrelets in Southeast Alaska*. Division of Wildlife Conservation, Juneau, AK.

Alaska Shorebird Group. 2008. *Alaska Shorebird Conservation Plan*. Version II. Anchorage, AK. http://alaska.fws.gov/mbsp/mbm/shorebirds/plans.htm.

Armstrong, R.H. 2008. *Guide to the birds of Alaska*. 5th Edition. Alaska Northwest Books, Portland, OR.

Carstensen, R. 2000. *A Discovery guide to common birds of Southeast Alaska*. Discovery Southeast, Juneau, AK.

De Santo, T. and M. Willson. 2001. Predator abundance and predation of artificial nests in natural and anthropogenic coniferous forest edges in Southeast Alaska. *Journal of Field Ornithology*. 72(1): 136–149.

Elphick, C., J. Dunning, and D. Sibley. eds. 2001. *The Sibley guide to bird life and behavior*. Alfred Knopf, NYC.

Gunn, D. and others. 2008. *Distribution of sea ducks in Southeast Alaska: Geographic patterns and relationships to coastal habitats*. SDJV Project 86. http://seaduckjv.org/studies/pro3/sdjv_project86_se_ak_sea_duck_distribution_final_report.pdf.

Heinl, S. 2010. *Birds of Southeast Alaska. An annotated list from Icy Bay south to Dixon Entrance*. Alaska Geographic, Anchorage, AK.

Hodges, J., D. Groves, and B. Conant. 2008. Distribution and abundance of waterbirds near shore in Southeast Alaska. 1997-2002. *Northwestern Naturalist*. 89: 85-96.

Hupp, J., J. Hodges, B. Conant, B. Meixell, and D. Groves. 2010. Winter distribution, movements, and annual survival of radiomarked Vancouver Canada Geese in Southeast Alaska. *Journal of Wildlife Management*. (74)2: 274–284.

Johnson, J., B. Andres, and J. Bissonette. 2008. *Birds of the major mainland rivers of Southeast Alaska*. General Technical Report. PNW-GTR-739.

King, J. 2008. *Attending Alaska's birds*. Trafford Publishing, Bloomington, IN.

Lebeda, C. S. and J. T. Ratti. 1983. Reproductive biology of Vancouver Canada Geese on Admiralty Island, Alaska. *Journal of Wildlife Management*. 47(2): 297-306.

Lyon, B. and R. Montgomerie. 2004. Dirty little secrets. *Natural History*. 113(5): 18-22.

Mowbray, T., C. Ely, J.Sedinger, and R.Trost. 2002. *Canada Goose (Branta canadensis)*. The Birds of North America Online (Poole, ed.). Cornell Lab of Ornithology, Ithaca, NY. *http:// bna.birds.cornell.edu/bna/species/682doi:10.2173/bna.682*

Piatt, J., K. Kuletz, A. Burger, S. Hatch, V. Friesen, T. Birt, M. Armitsu, G. Drew, A. Harding, K. Bixler. 2007. *Status review of the Marbled Murrelet (Brachyramphus marmoratus) in Alaska and British Columbia*. USGS Open-file Report. 2006–1387.

Sibley, D. 2003. *The Sibley field guide to birds of western North America*. Alfred Knopf, NYC.

Stenhouse, I. 2007. "Bald Eagle." In Schoen and Dovichin. eds. 2007. *A conservation assessment and resource synthesis for the coastal forests and mountains ecoregion in Southeastern Alaska and the Tongass National Forest.* Audubon Alaska and the Nature Conservancy. Anchorage, AK.

Van Vliet, G. 1994. Kittlitz's murrelet: The species most impacted by direct mortality from the Exxon Valdez oil spill? *Pacific Seabirds*. 21(2).

Welty J. and L. Baptista. 1988. *The life of birds*. Harcourt Brace Jovanovich College Publishers, San Diego, CA.

West, G. 2008. *A birder's guide to Alaska*. American Birding Association, Colorado Springs, CO.

Willson, M.F. and K.M. Hocker. 2010. *American Dippers*. Cinclus Press, Juneau, AK.

Wright, B. and P. Schempf. eds. 2008. *Bald Eagles in Alaska*. Bald Eagle Research Institute. University of Alaska Southeast, Juneau, AK. *http://www.uas.alaska.edu/arts_sciences/docs/ bald-eagles-ak12-07.pdf.*

Amphibians

Armstrong, R. and M. Hermans. 2001. Newts in the rain forest. *Alaskan Southeaster*. November.

Brodie, E. III and E. Brodie Jr. 1999. Predator-prey arms races. *BioScience* 49: 557-568.

Carstensen, R., M.Willson, and R.Armstrong. 2003. *Habitat use of amphibians in northern Southeast Alaska*. Discovery Southeast for Alaska Department of Fish and Game. Juneau,AK.

Corkran, C.and C.Thoms. 1996. *Amphibians of Oregon, Washington and British Columbia*. Lone Pine Publishing, Auburn, WA.

Hodge, R. P. 1976. *Amphibians and reptiles in Alaska, the Yukon, and Northwest Territories*. Alaska Northwest Books, Anchorage, AK.

Kuchta, S. and A. Tan. 2005. Isolation by distance and post-glacial range expansion in the rough-skinned newt, *Taricha granulosa*. *Molecular Ecology*. 14(1): 225-244.

MacDonald, S. 2003. *The amphibians and reptiles of Alaska: A field handbook*. US Fish and Wild-life Service.

Neill, W. 1958. The occurrence of amphibians and reptiles in saltwater areas, and a bibliogra-phy. *Bulletin of Marine Science of the Gulf and Caribbean* 8(1).

Slough, B. 2005. *A guide to Yukon amphibians*. Government of Yukon.

Taylor, M. S. 1983. *The boreal toad (Bufo boreas boreas) as a successional animal in Glacier Bay, Alaska*. MS thesis. California State University, Hayward, CA.

Fish

Alaska Department of Fish and Game. 2009. *Sustaining Alaska's fisheries: Fifty years of statehood.* ADF&G, Anchorage, AK.

Armstrong, R. H. 1971. Age, food, and migration of sea-run cutthroat trout, *Salmo clarki*, at Eva Lake, southeastern Alaska. *Transactions of the American Fisheries Society.* 100(2): 302-6.

Armstrong, R. H. and J. E. Morrow. 1980. "The Dolly Varden charr, *Salvelinus malma*." In *CHARRS, Salmonid fishes of the genus Salvelinus.* Perspectives in Vertebrate Science. 1: 99-140.

Armstrong, R.H. 1996. *Alaska's fish: A guide to selected species.* Alaska Northwest Books, Anchorage, AK.

Armstrong, R.H. 1974. Migration of anadromous Dolly Varden (*Salvelinus malma*) in southeastern Alaska. *Journal of the Fisheries Research Board of Canada.* 31: 435-444.

Armstrong, R.H. 1984. "Migration of anadromous Dolly Varden charr in southeastern Alaska—a manager's nightmare." In L. Johnson and B.L. Burns eds. *Biology of the Arctic charr, Proceedings of the International Symposium on Arctic Charr.* May, 1981. University of Manitoba Press, Winnipeg.

Eschmeyer, W. N. and E. S. Herald. 1983. *A field guide to Pacific coast fishes of North America.* Houghton Mifflin Company, Boston, MA.

Gende, S., R. Edwards, M. Willson, and M. Wipfli. 2002. Pacific salmon in aquatic and terrestrial ecosystems. *BioScience.* 52: 917-928.

Gende, S., T. Quinn, M. Willson, R. Heintz, and T. Scott. 2004. Magnitude and fate of salmon-derived nutrients and energy in a coastal stream ecosystem. *Journal of Freshwater Ecology.* (19)1: 149-160.

Halupka, K., M. Bryant, M. Willson, F. Everest. 2000. *Biological characteristics and population status of anadromous salmon in Southeast Alaska.* USDA Forest Service, Pacific Northwest Research Station. General Technical Report. PNW-GTR-468. Portland, OR.

Lyman, J. 2002. *Alaska's wild salmon.* Alaska Department of Fish and Game. Juneau, AK.

Mecklenburg, C.W., T.A. Mecklenburg, and L.K. Thorsteinson. 2002. *Fishes of Alaska.* American Fisheries Society, Bethesda, MD.

Morrow, J. E. 1980. *The freshwater fishes of Alaska.* Alaska Northwest Books, Anchorage, AK.

Munk, K. 2001. Maximum ages of groundfishes in waters off Alaska and British Columbia and considerations of age determination. *Alaska Fishery Research Bulletin.* 8(1).

Pollard, J., G. Hartman, C. Groot, and P. Edgell.1997. *Field identification of coastal juvenile salmonids.* Harbour Publishing, Madeira Park, BC.

Willson, M., S. Gende, and B. Marston. 1998. Fishes and the forest. *BioScience.* 48(6): 455-462.

Willson, M.F., R.H. Armstrong, M.C. Hermans, and K. Koski. 2006. *Eulachon: A review of biology and an annotated bibliography.* Alaska Fisheries Science Center processed report 2006-12.

Invertebrates

Baldwin, A. 2013. *Common seashore animals of southeastern Alaska: A field guide.* http://goo.gl/M2RTu4

Barr, L. and N. Barr. 1983. *Under Alaskan seas: The shallow water marine invertebrates.* Alaska Northwest Books, Anchorage, AK.

Black, B., C. Copenheaver, D. Frank, M. Stuckey, and R. Kormanyos. 2009. Multi-proxy reconstructions of northeastern Pacific sea surface temperature data from trees and Pacific geoduck. *Palaeogeography, Palaeoclimatology, Palaeoecology.* 278: 40-47.

Haggard, P. and J. Haggard. 2006. *Insects of the Pacific Northwest*. Timber Press Field Guide, Portland, OR.

Hocker, K. 2013. *A Discovery guide to intertidal animals of Southeast Alaska*. Discovery Southeast, Juneau, AK.

Holsten, E. H., P. E. Hennon, and R A. Werner. 1985. *Insects and diseases of Alaskan forests*. US Forest Service, Alaska Region. Report 181.

Hudson, J. and R. H. Armstrong. 2010. *Dragonflies of Alaska*. Nature Alaska Images, Juneau, AK.

Hudson, J., K. Hocker, and R.H. Armstrong. 2012. *Aquatic insects in Alaska*. Nature Alaska Images, Juneau, AK.

Kozloff, E. N. 1983. *Seashore life of the northern Pacific Coast: An illustrated guide to Northern California, Oregon, Washington, and British Columbia*. University of Washington Press, Seattle, WA.

Marshall, S. A. 2009. *Insects: Their natural history and diversity*. Firefly Books, Buffalo, NY.

McCafferty, P. 1998. *Aquatic entomology*. Jones and Bartlett Publishers, Sudbury, MA.

O'Clair, R. and C. O'Clair. 1998. *Southeast Alaska's rocky shores: Animals*. Plant Press, Auke Bay, AK.

Fungi and lichens

Arora, D. 1986. *Mushrooms demystified: A comprehensive guide to the fleshy fungi*. Ten Speed Press, Berkeley, CA.

Brodo, I., S. Sharnoff, and S. Sharnoff. 2001. *Lichens of North America*. Yale University Press, New Haven, CT.

Derr, C.C. and R.H. Armstrong. 2010. *Lichens around Mendenhall Glacier*. Nature Alaska Images, Juneau, AK.

Geiser, L.H., K.L. Dillman, C.C. Derr, and M.C. Stensvold. 1998. "Lichens and allied fungi of Southeast Alaska." In Glenn, Harris, Dirig and Cole. eds. *Lichenographia Thomsoniana: North American Lichenology*. in Honor of John W. Thomson. Mycotaxon Ltd., Ithaca, NY.

Plants

Alaska Exotic Plants Information Clearinghouse (AKEPIC) *http://aknhp.uaa.alaska.edu/botany/akepic/*

Hall, J. 2010. *Native plants of Southeast Alaska*. Windy Ridge Publishing, Haines, AK.

Hitchcock, C. and A. Cronquist. 1973. *Flora of the Pacific Northwest*. University of Washington Press, Seattle, WA.

Hocker, K. 2001. *A Discovery Guide to common flowers of Southeast Alaska*. Discovery Southeast, Juneau, AK.

Hultén, E. 1968. *Flora of Alaska and neighboring territories*. Stanford University Press, Palo Alto, CA.

Kimmerer, R. 2003. *Gathering moss: A natural and cultural history of mosses*. Oregon State University Press, Corvallis, OR.

Klinka, K., V Krajina, A. Ceska, and A. Scagel. 1989. *Indicator plants of coastal British Columbia*. University of British Columbia Press, Vancouver, BC.

Lamb, M. and M. Shephard. 2007. *A snapshot of spread locations of invasive plants in Southeast Alaska*. Forest Health Protection State and Private Forestry. R10-MB-597.

Lindeburg, M. and S. Lindstrom. 2012. *Field guide to seaweads of Alaska*. Alaska Sea Grant. University of Alaska Fairbanks, AK.

Lindstrom, S. 2008. The biogeography of seaweeds in Southeast Alaska. *Journal of Biogeography*, 36(3): 401–409.

O'Clair, R.M., S.C. Lindstrom, and I.R. Brodo. 1996. *Southeast Alaska's rocky shores: Seaweeds and lichens*. Plant Press, Auke Bay, AK.

Pojar, J., and A. MacKinnon. 1994. *Plants of the Pacific Northwest Coast: Washington, Oregon, British Columbia and Alaska*. Lone Pine Publishing, Redmond, WA.

Schofield, J. J. 1989. *Discovering wild plants*. Alaska Northwest Books, Seattle, WA.

Schofield, W. 1992. *Some common mosses of British Columbia*. Royal British Columbia Museum, Victoria, BC.

Schrader, B. and P. Hennon. 2005. *Assessment of invasive species in Alaska and its National Forests*. USFS Regional Office and Forestry Sciences Labs, Juneau, AK. *http://www.msb.unm. edu/mammals/ISLES_website_final_20091028/EXOTICS%20table.pdf*

Tandy, G. and R. Lipkin. 2003. *Wetland sedges of Alaska*. Alaska Natural Heritage Progam for the US Environmental Protection Agency.

Traveset, A. and M. Willson. 1997. Effect of birds and bears on seed germination of fleshy-fruited plants in temperate rainforests of Southeast Alaska. Nordic Society. *Oikos*. 80: 89-95.

Viereck, L.A., and E.L. Little Jr. 1972. *Alaska trees and shrubs*. USDA Forest Service. Agriculture Handbook 410.

Vitt, D., J. Marsh, and R. Bovey. 1988. *Mosses, lichens and ferns of Northwest North America*. Lone Pine Publishing, Edmonton, Alberta.

Worley, I. 1972. *The bryo-geography of southeastern Alaska*. PhD thesis, University of British Columbia, Vancouver, B.C.

INDEX

Page numbers in **boldface** indicate drawing, photo or map. Most place-names mentioned in *The Nature of Southeast Alaska* are mapped on pages 14 and 15.

ABOUT THE AUTHORS

Richard Carstensen moved to Southeast Alaska in 1977. He's a writer, illustrator, cartographer, environmental consultant, and instructor for Discovery Southeast, a not-for-profit group offering hands-on learning from nature for youth, educators, and families. "Discovery has been my professional home for a quarter century. The commitment of our members, staff and board to ardent nature study and kids outdoors is what keeps me here when it's raining sideways and the sun comes up, sort of, after 9 AM." Richard is coauthor of *The enduring forests* (1996), *Book of the Tongass* (1999), *The coastal forests and mountains ecoregion* (Schoen & Dovichin, eds. 2007), *Salmon in the trees* (2010), and *Natural history of Juneau trails* (2013). For Discovery Southeast, he's building a natural-and-cultural history website at *www.juneaunature.org*.

Bob Armstrong has pursued a career in Alaska as a biologist, naturalist, and nature photographer since 1960. From 1960 to 1984, he was a fishery biologist and research supervisor for the Alaska Department of Fish and Game, an assistant leader for the Alaska Cooperative Fishery Research Unit, and Associate Professor of Fisheries at the University of Alaska Fairbanks. Since retirement from the State of Alaska in 1984 he has authored or coauthored seventeen books and helped write numerous popular and scientific articles about Alaska's nature. "I really enjoy picking a subject I know little about and inviting experts to join me in writing a book about the subject." This has resulted in the books *Dragonflies of Alaska* and *Aquatic Insects in Alaska*. In addition he has written *A Guide to the Birds of Alaska*, which is now in its fifth edition, and *Photographing Nature in Alaska*. He also coauthored *Southeast Alaska's Natural World* and his most recent endeavor *Natural Connections in Alaska*.

From 1978 to 2000, Rita M. O'Clair taught a wide variety of biology courses at the University of Alaska Southeast, Juneau, where she was an associate professor of biology. She received a Ph.D. in zoology from the University of Washington, Seattle, in 1973. An honorary lifetime member of The Nature Conservancy, she belongs to numerous professional organizations. She has studied and photographed natural habitats around the world. She retired in 2000 and moved to Washington State.

Printed in the USA
CPSIA information can be obtained
at www.ICGtesting.com
JSHW012020140824
68134JS00033B/2791